£ 10.95

19
SCA

Sociological Theory and Medical Sociology

Sociological Theory and Medical Sociology

Edited by
GRAHAM SCAMBLER

Tavistock Publications: London and New York

First published in 1987 by
Tavistock Publications
11 New Fetter Lane, London EC4P 4EE

Published in the USA by
Tavistock Publications
in association with Methuen, Inc.
29 West 35th Street, New York NY 10001

Printed in Great Britain by Richard Clay
(The Chaucer Press) Ltd.,
Bungay, Suffolk

British Library Cataloguing in Publication Data
Sociological theory and medical sociology.
1. Social medicine
I. Scambler, Graham
306'.46   RA418

ISBN 0 422 60630 8
0 422 60640 5 Pbk

Library of Congress Cataloging in Publication Data
Sociological theory and medical sociology.
Includes bibliographies and index.
1. Social medicine.   2. Sociology – Philosophy.
I. Scambler, Graham.   [DNLM: 1. Social Medicine.
2. Sociology, Medical.   WA 31 S6793]
RA418.S6735   1987   306'.46   87–10207
ISBN 0–422–60630–8
0–422–60640–5 (pbk.)

Contents

Notes on contributors

David Armstrong is Senior Lecturer in Sociology Applied to Medicine at United Medical and Dental Schools – Guy's Campus. He is the author of *An Outline of Sociology as Applied to Medicine* (2nd edn 1984) and *Political Anatomy of the Body* (1983). His primary interest is in the sociology of medical knowledge and he has published numerous articles in this area.

Clive Ashworth is Lecturer in Sociology at the University of Leicester. He is an author of *The Structure of Social Theory* (1984) and has written articles on social theory and the sociology of religion.

David Blane is Lecturer in Sociology at Charing Cross and Westminster Hospital Medical School. He is particularly interested in social inequality and health, an area in which he has published, and is currently researching issues in occupational health.

Karl Figlio has held posts in History of Medicine at Cambridge University and in Medical Sociology at Charing Cross and Westminster Hospital Medical School and University College London. He now practises as a psychotherapist and is managing editor of *Free Associations: Psychoanalysis, Groups, Politics, Culture*.

Ray Fitzpatrick is Fellow of Nuffield College and University Lecturer in Medical Sociology at the University of Oxford. He is an author of *The Experience of Illness* (1984) and joint editor of a new series of volumes on chronic illnesses. Among his present interests are research studies on rheumatoid arthritis and AIDS.

Uta Gerhardt is Professor of Medical Sociology and Director of the Institute of Medical Sociology at the University of Giessen, West Germany. She has published many articles on social theory and health and has recently been joint editor of *Stress and Stigma* (1985).

Sheila Hillier is Senior Lecturer in Sociology Applied to Medicine at The London Hospital Medical College and Medical College of St Bartholomew's Hospital. Her research interests include rural health care, especially in the People's Republic of China. She has published on these subjects and is joint author of *Health Care and Traditional Medicine in China 1800–1982* (1983).

Graham Scambler is Senior Lecturer in Sociology at University College and Middlesex Hospital School of Medicine. He is joint editor of *Sociology as Applied to Medicine* (2nd edn 1986) and an author of *The Experience of Illness* (1984). He has a particular interest in the philosophy of the social sciences and in stigma theory.

Steve Taylor is Lecturer in Medical Sociology and Medical Law at King's College and the London School of Economics. He is author of *Durkheim and the Study of Suicide* (1982). Apart from social theory, his current interests include research on child abuse.

Simon Williams is a Ph.D. student at Royal Holloway and Bedford New College. He has published work on Goffman and is particularly interested in the realm of chronic illness and disability. He is currently engaged in a study of chronic obstructive airways disease.

Introduction

GRAHAM SCAMBLER

When sociologists have been invited or felt the need to comment on the current state of medical sociology in Britain, they have almost invariably included a lament on its theoretical impoverishment. This has generally been attributed to its detachment from mainstream social theory, which has in turn been explained by reference to medical sociology's emergence in Britain as a close ally of the essentially practical or applied disciplines of social epidemiology and health policy. A brief consideration of these themes will help put the present volume into context and, at the same time, pave the way for a statement on the thoughts and discussions which gave rise to it.

Medical sociology, as it is understood today, is normally regarded as a post-Second World War phenomenon, and as originating in the USA. But in Europe, and especially in France, Germany, and Britain, social aspects of health and disease had been studied within disciplines like social medicine, public health, and anthropology since the late eighteenth century.

> Theoretical treatises (and often empirical studies) of physicians, anthropologists, philosophers and social activists such as Edwin Chadwick, Rudolf Virchow, Salomon Neumann, Henry E. Sigerist, Viktor von Weizsacker, Alfred Grotjahn, Cabanis, Louis-René Villerme and others, could all be labelled premedical sociology. In Europe, premodern medical sociology grew from there through social epidemiology and public policy.
>
> (Claus 1983: 1592)

Modern medical sociology in Britain and most other European countries bears the stamp of its antecedent or 'premodern' phase. Most notably, according to Claus, its disciplinary boundaries are broad and ill-defined, it has an 'applied' character, and it is heavily oriented towards health policy-making.

The genesis of medical sociology was very different in the USA. It began to grow shortly after the Second World War when structural-functionalism was the discipline's dominant paradigm. Chapter X of

Parsons's *The Social System* (1951) firmly established health, disease, and medicine on the agenda for mainstream theorists. His statement has probably provoked more discussion in medical sociology than any other, but disciples of structural-functionalism were to prove more fitful contributors to medical sociology than those working within the principal rival paradigm of interactionism, who were extremely active from the late 1950s (interestingly Lemert's *Social Pathology*, an important inspiration to interactionists to turn their attention to health and disease, was also published in 1951). And as Johnson has remarked, 'once the field of medicine had become a noted area for the two dominant schools of theoretical thinking, medical sociology took off (in the US) into a period of unprecedented growth' (1975: 229). In the early 1960s Goffman, in particular, continued the dialectical interplay between mainstream theory and medical sociology and broke new ground with his analysis of 'total institutions' in *Asylums* (1961). Importantly all of these early theorists remained in post in university departments of sociology and enjoyed only fleeting contacts with physicians and other health professionals.

While the different origins of medical sociology in Britain and the USA have had long-term implications, it would be a mistake to simply assume that – to use Straus's (1957) well-known dichotomy – Britain has developed a sociology *in* medicine and the USA a sociology *of* medicine. After a decade or so of sporadic interest in and dependence on structural-functionalist and interactionist theory from the USA, younger British sociologists began to contribute their own middle-range theories and concepts in the early 1970s (Stacey 1978). And in the USA medical sociologists became increasingly involved in government-funded 'problem-solving' in collaboration with researchers from medicine and other health-related disciplines. Their biases may still be discernibly different, but contemporary medical sociology in both Britain and the USA is now a mixture of sociology *in* and *of* medicine.

British medical sociology's traditional proximity to medicine and to health policy and practice has been a help and a hindrance. It has certainly facilitated claims of relevance and led to an abundance of worthwhile research; moreover, the association with the medical profession in particular, which has long dominated access and resources in the area of health and illness, has been a key factor in medical sociology's consolidation. It is indeed ironical that this largest sub-discipline of sociology, which owes much of its salience to medicine's enlarged role in the twentieth century, has furnished a number of critiques of 'medical imperialism' (Strong 1979).

Paradoxically medicine has been held partly responsible for both the post-war expansion of medical sociology in Britain and its modest theoretical accomplishments. It has been argued that many of the sociologists working for or with physicians have become tame in the process. This is an argument which it is easy to exaggerate, but it is perhaps worth noting two ways in which medical sociology may be said to have paid a price for its patronage by the medical profession. First, sociologists have surrendered much of the responsibility for selecting topics for investigation. Often they are hired or otherwise approached to address their expertise to the solution of physician-defined problems. This can lead to considerable role strain:

> on the one hand they are required to maintain a close relationship with health professionals and contribute to health policy or clinical practice, and on the other hand to maintain a sociological perspective and approach to problems in the health field, which often involves uncovering and questioning unspoken assumptions.
>
> (Morgan *et al.* 1985: 287)

Not infrequently they feel compelled to suspend their commitment to their discipline and consent, for example, to treat medicine's diagnostic categories as unproblematic rather than as historico-social constructions meriting analysis in their own right. Moreover the combination of government cutbacks in research funding in the 1980s and its continuing commitment to the more efficient allocation of health resources is likely to lead to the employment of a rising proportion of medical sociologists on studies directly related to clinical practice and health-policy-making. Morgan, Calnan, and Manning foresee medical sociologists over the next decade becoming increasingly involved in 'applied' research, especially evaluative studies.

Second, medical sociologists have frequently been constrained to conduct their investigations in accordance with the canons of scientific enquiry formalized initially by J. S. Mill and dubbed by the Willers 'systematic empiricism' (Willer and Willer 1973). In other words, their studies tend to be acceptable – as 'scientific' – in so far as they produce a more or less sophisticated set of empirical generalizations based on correlations between observables. As C. Wright Mills (1963) has argued, systematic (or 'abstracted') empiricism subordinates theory to methodological technique in the formulation of explanations.

> For example, the analysis of suicide and its 'causes' ceases to exist as a significant theoretical problem for the abstracted empiricist. Suicide is merely to be related to a number of factors – religious affiliation, marital status, residence, income, occupation, sex, age, etc. – the list has no logical limits – in order to determine whether the correlation between suicide (the dependent variable) and a selection of these factors (independent variables) are significant or spurious
>
> (Johnson *et al.* 1984: 39)

If the correlation between suicide and, say, marital status is found to be significant, this is generally taken as justifying a statement that these two social phenomena are related. Yet, as the Willers point out, the case is not made. The fact that the correlation is significant does not justify a positive statement that marital status is more important than any other factor. What about all those factors left unexamined? And what are the criteria for deciding which of an infinite number of potentially important independent variables should be under investigation? It is not surprising that systematic empiricism is characterized by a high degree of indeterminacy.

It is particulary disappointing that so much research on social class and health has been influenced by systematic empiricism. Sometimes medical sociologists have been pressurized into accepting this influence, but on other occasions they have seemed content to follow the lead of those from other disciplines, notably social epidemiology and social medicine. Two comments might be made here. First, systematic empiricism is flawed principally because it involves no interplay or dialectic between theory and observation. It is not that theory is absent – for example, the decision to include some variables and omit others in the search for correlations with suicide 'ultimately depends on some *ad hoc* appeal to, or unstated acceptance of, theoretical ideas' (Johnson *et al*. 1984: 39). It is rather that its presence is unacknowledged and fortuitous. It would be wrong to insist that there has been *no* worthwhile return on the enormous research investment in systematic empiricism. But the return for medical sociology has been smaller than that for social epidemiology and statistics. Systematic empiricism does not lend itself to the study of what Illsley identifies as sociology's primary concern: 'social structure, social relationships, and social processes' (1980: 12).

Second, systematic empiricism has led to the reification of social class. The notion routinely used in this area of research derives from the office of the Registrar General and involves a 'pragmatic aggregation of occupations into social classes' which is intended to reflect the 'lifestyle' shared by different occupational groups (Illsley 1980: 15). The main ground for sticking with this vague and unvalidated measure is that almost everybody else uses it. It seems astonishing that so few medical sociologists have sought either to substitute their own measures, grounded in mainstream sociological theories of stratification, especially neo- or post-Marxist theories of social class, or even to utilize measures already developed and tested outside the sub-discipline (e.g. at Nuffield College, Oxford).

There would be general agreement amongst medical sociologists that the sub-discipline should aspire to more than 'applied' research and the methodology of systematic empiricism. Nor would many object to the proposition that it is precisely sociology's commitment to theoretical activity that differentiates it from grosser forms of social accounting. Fundamental disagreements would arise, however, over the criteria of acceptable theoretical activity. Many would probably wish to draw the line at Merton's (1963) generalizations of the 'middle range'; and since the early 1970s there has been a steady trickle of middle-range medical sociological theories which have both profited from and profited the sociologies of encounters, the professions, the family, organizations, and so on. A personal, and perhaps minority, preference would be to accept a role also for 'grand theory' (the other main object of C. Wright Mills's contempt), at least as providing an orientation for middle-range theoretical activity. While arguing that sociologists have often been overly constrained by the grand theories of the discipline's nineteenth-century 'founding fathers', Giddens has recently sought to defend 'some of the ends to which they aspired'. He writes:

> We live in a world in which the pace of social change, if anything, has accelerated since the turn of the present century. It is a world increasingly defined by its overall 'systemness'. How can we hope to come to terms with the nature and implications of these phenomena if we try to refrain from any portrayals of social institutions save miniatures painted with a fine-grained brush.
>
> (1987: 43)

If this view is correct, it has implications for each of the sub-disciplines of sociology.

The aim of this collection is to further the links between the substantive and often highly focused work of many medical sociologists and mainstream sociological theory. It is hoped that it will serve as a catalyst, that it will encourage and provoke others to elaboration or critique. The contributors were selected as medical sociologists with particular interests – and experience, through writing and/or teaching – in sociological theory. Each was invited to focus on an aspect of the work of a prominent theorist which was relevant to, and stood to illuminate, the contemporary study of health, disease, and medicine. The directions taken and arguments deployed very much reflect the special interests and expertise of the individual authors.

In Chapter 1 David Blane considers McKeown's thesis that rising living standards have been primarily responsible for the fall in British mortality rates and asks whether it might be usefully recast in terms of Marxist theory, with Marx's theoretical concept of the value of labour-power replacing McKeown's atheoretical concept of rising living standards. He explores this possibility through a detailed assessment of the period 1870–1914. Steve Taylor and Clive Ashworth (Chapter

2) set out to debunk popular myths about the nature of Durkheim's sociology. They explore the possibility of a genuinely Durkheimian approach to society and disease, largely through a consideration of the social support literature. They also examine some of the tensions within Durkheim's sociology and the extent to which these have been overcome within theoretical traditions of particular salience to contemporary medical sociology. In Chapter 3 David Armstrong's preliminary discussion of the boundary disputes between biology and sociology leads into an exposition of some of the principal theses of Foucault. Using Foucault's notions of 'power and the body', he invites medical sociologists to ask 'strategic' questions about the field of knowledge in which what he sees as 'the medical-sociological alliance' is cast.

Karl Figlio (Chapter 4) argues that both the medical model and the tradition of social medicine, which has been so important in the genesis of medical sociology in Britain, have largely displaced the subjective aspect of human experience. Reflecting on the influence of psychoanalysis on the work of the Chicago School and Parsons, he examines medical sociology's potential to reintegrate the subjective side of life into a 'properly sociological epidemiology'. Uta Gerhardt in Chapter 5 defends Parsons against those who have consistently misunderstood or misinterpreted his conceptualization of the sick role. She notes the general neglect of his 'deviance paradigm', which draws upon psychoanalytic thinking, and shows the significance of this paradigm for the analysis of both physician–patient interaction and the medical professions' role in modern society. Simon Williams (Chapter 6) gives a clear and comprehensive guide to Goffman's views on stigma and follows this with an exploration of the use made of the notions of stigma and stigma management within medical sociology. He also discusses some of the key implications of Goffman's analysis for health policy and for practising physicians.

In Chapter 7 I offer an outline of the ever-evolving 'Habermasian project' and suggest some ways in which his latest theories of rationalization in modern society, involving both system rationalization and the rationalization of the lifeworld, may contribute to our understanding of the nature of the power associated with medical expertise. This is illustrated throughout by reference to modern obstetric practice. Sheila Hillier (Chapter 8) draws on Weber's analysis of rationalization and his classification of types of action to examine the rationality and irrationality associated with scientific medicine. She then concentrates on the bureaucratic organization of health care, at both hospital and policy levels, with the tension between *wertrationalitat* and *zweckrationalitat* serving as a major theme. Finally in Chapter 9, Ray Fitzpatrick considers recent rival – conservative and Marxist – analyses of the 'crisis of the welfare state'. He focuses on the view of the welfare state propounded by Offe, and asks how relevant this is for understanding the difficulties currently besetting the British National Health Service.

Although each chapter should be regarded as discrete, the collection as a whole covers a reasonably wide range of sociological theorists and areas and topics within medical sociology. This is not to say that it is comprehensive: indeed it is clearly not. Its primary purpose will have been served if, by constructing a few bridges between mainstream sociological theory and medical sociology, it helps sustain and further theoretical endeavour through years which are less than propitious.

References

Claus, L. (1983) 'The development of medical sociology in Europe', *Social Science and Medicine* 17: 1,591–7.

DHSS (1980) *Inequalities in Health*, London: HMSO.

Giddens, A. (1987) *Social Theory and Modern Sociology*, Cambridge: Polity Press.

Goffman, E. (1961) *Asylums*, New York: Doubleday & Anchor.

Illsley, R. (1980) *Professional or Public Health? Sociology in Health and Medicine*, London: Nuffield Provincial Hospitals Trust.

Johnson, M. (1975) 'Medical sociology and sociological theory', *Social Science and Medicine* 9: 227–32.

Johnson, T., Dandeker, C., and Ashworth, C. (1984) *The Structure of Social Theory*, London: Macmillan.

Lemert, E. (1951) *Social Pathology*, New York: McGraw-Hill

Merton, R. (1963) *Social Theory and Social Structure*, Glencoe: Free Press.

Mills, C. W. (1970) *The Sociological Imagination*, Harmondsworth: Pelican.

Morgan, M., Calnan, M., and Manning, N. (1985) *Sociological Approaches to Health and Medicine*, London: Croom Helm.

Parsons, T. (1951) *The Social System*, New York: Free Press.

Stacey, M. with Homans, H. (1978) 'The sociology of health and illness: its present state, future prospects and potential for health research', *Sociology* 12: 281–307.

Straus, R. (1957) 'The nature and status of medical sociology', *American Sociological Review* 22: 200.

Strong, P. (1979) 'Sociological imperialism and the profession of medicine: a critical examination of the thesis of medical imperialism', *Social Science and Medicine* 13A: 199–215.

Wilkinson, R. (ed.) (1986) *Class and Health: Research and Longitudinal Data*, London: Tavistock.

Willer, D. and Willer, J. (1973) *Systematic Empiricism: A Critique of a Pseudo-Science*, Englewood Cliffs, NJ: Prentice-Hall.

1

The value of labour-power and health

DAVID BLANE

Introduction

Marxism has always been concerned with some of the phenomena which are now seen as the subject matter of medical sociology. Engels, for example, described the effect of environmental factors on workers' health (Engels 1845), and Marx drew attention to the consequences of overwork by comparing the health of workers in industries covered by the Factory Acts with those in industries not protected in this way (Marx 1867). While these early 'founding fathers' concentrated on the effects of living standards on health, later contributors from within the Marxist tradition have also examined the provision of medical services. Tudor Hart (1971), for example, has analysed the effects of private medicine on the distribution of medical care, and Robson has examined the effects of the drug industry (1972) and professions (1977) on the NHS. Finally, some medical sociologists such as Navarro (e.g. 1978) and Doyal (e.g. 1979) are at present working within an explicitly Marxist framework.

However, it is not the intention of this chapter to review further these contributions to medical sociology. Instead an attempt will be made to explore the way in which Marxist theory and medical sociology can contribute to one another, by examining an obvious area of overlap between these two schools of thought.

McKeown's thesis (McKeown and Lowe 1966; McKeown 1976; McKeown 1979), that rising living standards have been primarily responsible for the fall in British mortality rates, has had a profound influence on medical sociology. In his treatment of this issue, however, 'rising living standards' appears as an atheoretical and taken-for-granted concept. In Marx's analysis of capitalism, in contrast, this concept, in the guise of the value of labour-power, appears as one factor in a fully developed theoretical scheme. This chapter proposes to examine the issue from both points of view. Starting with an examination of Marx's analysis of the value of labour-power and, then, the 'McKeown Thesis', it goes on to focus upon the period 1870–1914, and ends by re-examining both Marx's and McKeown's contributions in the light of events during this period.

The value of labour-power

The status of the producer is central to Marxism. Thus the defining characteristic of capitalism is not the search for profit nor factory production, but the existence of labourers who are 'doubly free'. 'Free', first, of the means of production; that is dispossessed of the means needed to produce the necessities of life, and hence forced to sell their labour in order to buy these necessities. Second, 'free' to dispose of their labour; in the sense of being citizens under formal democracy, who have the right to make a contract with any other citizen. The former 'freedom' resulted from the enclosures, which deprived peasants of their land; the latter from the growth of 'civil society' which abolished the feudal law tying peasants to their lords' lands. Only under these historically specific political and economic conditions did labour, or more precisely labour-power, become a commodity and the producer become a proletarian or worker who must sell his or her labour-power in order to live. Capitalism is thus a system of 'generalized commodity production', in which the commodity form has been extended to include the labourer's ability to work.

In general, the value, or more accurately the exchange value, of a commodity is established by the labour-time which is normally necessary for its production at any particular stage in the development of the productive forces. In the early volumes of *Capital* Marx argued that commodities are exchanged on the quantitative basis of equal labour-times, and although he amended this initial formulation in the third volume, when dealing with the transformation of value into prices, it remains the case that exchange values are the basis upon which commodity prices are formed.

The value of labour-power is established in the same way as that of any other commodity; that is by the labour-time necessary for its production. As labour-power, or the ability to work, cannot be separated from the existence of the labourer, the value of labour-power equals the value of those commodities necessary for the worker's existence. Marx analysed this value in terms of three components. First, the value of the means of subsistence necessary to maintain the worker as a labouring individual. Second, as the labourer is mortal but capital requires a continuous supply of labour-power, the value of the commodities necessary to raise the worker's replacements. Third, the value of the commodities necessary to support the worker during the training which is appropriate to any particular type of work within the division of labour. Each of these three components will now be considered in more detail.

Subsistence

Marx was emphatic that the first of these components was neither a fixed value nor tied to a physiological minimum:

> the number and extent of his [i.e. the labourer's] so-called wants, as also the modes of satisfying them, are themselves the product of historical development, and depend therefore to a great extent on the degree of civilisation of a country, more particularly on the condition under which, and consequently on the habits and degree of comfort in which, the class of free labourers has been formed. In contradistinction therefore to the case of other commodities, there enters into the determination of the value of labour-power a historical and moral element.

(Capital 1: 171)

Similarly, and following from this, while the minimum limit may be formed by the value of those means of subsistence which are physically indispensable, 'If the price of labour-power falls to this minimum, it falls below its value, since under such circumstances it can be maintained and developed only in a crippled state. But the value of every commodity is determined by the labour-time requisite to turn it out so as to be of normal quality' (1: 173).

While these passages are ignored at their peril by those who argue that rising living standards are in some way incompatible with Marxism, they still leave important questions unanswered. Most importantly, how is the value of the means of subsistence established, given that it is above the physiological minimum, and how is it increased? All Marx had to say in answer to the former of these questions was 'in a given country, at a given period, the average quantity of the means of subsistence necessary for the labourer is practically known' (1: 171), which begs the questions 'known by whom, and how?', although the use of the term 'practically' suggests that it is an empirical issue which is resolved in practice, perhaps, during wage bargaining between workers and employers. Marx did not deal with the question of how 'the historical and moral element' in the labourer's standard of living is increased, although, in what may be taken as a parallel instance, he showed that 'the determination of what is a working day presents itself as the result of a struggle, a struggle between collective capital, i.e. the class of capitalists, and collective labour, i.e. the working class' (1: 235). The problem with this analogy, however, lies in the difference between the length of the working day, which was established by class-wide legislation, and the generally accepted standard of living of labourers, which emerges from myriad local wage negotiations.

In a more polemical treatment of the question of wages Marx seems to imply that this difference is not important:

> The maximum of profit is, therefore, limited by the physical minimum of wages and the physical maximum of the working day. It is evident that between the two limits of this maximum rate of profit an immense scale of variations is possible. The fixation of its actual degree is only settled by the continuous struggle between capital and labour, the capitalist constantly tending to reduce wages to their physical minimum, and to extend the working day to its physical maximum, while the working man constantly presses in the opposite direction. The matter resolves itself into a question of the respective powers of the combatants.
>
> (1865: 51–2)

In this work at least, Marx was pessimistic about the workers' chances of success, concluding that

> their struggles for the standard of wages are incidents inseparable from the whole wages system, that in 99 cases out of 100 their efforts at raising wages are only efforts at maintaining the given value of labour, and that the necessity of debating their price with the capitalist is inherent in their condition of having to sell themselves as commodities.
>
> (1865: 54)

He explained this general balance of class forces ('in its merely economic action capital is the stronger side') by arguing that capital always has the option of replacing labour with machines: 'machinery is in constant competition with labour, and can often be only introduced when the price of labour has reached a certain height' (1865: 53).

Reproduction costs

The second component in the value of labour-power consists of the commodities necessary to raise the next generation of workers.

> The labour-power withdrawn from the market by wear and tear and death must be continually replaced by, at the very least, an equal amount of fresh labour-power. Hence the sum of the means of subsistence necessary for the production of labour-power must include the means necessary for the labourer's substitutes, i.e. his children, in order that this race of peculiar commodity owners may perpetuate its appearance in the market.
>
> (1: 172)

This component is often referred to as 'reproduction costs'.

Marx was not claiming that all wages included adequate reproduction costs, indeed he explicitly recognized that 'Individual workers, millions of workers, do not get enough to be able to exist and reproduce themselves' (1847: 79), but that the continuity of capitalist production demanded that the value of the labour-power of the class as a whole contained these reproduction costs. Anticipating a later discussion, it is also worth noting that he recognized labour-power may be paid below its value, with the difference being made up by the state. For example, 'the honest English farmers ... depressed the wages of the agricultural labourers even beneath the mere physical minimum, but made up by the Poor Laws the remainder necessary for the physical perpetuation of the race' (1865: 51).

This aspect of Marx's analysis of reproduction costs has been subjected to a vigorous critique by socialist feminists. Barrett and McIntosh (1980), for example, have argued that 'there is one point that is certain: this notion does not serve as an accurate description of the means by which the working class has been supported and reproduced'. In place of a 'family wage' (that is a male wage which includes adequate reproduction costs) these authors have stressed that the production of the next generation of workers crucially depends on unpaid female labour within the home and on subsidies from the state.

It is in fact possible to see these two means of subsidizing reproduction costs not as alternatives, but as historical accretions. Hewitt (1958) has described how married female workers during the early nineteenth century, while accepting the obligations of mother and housewife, had begun to develop a way of discharging these obligations through the market, by hiring young girls, old women, and industrially maimed people to nurse, child-care, cook, clean, and wash. The logical development of this system would have involved, among other things, reproduction costs ('the family component' of wages) being transferred from the value of male labour-power to that of female workers. Instead of this, as Hewitt documents, moral entrepreneurs, often supported by male workers, launched a veritable propaganda campaign designed to transfer married women from paid employment into unpaid domestic labour. A prominent feature of this campaign was the supposed effect of maternal employment on infant and child health, and, although the effectiveness, in this respect, of professional nursery care and paid maternity leave had already been demonstrated in France, these lessons were ignored in Britain. Whether or not as the result of this campaign, the proportion of married women in paid employment fell throughout the second half of the nineteenth century, and reached an historic low by 1900. As a solution, at least to the problem of poor infant and child health, this form of subsidizing reproduction costs proved a failure, as was shown by the unchanging infant mortality rate up to 1900 and by the high rate of rejects among army recruits for the Boer War.

The response to this failure is relevant to Marx's analysis of reproduction costs. Land (1976) has shown that the working class, via its socialist and feminist organization, demanded state support for wages in the form of family allowances. The response of the capitalist class was similarly via the state, in the form of free school meals to subsidize childhood nutrition. Neither class demanded that male wages should be increased to include adequate reproduction costs. Indeed, in what has become the generally held view, Eleanor Rathbone's Family Endowment Society argued that childhood poverty resulted from the attempt to support families of various sizes and stages of dependency by means of a relatively homogeneous adult male wage. Rathbone's solution was state subsidies which would be sensitive to the number of children in a family and their level of dependence (Barrett and McIntosh 1980), and this rationale can be seen as underlying the present system in which reproduction costs are subsidized by the state through a complex of family allowances, family income supplement, and income tax concessions (Land 1979).

It would seem, therefore, that the end of the nineteenth century saw inadequate working-class reproduction change from being a cause of concern for moral entrepreneurs into a problem which demanded effective action. Part of the background to this shift in emphasis was the loss at this time of the main supply of 'green' labour, as a consequence of rural areas having been more or less fully drained of surplus agricultural labourers. As a result capital needed to improve working-class reproduction in the towns, and achieved this via the state which progressively subsidized reproduction costs. De Brunhoff (1978) has argued that it was necessary for capitalism to subsidize reproduction costs via the state, as opposed to paying an adequate 'family wage', because to pay a worker according to the number of his children, and whether or not his wife was financially dependent, would have broken the illusion that wages are payment for labour, and exposed the underlying reality that wages are the price of the worker's means of subsistence. De Brunhoff's argument, then, is consistent with Marx's work in the sense that she sees the wages system, and the opacity of the process by which profit is extracted from workers' labour-power, as central to capitalism's stability. She amends his analysis of the value of labour-power, however, by reasoning that this stability requires that reproduction costs come from the state rather than via wages. One can in fact take this argument further, and in the process bring it closer to Marx's analysis, by including the net effect of working-class taxation and state subsidies, which is to redistribute income within the class. In this sense, Marx's assertion about reproduction costs becomes justified at the level of the working class as a whole.

Training

The third and final component in the value of labour-power consists of the means of subsistence necessary to support the labourer during whatever period of education or training is required to turn simple labour-power into labour-power of a specific type. As a result the labour-power of a technical worker has greater value than that of a skilled worker, which in turn has greater value than that of an unskilled worker, and it is these pay differentials which form the economic basis of the main division within the working class.

Capitalist development, which involves progressive mechanization, subjects this component in the value of labour-power to conflicting tendencies. On the one hand, machinery, by simplifying or de-skilling tasks, reduces the length of apprenticeship needed to master a trade, and thus reduces the value of skilled labour-power. At the same time, however, mechanization, by displacing labour, requires greater flexibility of workers. Modern industry, therefore, is accompanied by compulsory universal education, which increases the value of labour-power. Thus, while the value of labour-power goes down because of progressive mechanization, the length of basic general education increases, causing the value of labour-power to rise again.

Some unresolved issues

The preceding sketch of Marx's analysis of the value of labour-power has left many issues unresolved, and two of these will now be considered in more detail; the sexist character of Marx's assumptions about the value of female labour-power and relations within the nuclear family, and second, how Marx accounted for rising living standards.

There is an ambiguity in Marx's treatment of the value of labour-power which he does not seem to have recognized. The main thrust of his analysis was that the value of male labour-power includes reproduction costs, that is the cost of raising children. In places, however, he extended this to include a financially dependent wife – for example, 'The value of labour-power was determined, not only by the labour-time necessary to maintain the individual adult labourer, but also by that necessary to maintain his family' (1: 395) – and it was this version which allowed him to argue that mechanization lowered the value of male labour-power because it enabled women and children to enter the work-force, thus spreading the family's expenses across all its members.

While Marx argued that women entering paid employment lowered the value of male labour-power, some modern feminists, such as Gardiner (1975), have reasoned that women's unpaid domestic labour also has this effect as the result of housewives' producing use values in the home. It would seem, then, that female labour lowers the value of male labour-power irrespective of whether this is paid employment which spreads the cost of family expenses, or unpaid domestic labour which supplies some of the means of subsistence in a non-commodity form.

Beechey (1978) has pointed out that within Marx's framework there are only two ways of accounting for the lower value of female labour-power. One way would be that female labour-power is predominantly unskilled, and therefore involves lower training costs; the other that, by virtue of the existence of the family, women are not expected to provide reproduction costs. These are both historically specific forms, which assume the existence of a family containing a wife who is financially dependent for most of the time. While this may have seemed a plausible assumption in the mid-nineteenth century, with its high birth-rate and shorter life expectancy, it is strange that Marx, who in other respects was so astute at identifying numerically small but historically decisive tendencies, should have ignored the experience of married female workers in the advanced industries who, as was noted earlier, were discharging their domestic and maternal obligations through the market. From this perspective, which is entirely consistent with the logic of capitalist development, reproduction costs should have been attached to the value of female, and not male, labour-power.

The second issue to be considered concerns the problem of accounting for rising standards of living in a way which is consistent with Marx's treatment of the value of labour-power. At first sight there seems to be little room for such improvements. Although the 'historical and moral element' in the means of subsistence takes this component above the physiological minimum, Marx saw it as relatively unresponsive to workers' struggles, arguing that the vast majority of these were defensive in nature, being designed to maintain the existing value of labour-power under changing conditions in the labour market. As was similarly noted above, neither of the other two components seems able to account for this phenomenon, improved reproduction costs being subsidized by the state, and changes in training costs tending to cancel each other out as mechanization progresses.

A possible solution to this problem is to be found in Marx's analysis of the effects of the increase in productivity which results from the growing mechanization of production. To the extent that this process transforms those branches of industry which produce the workers' means of subsistence, the value of the commodities which comprise this means of subsistence will fall. 'The value of labour-power is determined by the value of a given quantity of necessaries. It is the value and not the mass of these necessaries that varies with the productiveness of labour' (1: 523). Under such conditions, say a doubling of productivity, the price of labour could fall, in this example by half, while leaving the value of labour-power, 'the mass of necessaries', unchanged. If the price of labour falls by less than the increase in productivity, however, the value of labour-power, the mass of necessaries, and hence workers' living standards, will increase. 'In this way it is possible with an increasing productiveness of labour, for the price of labour-power to keep on falling, and yet this fall to be accompanied by a constant growth in the mass of the labourer's means of subsistence' (1: 523).

To account for rising living standards in this way, it is only necessary to add a mechanism which prevents the price of labour-power from falling fully in line with rises in productivity. Such a mechanism is provided by the worker who, because of the opacity of the process by which profit is extracted, sees wages as the price of labour, not the cost of his means of subsistence. As the labourer is likely to be performing at least as much work under the new, more productive, regime, a fall in wages will be seen as unwarranted. Once workers collectively organize themselves into trade unions, therefore, they will attempt to minimize the fall in wages which, according to the law of value, could legitimately accompany a rise in general productivity and in the process raise the value of their labour-power, and hence their standard of living.

The McKeown thesis

The notion that a population's standard of living has an important effect on its health is not of recent origin. In the mid-nineteenth century, for example, William Farr (1843) produced an equation: $M_1 = M \times D \times 0 \times S$ in which M_1 is the observed mortality rate in an area, M the ideal rate (the rate under perfect conditions), D the population density, O atmospheric pollution with organic particles, and S the population's ability to procure the necessities of life – measured as C/N, where C is the market-price of the necessities of life, and N the population's mean income.

Some fifty years later Newsholme (1906) used ecological and time-series correlations to examine variations in the tuberculosis ('phthisis') death-rate. He found that the phthisis death-rate varied with the cost of living and, particularly, with the cost of wheat and other foods, as well as with housing quality and the degree of overcrowding, the level of pauperism and the institutional segregation of those with phthisis.

Fifty years on again, McKeown and Lowe (1966) used the previous one hundred years' mortality statistics to show that the bulk of the fall in mortality was due to a fall in deaths from infectious diseases, and that this had overwhelmingly occurred before antibiotics and immunization became available. Their work differed in three important respects from earlier studies in this field. First, they were able to use the time-series mortality data which had been accumulated over the previous century or more. This allowed them to map changes in the death-rate due to any specific disease, and relate these changes to social events such as the introduction of antibiotics or the nineteenth-century sanitary reforms. The registration of death, on which these time-series data are based, is generally regarded as being virtually complete from around 1850, and although Bartley (1985), Prior (1985), and others (e.g. Figlio 1978) have suggested that we should be wary of the accuracy of the cause of death as registered on a death certificate, it is difficult at present to quantify the importance of this insight and in any case the problem can be entirely avoided by the use of mortality rates due to all causes of death combined.

Second, McKeown and Lowe's work gained in credibility as the result of developments in the sciences of nutrition and immunology which provide a linking mechanism in the causal chain relating standard of living to deaths due to infectious diseases. Although the textbooks tend to be rather coy on this subject, the science of nutrition, for example, recognizes that malnutrition adversely affects many elements of the immune system and that 'These changes lead to decreased resistance to infections' (Davidson et al. 1979: 262). Immunology similarly acknowledged that 'clinical impression and epidemiological studies lend support to the concept that nutritional deficiency increases the frequency and severity of infection' (Chandra 1980: 76) and 'Thus nutrition appears to be a critical determinant of susceptibility to infection' (77).

Finally, McKeown and Lowe attempted to rank the relative importance of the various factors which might account for the fall in mortality from infectious diseases. Medical intervention was judged to be of minor importance on the grounds that the largest fall in deaths due to infectious diseases had preceded the introduction of antibiotics and immunization. The sanitary reforms were considered to be of intermediate importance because although they would have reduced mortality due to water-borne infections, they would have had little effect on infections spread through the air, and these were responsible for the majority of infectious deaths. By excluding the alternatives in this way, McKeown and Lowe were able to argue that increased living standards were of greatest importance, and they singled out improved levels of nutrition as being of particular importance in this respect.

The logical flaw in such 'argument by exclusion' has been criticized by Woods and Woodward (1984), who point out that it depends upon the assumption of all possibly relevant factors being known. Rather than pursue this line of thought here, however, it is proposed to examine in detail the relationship between falling mortality and rising living standards during one specific period. By doing this, it is hoped both to test McKeown's thesis, and to relate it to Marx's analysis of the value of labour-power. McKeown and Lowe's graphs of changes in the mortality rate from the main infectious diseases have been used to select the period for detailed examination, and as all of these show a dramatic fall somewhere between 1870 and 1914, this period in England and Wales has been chosen for further study.

Mortality 1870–1914

The Registrar General's Statistical Review of England and Wales for 1921 contains age-specific rates of mortality from all causes combined for the period 1870 to 1914 (in the form of five-yearly means). The data are of course national averages, and thus capable of hiding wide variation. Indeed it is known from Chadwick (1842), before this period, and from Stevenson (1923), soon after its end, that mortality rates were far higher than the national average among the poorest sections of the population, and that these rates fell as one moved up the social hierarchy, with the population's richest sections experiencing mortality rates which were much lower than the national average. It is important to bear in mind therefore that the poorer sections of the population made a quite disproportionate contribution to national averages of mortality.

The data show that the improvements in health, or at least the changes in mortality rates, were different for the various age-groups. The mortality rates of those aged 5–45 years fell steadily from 1870 to 1914, having approximately halved during this time. The mortality rates of those aged less than 5 years and those aged more than 45 years, however, showed a different pattern. The former remained relatively unchanged for the first two-thirds of the period, and started to fall only after 1896–1900; the latter were similarly static at the beginning of the period, although they started to fall somewhat earlier, in 1890–5. The difference in pattern is in fact greater if only the extremes of age are examined. The mortality rate of those under 1 year old actually rose from 1881–5 to 1896–1900, before it fell; similarly the mortality rates of those over 65 years rose from 1881–5 to 1891–5, before starting to fall. To the extent therefore that it is legitimate to use mortality rates as an indicator of a population's health, these data present a picture in which the health of adolescents and young adults improved steadily from 1870 to 1914, with parallel improvements in the health of other age groups being delayed by some twenty-five years.

Unfortunately the only other available measure of the population's health, apart for mortality rates, does not unambiguously support this picture. The medical examination of volunteers during the Boer War and conscripts during the First World War can be seen as a form of 'mass screening' of the young adult male population in 1900 and 1914 respectively. In the Boer War the minimum height for recruits was 5 feet, 40 per cent of volunteers were judged 'physically unfit for service', and there was a shortage of 'fit young men'. In the First World War the previous minimum height was reduced by the formation of 'bantam battalions' of men under 5 feet, some 40 per cent of conscripts were judged 'physically unfit for service', and only one-third were fit young men (Oddy 1982). Bearing in mind that the age-groups 'screened' in these two wars were those which have the lowest mortality rates, these results suggest a sombre picture of the population's health at the beginning and at the end of the final third of the period under examination. These results also put into perspective the improvements in health, as judged by mortality rates, which took place during the first two-thirds of this period.

The apparent inconsistency between an identical reject rate in both 1900 and 1914, on the one hand, and falling mortality rates for young men between these dates, on the other, is probably best explained by the 'screening' having been more complete on the latter occasion. Conscription and abolition of the minimum height during the First World War would have, in combination, extended the 'mass screening' to the least healthy section of the age group. If similar regulations had been in force during the earlier war, the reject rate would probably have been higher. Thus although the 'screening' data do not unambiguously support the mortality data, it seems reasonable to conclude that they do not undermine the credibility of the picture of the population's health which is suggested by the falling mortality rates.

The delay in the fall of the infant mortality rate has already attracted attention. Glass (1959) has shown that this was unlikely to have been due to technical factors, such as changes in the registration of infant deaths. He considered registration to have been virtually complete after 1874, when registration of infant deaths was made the legal responsibility of parents, and demonstrated that any residual under-registration after this date would have made a negligible difference to the infant mortality rate. There is no agreement, however, about the 'real' causes of this phenomenon. Tatham (1904) and Smith (1979) have pointed to the serious inadequacies of the first proprietary infant foods which became available towards the end of the nineteenth century. McKeown (1976) has attributed the delay to the time-lag involved in a generation of healthier females reaching fertility. And, although McKinlay (1928) long ago disputed the point, Smith (1979) also saw the delay as resulting from the slow diffusion of knowledge about infant hygiene which reached poor families only with the development of the health visitor movement around 1900.

The problem with these explanations, however, is that they ignore the similarity between the mortality experience of those under 5 years and those over 45 years. Compared with the rest of the population, the fall in the mortality rates of both these age groups was delayed, and this suggests the possibility of a single factor which can account for both the similarity between these groups and their delay when compared with the rest of the population. This possibility will be explored by examining the way in which working-class living standards changed during the period 1870–1914.

The working class 1870–1914

The period under examination was preceded by two important pieces of legislation. In 1867 the franchise was extended to include the vast majority of male workers, so adding a parliamentary dimension to their struggles. Second, the Education Act, 1870, enforced primary education for all children, up to the age of 11, so finally removing most children from the labour market. The period itself has been characterized by Hobsbawm (1954) as involving two distinct phases in the development of capitalism. The first, which lasted from the early 1870s to the late 1890s was called at the time the 'Great Depression'. It coincided with the end of Britain's industrial supremacy in world markets, as the result of growing competition from particularly German and US capital. The second phase, lasting from the late 1890s to the start of the First World War, covered the years of the 'Edwardian Boom' and had as its economic basis changes which had been gathering pace during the Great Depression, most importantly the reorganization of industry on a larger scale and the development of protected colonial markets. In Marxist terms, therefore, the period 1870–1914 involved the transition from *laissez-faire* capitalism to monopoly capitalism and imperialism.

Various factors which are relevant to the standard of living of the working class were affected by this process. Prices fell during the Great Depression, and rose again during the Edwardian Boom. It is difficult to quantify these price movements precisely, not only because the various time-series which are available include different items, but also because the change in the price of particular commodities varied in both timing and extent (Mitchell and Deane 1962). Nevertheless, it is probably true to say that the overall index of wholesale prices fell by some 40 per cent during the Great Depression, and subsequently increased by 20 per cent during the Edwardian Boom. By excluding capital goods, and only counting those commodities which comprise the means of subsistence, it is possible to quantify changes in the cost of living. Phelps Brown and Browne's (1968) cost of living index for this period shows changes which are very similar to those described for all prices (that is a 40 per cent fall, followed by a 20 per cent rise), and the few available data based on the retail price of individual commodities also conform to this pattern (Mitchell and Deane 1962).

One would expect unemployment to have risen during the Great Depression, and fallen again during the Edwardian Boom. Unfortunately the available data on levels of unemployment during this period are so flawed as to be of little use for present purposes. National data were not collected until 1922; certain trade unions reported the proportion of their members who were unemployed, but these results fail to distinguish between those who had re-entered employment and those who had left their union because of continued unemployment; finally even this inadequate information is available only for the trade unions of skilled workers (Mitchell and Deane 1962). This last point is of particular importance, because, as has been found during the current recession (Stern 1979; Smee 1980), unemployment at such times is concentrated among the unskilled. The available data, then, are likely to underestimate greatly the levels of unemployment during the period 1870–1914 and are probably better at reflecting short-term trade fluctuations, of the type which would persuade a temporarily unemployed skilled worker to maintain trade union membership, than at measuring the lengthy disruption of employment involved in a major restructuring of production. Nevertheless, even these extremely unreliable data do show that unemployment was higher during the Great Depression than during the Edwardian Boom, although both periods contained good and bad years.

Hinton has documented the changes in production which occurred during the Great Depression (that is between 1873 and 1896) and summarized these as 'the growing predominance within the working class of regular industrial wage-earners, concentrated in substantial work units' (1983: 26). By 1900 the factory had replaced home working and small workship production in all industries. Manufacturing industry maintained its share of the work-force, at 40 per cent, with the relative decline of textiles and clothing being balanced by the rapid growth of metal working and food production. The proportion of the work-force engaged in agriculture fell from 15 to 7.5 per cent, while mining, transport, especially railways, and to a lesser extent chemicals grew rapidly. There was, thus, a tendency for regular, better-paid employment to replace casual low-paid work. Hinton argues that the growth of mines, transport, and factories 'swelled the intermediate strata of the working class, and these strata were the chief beneficiaries of the great price fall between 1873 and 1896' (1983: 27). He continues

> Poverty was endemic among the unemployed, casual and seasonal workers, or simply low-paid regular wage earners. ... The largest con-centrations of poverty were found where casual labour prevailed. ... The old suffered worst, and women and children. While a casual labourer might get sufficient food to maintain physical efficiency, his wife and children would go without.
>
> (1983: 29–30)

When industrial growth resumed during the Edwardian Boom, it did so on the basis which had been established during the Great Depression, and would have furthered the changes within the working class which Hinton has described.

Strata within the working class

Hobsbawm (1954) has characterized and attempted to quantify the various strata within the working class during this period. At the top was a 'labour aristocracy', comprising some 15 per cent of the class, whose defining characteristic was good and, of equal importance, regular wages. Beneath them were ordinary skilled men, better-paid labourers, and the growing body of semi-skilled workers; together these comprised some 45 per cent of the class. At the bottom were the unskilled, most of whom were living on or below the harshest poverty line, and some two-thirds of whom, mainly in old age, became paupers. Pay differentials provide a guide to the relative position of these strata. Knowles and Robertson (1951) have shown that the differential between skilled and unskilled workers widened somewhat up to 1880, but remained virtually unchanged from then until 1914, with the unskilled receiving some half to two-thirds of the skilled rate, depending upon the industry involved. The transfer of workers from the lowest to the intermediate stratum was therefore more important than any shift in the relative position of these strata.

Trade union membership increased rapidly during this period, from 4 per cent of the work-force in 1880 to 15 per cent in 1914 (Hinton 1983). Although strikes were, as always under capitalism, a constant feature of this period, two great strike waves stood out from the rest. These were referred to by contemporaries as the 'New Unionism' and the 'Great Unrest', and to some extent they involved different strata of the working class. The former primarily involved unskilled workers, occurred 1889–91, and was greatly influenced by Marxists (Hunt 1981). What was 'new' about the New Unionism was not only the unionization of the unskilled, but also its industrial militancy and socialist politics, both of which profoundly influenced the labour movement (Murphy 1934). The Great Unrest, in contrast, primarily involved the intermediate stratum, took place in 1908–14, and was often led by syndicalists. It was temporarily brought to an end by the start of the First World War (Holton 1976).

As would be expected these two strike waves affected the level of wages. Phelps Brown and Browne (1968) have charted the change in money wages during this period. Wages fell at the start of the Great Depression, and remained at this low level until 1890, when, coincident with the New Unionism, they were more than restored to their earlier level. They then remained at this new level until they rose again in the late 1890s, at the start of the Edwardian Boom. Subsequently they fell slightly, but rose once more at the time of the Great Unrest.

Real wages

From the point of view of living standards, however, real wages are of greater importance than money wages; that is money wages have to be seen in relation to prices. As was noted earlier, prices fell steadily during the Great Depression, and rose during the Edwardian Boom. Phelps Brown and Browne (1968) produced an index of real wages by calculating the net effect of changes in money wages and prices. Although they drew attention to its weaknesses as a measure of living standards the index showed that real wages increased by 66 per cent between 1870 and 1900, and this figure is broadly in line with the much earlier estimates of Bowley (1900) and Wood (1909). Interestingly Wood tried to separate the effects of rising money wages and falling prices from those of the shift in the nature of production which was described earlier. He estimated that some 60 per cent of the rise in real wages was due to the combination of rising money wages and falling prices, while the remaining 40 per cent of the rise in real wages was due to the 'shifting up of industrial employment', particularly the transfer of labour from agriculture and textiles to the engineering, mining, and building industries.

The indices of Bowley and Phelps Brown and Browne also cover the years of the Edwardian Boom. They are in broad agreement, and both indicate that real wages were virtually unchanged or, more accurately, fell slightly during the period 1900–14. However, as Hunt (1981) has pointed out, this average disguised a much larger fall in the real wages of workers in some industries in some years. Of the industries he mentions as being particularly affected, some such as railways and coal-mining were also at the forefront of the Great Unrest. This suggests that, just as the New Unionism can be seen as the unskilled's attempt to share the rising living standards of the Great Depression, so the Great Unrest appears to be the effort of the intermediate stratum to maintain this standard of living during the Edwardian Boom.

It would be wrong, however, to assume that the rising real wages of the Great Depression were transferred *in toto* to the increased purchase of commodities. Phelps Brown and Browne note that the 'pressure for shorter hours had itself been both permitted and instigated by the rise in real rates of pay, and the same effect was seen in a reduction of effort by pieceworkers who did not need to produce so much as before in order to obtain a given real weekly wage' (1968: 185). They also note that absenteeism increased, and partly explain this by the exhaustion of 12-hour shifts. It seems, therefore, that workers 'spent' some of the rising real wages of the Great Depression on a less physically punishing work regime, and on more rest when they deemed it necessary.

An individual's standard of living, in addition, depends upon the number of financially dependent individuals per household as well as on the level of real wages. It seems likely that the number of such individuals was growing during the period 1870–1914, as the result of women and children leaving the labour-market. The effect of the Education Act, 1870, in this respect has already been mentioned, although as Hobsbawn (1954) has pointed out, children still provided 5 per cent of the total occupied population in 1881. This increase in child dependants, however, was to some extent counterbalanced by a fall in the birth-rate, by more than one-third between 1870 and 1914 (OPCS 1974).

Married women were also leaving paid employment during this period. Unfortunately the nineteenth-century data are far from complete; nevertheless the 1851 census found that one-quarter of all wives were in paid employment, while the comparable figure in 1911 was 10 per cent (Hakim 1985). The economic activity rate of unmarried women seems to have remained relatively unchanged. To some extent, however, the downwards effect on household incomes of married women's progressive exclusion from the work-force was offset by a change in the nature of the employment of those still in work. Hobsbawm (1954) has described how this involved a shift from poorly paid domestic industries, such as lace- and ribbon-making, to better-paid industrial production, often in the new food industries. It seems reasonable to conclude, then, that the number of financial dependants per household increased between 1870 and 1914, but that this tendency was restricted by countervailing factors, such as the falling birth-rate, the continuation of child labour, and the improved chances of married women finding better-paid work.

It is now possible to consider directly the changes in working-class living standards which took place between 1870 and 1914. Real wages rose by some two-thirds between 1870 and 1900, and were subsequently static up to 1914, but one cannot assume that individual per capita consumption rose by an equivalent amount because some of the rising real wages were 'spent' at work, in the form of shorter hours, and because each real wage was almost certainly having to support an increased number of household dependants. Similarly Phelps Brown and Browne caution against a simple equation of real wages with living standards, on the grounds that the former ignores

> the hours of work, the physical and social conditions of the work place, the quality of housing, the means of meeting misfortunes such as sickness and unemployment, the prevailing level of health, the squalor and the amenities of the towns; as well as the number of dependants in the household
>
> (1968: 157)

all of which are relevant to the standard of living. Some of these (hours of work and household dependants) have already been considered. While one would expect that some of the remaining items, such as urban amenities and work-place conditions, would have depended more upon workers' collective political power than upon their individual purchasing power, it seems reasonable to think that others, such as improved housing and Friendly Society insurance against sickness and unemployment, would have further diverted rising real wages away from direct consumption. The question of the extent of changes in workers' nutrition, therefore, needs to be considered further.

The dietary surveys which were undertaken at the end of the nineteenth century, that is at the end of the rise in real wages, provide a solid basis from which to examine this issue. Rowntree (1901), for example, collected the weekly family budgets of eighteen families drawn from 'the steady, respectable section of the labouring classes', which in practice meant excluding families which regularly consumed beer and spirits. Among families earning 26 shillings (£1.30) or less per week he found that in every case the diet was inadequate, specifically being on average 17 per cent below standard in terms of calories and 29 per cent below standard in terms of protein. Even the remaining working-class families, that is those earning above 26 shillings per week, were on average 10 per cent below standard on protein, although their calorie intake was more or less adequate. Bowley's

(1900) data on wage rates at the end of the nineteenth century reveal that most agricultural labourers, seamen, and wool-spinners were earning less than 26 shillings per week at this time, as were a significant proportion of cotton-spinners and weavers and engineering workers. Rowntree's findings, then, suggest that malnutrition was endemic among the lower-paid sections of the working class. This conclusion becomes even firmer when those families which regularly consumed alcohol are included. Dingle (1972) has suggested that at least 50 per cent of families behaved in this way, making it normal and customary behaviour. Dingle further reports average expenditure per head per year on alcoholic drinks as being 4 pounds (£4) in 1899. Concentrated into the 50 per cent of families which actually drank, this amounts to 3 shillings (15p) per week, which would raise Rowntree's malnutrition line for those who 'drank' from 26 to 29 shillings (from £1.30 to £1.45) per week. At this level, and again using Bowley's data, the earlier identified workers would be joined by some compositors, the remaining cotton-weavers, and more cotton-spinners and engineering workers.

Oddy (1970) has compared Rowntree's findings with those of the five other similar studies which were undertaken during the final decade of the nineteenth century. The six studies, which involved a combined total of 151 families, were found to have produced remarkably consistent results. These suggest that 30 shillings (£1.50) per week was a better guide to the level of wages necessary to support adequate family nutrition, and at this level malnutrition would have been common among all casual workers and all lower grades of unskilled workers, as well as most other unskilled workers in regular employment.

In 1900, then, malnutrition would seem to have been common among the unskilled, to have been lapping at the door of the new intermediate stratum of the working class, and to have been safely absent only in the case of skilled workers. Using Hobsbawm's estimates, which were detailed earlier, this suggests that malnutrition would have been common among 40 per cent of the working class. This figure compares well with Rowntree's and Booth's estimates that 30 per cent of the total population was living in poverty, and it is identical with the reject rate among volunteers to the Boer War.

Burnett (1966) and Oddy (1970) have reviewed the dietary evidence which is available for the remainder of the period 1870–1914, and have found that it is, unfortunately, not of the same quality as that which has already been examined. Smith's study (quoted in Burnett 1966) in the early 1860s, for example, although based upon several hundred family budgets, was limited to agricultural labourers and the lowest-paid industrial workers. Its results do provide a reliable comparison with the studies done around 1900, but the comparison is limited to the lowest-paid workers. The two other relevant studies, that of 1881 and Flux's of 1909–13, were based upon details of national food production, which were simply divided by the total population size to give estimates of average individual food consumption. The results of these two studies, then, are based on a measure of individual food consumption which is less valid than the use of family budgets and, being expressed as national averages of food consumption, tell us nothing about how food consumption varied between the different social classes. However, as these three studies provide the only information which is available, their results need to be briefly examined.

Some idea of the changes in the diet of low-paid workers between 1862 and 1900 can be obtained by comparing Smith's results with those for the appropriate income group in the 1900 studies. This comparison shows that while the consumption of bread and potatoes fell, that of sugar increased; the consumption of meat also increased, although the extent of this increase was probably underestimated because of the progressive substitution of fresh meat for fatty bacon. These seemingly modest changes nevertheless suggest that the diet of low-paid workers became less carbohydrate-dependent and less protein-deficient during the years of the Great Depression.

This impression is supported by the results of the 1881 study which found that similar changes were taking place in the diet of the nation as a whole. Vegetables other than potatoes, eggs, fruit, and coffee also appear in the 1881 study which suggests an increasingly varied diet, at least for some groups within the population.

The results of Flux's study in the years immediately preceding the First World War suggest that these changes continued into the Edwardian Boom. The consumption of bread continued to fall, compared with 1900, while that of sugar increased; meat consumption also increased, as did the tendency towards a more varied diet.

Finally, MacKenzie's study (1921) must be mentioned. She attempted to assess the calorific adequacy of the diets of the different strata of the population in 1860, 1880, and 1914. Unfortunately the assumptions and 'guestimates', which she had to make as the basis of her calculations, place a question mark against her precise results. What is striking about these results, however, is the relatively minor improvements which they reveal. For example she calculated that the calorie intake of the top unskilled workers, who formed her median group in 1860 and her lower quartile group in 1914, increased by a mere 9 per cent between these dates. Her comparable figures for ordinary semi-skilled workers and for the bottom layer of unskilled workers are similarly below 10 per cent.

When the results of these dietary studies are placed together, they suggest the following picture of working-class nutrition between the years 1870 and 1914. At the end of the nineteenth century some 40 per cent of the working class was malnourished, with the protein deficiency being more serious than the deficiency in total calorie intake; although they were not measured, one can probably add that these diets were also vitamin deficient. Three decades earlier the proportion of the working class which was malnourished was almost certainly greater than 40 per cent and, although one cannot say by precisely how much, figures of over 50 per cent seem plausible. In addition the protein deficiency was probably more widespread. The increase in meat consumption during the intervening thirty years, however, suggests that protein deficiency fell faster during this period than the deficiency in total calorie intake, and it is therefore possible that the severity of the malnutrition may have changed more than its extent. Whether these changes were continued into the years 1900–14 is uncertain; on balance it seems probable that there was a small fall in both the extent and the severity of the malnutrition.

This picture reinforces the earlier caution against any direct equation of rising real wages with increased nutrition. The proportion of the increased real wage which was spent on nutrition bought a more varied diet rather than a larger amount of the same foods. The relatively small increase in total calorie intake between 1870 and 1914 is comprehensible in terms of the demand for calories being determined by immediate physical needs. In a sense, if calorie needs are consistently unmet, then workers would be unable to continue working; one would therefore not expect calorie intake to change greatly, and indeed it could safely fall to the extent that work is mechanized and heavy physical labour eliminated. The longer-term integrity of the body, in contrast, depends upon specific constituents, such as protein and vitamins, and these were increasingly present in the more varied diet which workers purchased out of their rising real wages.

This rough sketch of the experience of the working class during the period 1870–1914 has included the factors thought relevant to its standard of living. Although these issues have been considered separately, they are obviously interrelated. One cannot, for example, examine changes in the standard of living without also examining changes in the family structure, and this in turn, involves changes in unemployment and the organization of production. This point will be developed in the next section, which returns to the issue of the relationship between the standard of living and health.

The McKeown thesis re-examined

It is first necessary to attempt to justify this section's comparison of national mortality data, which are based on the whole population, with changes in working-class living standards, which refer to only part of the population. To some extent this involves assuming that upper- and middle-class mortality is affected by the same factors as working-class mortality, but the justification depends mainly on the fact that the working class contributed most to the total population's mortality. From Hobsbawm (1968: 139) it is possible to calculate that something like three-quarters of the population in the period 1870–1914 belonged to the working class, with the proportion falling between these dates from 77 per cent to around 70 per cent. When the working class's considerably higher mortality rates are also taken into account, it seems reasonable to assume that their contribution to the national mortality total was in the region of 80 to 85 per cent. It is hoped, therefore, that having ignored non-working-class living standards will prove to be of little significance.

In what follows the standard of living has been equated with real wages, which have the advantage of being approximately quantifiable, as well as allowing one to sidestep the issue of whether nutrition, the hours of work, or some other factor is of greatest importance. We have seen that real wages rose by some two-thirds during the Great Depression, and were static, or fell slightly, during the Edwardian Boom. Several modifying factors were identified, such as an increase in the number of household dependants and the shift of women workers away from low-paid domestic production, but it seems likely that these largely cancelled each other out, and resulted in no great net effect. It remains the case, therefore, that real wages rose substantially between 1870 and 1900, and were subsequently unchanged from 1900 to 1914.

A comparison of this change in real wages with the change in mortality rates reveals both agreements and disagreements with McKeown's thesis. Falling mortality rates were only accompanied by rising living standards in the case of the 5–45 age groups between the years 1870 and 1900. In contrast, unchanged mortality rates for the under-5s and the over-45s accompanied rising living standards between 1870 and 1900, and the mortality rates of all age groups fell from 1900 to 1914 when living standards were unchanged. In defence of the thesis, it can be argued that by holding for the 5–45 age groups between 1870 and 1900 it in fact proved an accurate guide for most of the population for most of the period being examined. Nevertheless, the departures from the thesis deserve further consideration.

It is, of course, possible that these discrepancies can be accounted for by factors which McKeown regarded as being of secondary importance. This, however, is unlikely to be the case. There is no reason for believing that the under-5s and over-45s were differentially excluded from the benefits of the sanitary reforms before 1900, and, in any case, the fall in mortality at all ages after 1900 primarily involved diseases which are spread through the air. Similarly medical measures remained largely ineffective throughout the whole period 1870–1914, and although Newsholme (1906) was optimistic about the effect of isolation on TB mortality, the practice was not widespread before 1911. It would seem, therefore, that if these discrepancies are to be reconciled with McKeown's thesis, it will have to be in terms of changes in the living standard of particular fractions of the population. One way of doing this involves taking account of the business cycle and changes in the labour market, and their differential impact on the various strata within the working class.

Unemployment figures before 1922 were earlier judged to be almost totally inadequate as a guide to anything but short-term changes in employment levels. In the absence of reliable data one is forced to assume that past business cycles affected the labour market in ways which are similar to today (Daniel and Stilgoe 1979; Moylan, Miller, and Davies 1984; Walker, Noble, and Westergaard 1985). If this assumption is granted, it follows that unemployment during the Great Depression was considerably higher than during the Edwardian Boom, that this unemployment was concentrated among the older workers and the unskilled sections of the working class, and that the rising real wages of the period mainly benefited the younger and healthier members of the skilled and intermediate strata of the class.

If this were the case, the national mortality rates of the Great Depression would contain conflicting tendencies, and whether they fell or remained static for any particular age group would depend upon the relative balance within that age group of those with access to, and those excluded from, the rising real wages of the period. With the return of economic growth during the Edwardian Boom, older workers and the unskilled would have been differentially reintegrated into the work-force, and although real wages were now static, a greater proportion of the population would have benefited from them.

Seen from this point of view, the apparent inconsistency among the 5–45 age groups, of static real wages combined with falling mortality between 1900 and 1914, becomes comprehensible in terms of the improved access of the unskilled during this period to higher, though now static, real wages, and hence an improved standard of living. One would therefore expect the mortality rate of these age groups to continue to fall because the standard of living of a significant proportion of unskilled workers in this age group continued to improve. The pattern of mortality of the over-45s becomes similarly comprehensible. Differentially excluded from the rising real wages of the Great Depression, their mortality rate remained unchanged; increasingly reintegrated into the work-force after 1900, their mortality rate fell because their standard of living increased.

The discrepancy of infant and early childhood mortality presents greater problems, and involves recognizing both the greater vulnerability of humans at these ages, and the enormously disproportionate contribution which is made to total mortality at these ages by the infants and young children of the unskilled. Seen in this way, the static mortality rates from birth to 5 years during the Great Depression were the net result of falling rates among families with access to the rising real wages, and rising rates among families, particularly the unskilled, who were denied such access. When the unskilled rejoined the work-force after 1900, the standard of living of their families improved, the mortality rate of their infants and young children fell into line with that of families who were employed during the Great Depression, and, relieved of this conflicting tendency, the national mortality rates at these ages started to fall rapidly.

In summary, then, the relationship between standard of living and health for most of the population for most of the period 1870–1914 straightforwardly follows the line predicted by McKeown's thesis. Three inconsistencies, however, can be identified, and it was argued that, in the main, these could not be accounted for by factors which McKeown regarded as being of secondary importance. Instead it was suggested that these discrepancies could be reconciled with McKeown's thesis by setting them in their economic context and seeing the ways in which the availability of employment affects the standard of living of different strata within the working class.

The value of labour-power re-examined

To recapitulate, the value of labour-power equals the value of those commodities which are necessary for the worker's existence, and these were analysed by Marx in terms of the three components of subsistence costs, reproduction costs, and training costs.

We have seen that the value of labour-power, in the quantifiable form of real wages, increased between 1870 and 1900. It is unlikely that this can be primarily accounted for by an increase in either training costs or reproduction costs. Reproduction costs, for example, may have been affected by the fall in the birth-rate, but the increased length of financial dependency after the Education Act, 1870, would have had a countervailing effect. Similarly the main change in the labour market, the shift of unskilled workers into the intermediate stratum of the working class, involved little extra training costs. Within the framework of Marx's analysis, therefore, this increase in the value of labour-power must be due mainly to an increase in 'the historical and moral element in the cost of subsistence'.

However, as we have also seen, Marx was arguing, a mere five years before the start of our period, that there was little chance of permanently enlarging this historical and moral element by any great extent. The rise in real wages during the Great Depression, and their maintenance during the Edwardian Boom, show that he was therefore wrong in this respect.

Marx's over-pessimistic conclusion was based on his observation that the balance of power in the economic sphere lay with the capitalists, because they always had the option of replacing workers with machines. With the advantage of hindsight, it is possible to see that, while this may be true for the workers directly affected, it does not necessarily follow for the class as a whole. In particular, the new machines still need workers, and the scale of investment involved usually means that they are brought together in large numbers. The industrial basis of workers' collective existence and organization therefore continues.

Events during the period 1870–1914 fit better with this alternative conclusion. Living standards rose between 1870 and 1900 primarily as the result of money wages failing to fall in line with the price of other commodities. At the same time, changes in the sphere of production actually increased the workers' industrial power. For example factory production increasingly replaced production in the home and small workshop; the new industries, such as the railways, were large scale and labour intensive; the intermediate stratum within the working class grew at the expense of casual, unskilled work. Such changes meant that a growing proportion of the working class was in steady employment alongside large numbers of other workers. This situation encourages the development of a collective consciousness, and, in time, makes trade union organization possible. Changes in the sphere of production therefore made it increasingly possible for workers to prevent a fall in money wages.

The rising organic composition of capital (that is its in-built tendency towards large-scale, mechanical production) can be seen as responsible for both these developments. On the one hand, via the concentration and centralization of capital, it created the industrial conditions which foster workers' collective resistance. On the other hand, via increased productivity in, amongst others, the consumption goods sector, it cut the cost of the workers' means of subsistence. It was not a coincidence, therefore, that the cost of living fell at the same time as workers' ability to resist wage cuts increased. The net result was a steady increase in living standards throughout the Great Depression. The steady cumulative nature of the increase in living standards further supports this analysis, because it suggests an underlying tendency, which would have affected different industries and different localities at various times over decades rather than a specific event such as the New Unionism.

This analysis is also consistent with both the mortality data and the little which Marx did say about the historical and moral element. The growth of large-scale production meant, for those in work at least, the chance to resist wage cuts during the Great Depression, and, with the New Unionism, even to increase money wages at this time of falling prices. The standard of living of those in work therefore increased.

This process established levels of living standards which were, in time, generally accepted as appropriate to the various strata within the working class. When the work-force expanded during the Edwardian Boom, the new workers were taken on at these levels of real wages. Real wages increased no further; in fact workers were hard pressed to increase money wages in line with rising prices. These levels of real wages, however, became available to a greater proportion of the population, and, for the individuals involved, the increase in their standard of living must have been marked.

The conclusion of this analysis is that Marx underestimated the effect on the working class of the rising organic composition of capital, in particular the way in which large-scale production would affect the balance of class power in the economic sphere. Marx did not have the opportunity to develop his analysis in the light of these changes, but this task remained a central concern of both the syndicalists (Holton 1976) and the Third International (Trotsky 1972).

Acknowledgements

I should like to thank M. Bartley, G. Betts, A. MacFarlane, and J. Ure for their comments on an earlier draft. I am also grateful to L. Jagger and S. Jefferys for giving me important references.

References

Barrett, M. and McIntosh, M. (1980) 'The "Family Wage": some problems for socialists and feminists', *Capital and Class* 11: summer.

Bartley, M. (1985) 'Coronary heart disease and the public health 1850–1983', *Sociology of Health and Illness* 7, 3: 289–313.

Beechey, V. (1978) 'Women and production', in A. Kuhn and A. Wolfe (eds) *Feminism and Materialism*, London: Routledge & Kegan Paul.

Bowley, A. L. (1900) *Wages in the United Kingdom in the Nineteenth Century*, Cambridge: Cambridge University Press.

Burnett, J. (1966) *Plenty and Want*, London: Scolar Press.

Chadwick, E. (1965) *The Sanitary Condition of the Labouring Population of Great Britain: Report 1842*, Edinburgh: Edinburgh University Press.

Chandra, R. K. (1980) *Immunology of Nutritional Disorders*, London: Edward Arnold.

Daniel, W. W. and Stilgoe, E. (1979) 'Where are they now?' *Political and Economic Planning*, London.

Davidson, S., Passmore, R., Brock, J. F., and Truswell, A. S. (1979) *Human Nutrition and Dietetics*, Edinburgh: Churchill Livingstone.

De Brunhoff, S. (1978) *The State, Capital and Economic Policy*, London: Pluto Press.

Dingle, A. E. (1972) 'Drink and working-class living standards in Britain 1870–1914', *Economic History Review* 25: 608–22.

Doyal, L. with Pennell, I. (1979) *The Political Economy of Health*, London: Pluto.

Engels, F. (1845) *The Condition of the Working Class in England*, London: Granada (1969 edn).

Farr, W. (1843) *5th Annual Report of the Registrar-General*, *Parliamentary Papers* xxi: 202–3, 210.

Figlio, K. (1978) 'Chlorosis and chronic disease in nineteenth-century Britain', *International Journal of Health Services* 8: 589–617.

Gardiner, J. (1975) 'Women's domestic labour', *New Left Review* 89: 47–58.

Glass, D. V. (1959) 'A note on the under-registration of births in the nineteenth century', *Population Studies* 5: 70–85.

Hakim, C. (1985) 'Social monitors: population censuses as social surveys', in M. Bulmer (ed.) *Essays on the History of British Sociological Research*, Cambridge: Cambridge University Press.

Hewitt, M. (1958) *Wives and Mothers in Victorian Industry*, London: Rockliff.

Hinton, J. (1983) *Labour and Socialism*, Brighton: Harvester.

Hobsbawm, E. J. (1954) 'The Labour aristocracy in 19th century Britain', in J. Saville (ed.) *Democracy and the Labour Movement*, London: Macmillan.

—— (1968) *Industry and Empire*, Harmondsworth: Penguin.

Holton, B. (1976) *British Syndicalism 1900–1914*, London: Pluto Press.

Hunt, E. H. (1981) *British Labour History 1815–1914*, London: Weidenfeld & Nicolson.

Knowles, G. L. and Robertson, D. J. (1951) 'Differences between the wages of skilled and unskilled workers 1880–1950', *Bulletin of the Oxford University Institute of Statistics* April: 109–23.

Land, H. (1976) 'Women: supporters or supported?' in D. L. Barker and S. Allen (eds) *Sexual Divisions and Society*, London: Tavistock.

—— (1979) 'The boundaries between the state and the family', in C. Harris (ed.) *The Sociology of the Family*, Monograph 28, University of Keele.

McIntosh, M. (1979) 'The welfare state and the needs of the dependent family', in S. Burman (ed.) *Fit Work for Women*, London: Croom Helm.

MacKenzie, W. A. (1921) 'Changes in the standard of living in the United Kingdom 1860–1914', *Economica* 1, 3: 211–30.

McKeown, T. (1976) *The Modern Rise of Population*, London: Edward Arnold.

—— (1979) *The Role of Medicine*, Oxford: Blackwell.

McKeown, T. and Lowe, C. R. (1966) *An Introduction to Social Medicine*, Oxford: Blackwell.

McKinlay, P. L. (1928) 'The decline in infant mortality', *Journal of Hygiene* 27: 424–37.

Marx, K. (1849) 'Wage labour and capital', in *Marx and Engels Selected Works* London: Lawrence & Wishart (1968 edn).

—— (1865) 'Wages, price and profit', in *Marx and Engels Selected Works* London: Lawrence & Wishart (1968 edn).

—— (1867) *Capital; Volume I* Moscow (1965 edn).

Mitchell, B. R. and Deane, P. (1962) *Abstract of British Historical Statistics*, Cambridge: Cambridge University Press.

Moylan, S., Miller, S., and Davies, R. (1984) *For Richer, for Poorer*, DHSS Cohort Study of Unemployed Men, London: HMSO.

Murphy, J. T. (1934) *Preparing for Power*, London: Pluto Press.

Navarro, V. (1978) *The State, Medicine and the Class Struggle*, London: Martin Robertson.

Newsholme, A. (1906) 'An inquiry into the principal causes of the reduction in the death-rate from phthisis during the last 40 years', *Journal of Hygiene* 6, 3: 304–84.

Oddy, D. J. (1970) 'Working-class diets in late-nineteenth-century Britain', *Economic History Review* 23: 314–22.

—— (1982) 'The health of the people', in T. Barker and M. Drake (eds) *Population and Society in Britain 1850–1980*, London: Batsford.

OPCS (Office of Population Censuses and Surveys) (1974) *Birth Statistics (England and Wales)*, Series FMI no. 1, London: HMSO.

—— (1985) *Mortality Statistics 1841–1980*, Serial Tables: Series DH1 no. 15, London: HMSO.

Phelps Brown, E. H. and Browne, M. H. (1968) *A Century of Pay*, New York: St Martin's Press.

Prior, L. (1985) 'The social construction of mortality statistics', *Sociology of Health and Illness* 7: 2.

Registrar General's Statistical Review of England and Wales (1921) No. 1, London: HMSO.

Robson, J. (1972) 'Take a pill', *Medicine in Society*.

—— (1977) 'Quality, inequality and health care', *Medicine in Society*.

Rowntree, B. S. (1901) *Poverty*, London.

Smee, C. H. (1980) 'Unemployment and poverty', presented at SSRC Workshop, Department of Employment, London, 6 June.

Smith, F. B. (1979) *The People's Health 1830–1910*, London: Croom Helm.

Stern, J. (1979) 'Who bears the burden of unemployment?', in W. Beckerman (ed.) *Slow Growth in Britain*, Oxford: Clarendon Press.

Stevenson, T. H. C. (1923) 'The social distribution of mortality from different causes in England and Wales 1910–1912', *Biometrika*, xv: 382–400

Tatham, J. (1904) 'English mortality in infants under one year of age', in *Report of the Inter-Departmental Committee on Physical Deterioration*, vol. I, Cmnd 2175, London: HMSO.

Trotsky, L. (1972) *The First Five Years of The Communist International*, New York: Monad Press.

Tudor Hart, J. (1971) 'The inverse care law', *Lancet* 1: 405–12.

Walker, A., Noble, I., and Westergaard, J. (1985) 'From secure employment to labour market insecurity', in B. Roberts, R. Finnegan, and G. Gallie (eds) *New Approaches to Economic Life*, Manchester: Manchester University Press; New York: Pathfinder Press (1972 edn).

Wood, G. H. (1909) 'Real wages and the standard of comfort since 1850', *Journal of Royal Statistical Society* 72: 91–103.

Woods, R. and Woodward, J. (eds) (1984) *Urban Disease and Mortality in Nineteenth-Century England*, London: Croom Helm.

2

Durkheim and social realism: an approach to health and illness

STEVE TAYLOR WITH CLIVE ASHWORTH

Introduction

None of the classical sociologists has been subject to more misrepresentation than Emile Durkheim and it is only relatively recently that a more carefully considered view of his work has begun to emerge in English-speaking sociology (Hynes 1975; Lukes 1973). In attempting to examine the relevance of Durkheim's work for the sociology of health and illness the first task, therefore, is to cut through some of the mythological accounts of Durkheim's work in order to establish how he viewed sociology.

Second, we shall compare Durkheim's sociology with the theoretical approaches currently dominant in medical sociology, offer some suggestions as to how Durkheim might have studied the relation between society and disease, and look at some work that we feel is closest to the Durkheimian tradition.

Third, we shall outline some of the tensions and contradictions inherent in Durkheim's sociology and examine the extent to which the main theoretical perspectives influential in medical sociology represent an 'advance' on Durkheim's ideas. It is important to emphasize that this essay offers what we believe to be a *Durkheimian* analysis of the sociology of health and illness, and should not be taken to imply that the authors necessarily concur with that view.

Durkheimian sociology

Judging by courses in sociology and general and theoretical texts on the subject, Durkheim would still appear to be one of the most influential figures in sociology. However, on closer inspection, this is misleading. Whether one looks at theoretical debates or empirical research in sociology, it is hard to identify much commitment to a 'Durkheimian' position. In the theoretical and general texts analysis is essentially historical (Giddens 1971; Thompson 1982). Scholars either look (admiringly) at Durkheim's contribution to the formation of the discipline and key areas within it (Fenton, Reiner, and Hamnett 1984), or (disparagingly) at his responsibility for a form of sociology (functionalism for example) to which the critic is opposed (Cuff *et al*. 1984).

In empirical research – especially into suicide, crime, law, and religion and, to a certain extent, health and illness – there are references to Durkheim, the use of concepts such as egoism and anomie and even claims to be developing or 'testing' Durkheim's ideas (Breault 1986). However, as we shall try to show later in the essay, not only are these students not following Durkheim, but they are also undertaking research in a manner to which he would be directly opposed. Thus, in short, while there are many who write about Durkheim, or cite his work in research projects, there are few 'Durkheimians' in the sense that there are 'Marxists' or 'Weberians' or even, since the rise of ethnomethodology, 'Shultzians'.

It is our view that this sense of having 'seen through' or 'progressed beyond' the kinds of issues with which Durkheim was concerned comes, at least in part, from a fundamental misunderstanding of his sociology. In fact so commonly misunderstood has Durkheim's work been that there have arisen around it a series of mythologies which have become a hardened part of the accepted wisdom of sociology. The conventional, textbook view of Durkheim is that he was the founding father of a positivist, functionalist, and determinist sociology (Bilton *et al*. 1972; Cuff *et al*. 1984), an interpretation of Durkheim that has filtered down to medical sociology (Atkinson 1978; J. Clarke 1981).

Let us take each element of this description in turn. First, was Durkheim a positivist? The term positivism has a long and varied history and is often used loosely (Giddens 1977). However, it may be properly defined as a philosophical position embodying an ontology grounded in a nominalist materialism; an epistemology holding that the only certain knowledge we can obtain comes either from the induction of nominalist theoretical constructs, or from the testing of deductions against experience; a variety of methodologies based on a belief in the unity of scientific practice, and a conviction that facts and values are not derivable from each other.

While a great deal of sociological research, including a body of research in medical sociology, makes precisely these assumptions, in important respects Durkheim's work was opposed to most, if not all of them. For Durkheim a social fact was not nominal; it was holistic, not given in experience but none the less real. Thus Durkheim sought to explain the relationship between suicide rates and rates of external association in terms of another order of facts – suicidogenic currents –

which stemmed from the forces of collective social life. The imbalance of egoism, altruism, anomie, and fatalism could not be perceived by sensory perception, but had to be penetrated by special (that is Durkheimian) methods. It should also have struck the many writers who label Durkheim as a positivist as curious that we do not find in Durkheim's works either the fact–value dichotomy, or the distinction between theoretical and observational categories that characterize positivist works. Whereas we do find Durkheim concerned with the explanation of the 'interior' world of ideas and meanings (Johnson, Dandeker, and Ashworth 1984).

Second, it is similarly misleading to equate Durkheim's use of structures with that of Parsonian functionalism (Parsons 1961). Whereas functionalists sought to explain relationships between observable parts of a social system, Durkheim was concerned with structures that lie behind observable phenomena. As we shall try to show later in relation to the specific context of health and illness, Durkheim's sociology has far more in common with a realist structuralism than with a nominalist functionalism. Durkheimian sociology sets out to show that societies are *really* something more than the sum of their apparent parts, while the positivist functionalists, apparently following in his 'tradition', reject such a notion and confine themselves to relationships between observable parts of society (Cresswell 1972).

Third, just as Durkheim's desire to make sociology scientific is interpreted as positivism, so his concern to establish the boundaries of social reality is seen as crude social determinism, where the individual becomes 'dissolved' into the group. In fact, contrary to a great deal of modern sociology, Durkheim's work *retains* the individual and specifically explores the relationship between the individual and society, which he conceived of as one of fluctuation and tension.

We shall develop these ideas in more detail, and in a more specific context, later in the essay when we apply a 'Durkheimian' critique to the positivist tradition in medical sociology. But, if Durkheim was not the founder of positivist sociology as we have argued above, then why should he be of interest to sociologists in general and medical sociologists in particular? Our short answer to that would be that in Durkheim's work we get a clearer articulation of the problem of whether or not there can be a science of society than we do with any of the other 'classical' sociologists. What characterized Durkheimian sociology, and distinguished it from attempts to ground the discipline in empiricism or German idealism, was the insistence that sociology would make no progress without the recognition that society was an irreducible reality in itself. Durkheim warned that those who doubt this and try to build explanations on the shifting sands of passing empirical associations, or individual consciousness, are in fact 'robbing sociology of the only object proper to it' (Durkheim 1952). In this context it is significant that with the intellectual collapse of the positivist and subjectivist paradigms, at least at the philosophical and theoretical level of sociological debate, theorists are returning to the 'Durkheimian' question of establishing the reality of the subject matter of sociology (Keat and Urry 1975; Bhaskar 1979).

For Durkheim, the reality of society – the subject matter of sociology – lay in a collective consciousness, a group mind, which existed both within individuals and yet which was also 'external' to them and influenced and constrained their activities. The nature of this social reality is not 'given' to us merely by membership of society; nevertheless, by its effects, its existence must be demonstrated empirically. This was the problem Durkheim set for himself in his empirical work, and this was the problem he clearly thought he had overcome in his major works on suicide (1952) and religion (1965).

Theory in medical sociology

Although there is relatively little explicit theoretical discussion in medical sociology, Johnson, Dandeker, and Ashworth (1984: 5) have observed that 'theorising enters into *any* sociological analysis', for the act of research necessarily involves making certain questionable assumptions about the nature of social reality and how it becomes intelligible to us. Medical sociologists do not avoid theorizing simply by claiming to reject it on the grounds that they are researchers concerned only with the real, or empirical, world. The theoretical assumptions that are made (explicitly or implicitly) structure the scope and nature of research, including what are considered as appropriate data and how those data are interpreted.

Most research in medical sociology implicitly adopts a *nominalist* view of social reality, and within this general frame of reference we can distinguish between what are usually considered to be the two dominant paradigms of medical sociology (Freidson 1983; Gerhardt 1985). First, there is a medical sociology grounded in positivism and empiricism, much of which tends to focus its attention on the influence of 'social' variables on the origins of disease. Second, there is a medical sociology loosely in the tradition of Dilthey and Rickert, which stresses the fundamental distinction between the study of the natural and the cultural world, and which employs essentially 'interpretive' methodologies of one sort or another to try to understand varying conceptions and experiences of illness. Thus for Dilthey, 'Nature, the subject matter of the physical sciences, embraces the reality which has arisen independently of the activity of the mind. Everything on which man has actively impressed his stamp forms the subject-matter of the human studies' (1976: 192).

Similarly in the context of medical sociology, Freidson (1970) makes a significant distinction between the biophysical phenomenon of disease and the social phenomenon of illness. While disease belongs to the world of objective sciences of the body and occurs independently of human evaluation, the various ways in which social groups respond to it and experience it are the legitimate concerns of sociological analysis. Thus research in this interpretative perspective tends to focus on the application of illness labels, and the (often stigmatizing) impact of these on individuals' identity and status (Scott 1969; Locker 1983; Scambler 1984).

While some medical sociologists work exclusively in one or other of these perspectives, either explicitly or implicitly seeing it as the 'legitimate' one, others either advocate a more eclectic approach, on the lines that both have their own value in explaining different problems (J. Clarke 1981; Freidson 1983; Morgan, Calnan, and Manning 1985), or look towards some sort of integration or synthesis (Gerhardt 1985).

In this context Durkheim would not see theoretical 'progress' coming from either some kind of 'accommodation' or 'synthesis' between the positivist and subjectivist approaches. In important respects, as we have already suggested, his sociology must be distinguished from both of them. As Durkheim's opposition to interpretative sociology is better known, we shall deal with that first. However, it is important to emphasize at this stage that, just as Durkheim was not as close to positivism as most commentators claim, he was also not as *far* removed from some of the concerns of interpretative sociology as many imply.

Durkheim shares with the interpretative subjectivists a concern with a meaningful social order, but differs from most of them in not assuming that this means making a rigid distinction between the natural and social sciences. He would also not accept forms of subjectivism that focus explanation on the *consciousness* of the subject. According to Durkheim, as the nature of social reality is not apparent to us, it follows that 'understanding' cannot emerge, or be constructed, from the meanings that individuals attach to their own or others' actions.

A Durkheimian analysis of the study of the 'interior', and the interpretation of experiences, approaches the problem in a rather different way. Let us illustrate this by looking at a topic of interest to medical sociology: social responses to death and dying.

Most sociological work in this area consists of 'micro' studies of awareness of death, communications with dying, or how individuals draw on certain taken-for-granted assumptions in its management (Glaser and Strauss 1965, 1968; Sudnow 1967). To illustrate a

Durkheimian approach we can turn to the work of his pupil Robert Hertz (1960). Death, Hertz observed, does not confine itself to the ending of bodily life, it also destroys the social being grafted on to the physical individual. It is thus a social event; its nature and consequences depend on how it is represented in the belief systems of society.

In modern society we tend to conceive death as the opposite to life. We treat it as an essentially individual interpersonal event, brought about by natural causes, and marked by a single ritual ceremony which signifies permanent withdrawal from 'this world'. These representations of death are not universal, but particular. For example notions of 'individuality' and 'natural causality' are products of highly differentiated societies.

In the 'primitive' societies examined by Hertz, death (other than by wounds) was not seen as a natural phenomenon, but as caused by spiritual powers, either because the deceased had violated a taboo or been the victim of an enemy sorcerer, in which case the death was part of a sinister plot. Further, in contrast to modern societies, the group had lost more than a unit, which even when alive was in important respects 'detached' and separate from the whole. In societies characterized by mechanical solidarity, the group loses a part of *itself* by death. As Hertz puts it: 'It seems the entire community feels itself lost, or at least directly threatened by the presence of antagonistic forces, and the very basis of its existence is shaken' (1960: 52).

However, the loss of the deceased is not permanent. The societies studied by Hertz have two burial rituals. The first represents the exclusion from visible society, while the second marks not a permanent departure, but a return to a parallel social existence symbolically linked to the everyday social world. The gravity and alarm of the social response varies depending on who has died. Whereas the death of a chief, for example, is met with profound terror and a long process of mourning, the death of a child provokes little grief, even from the parents, and there is no secondary burial.

Our modern 'child-centred' world might reflect on that as callousness and indifference on the part of a 'primitive mind'. Hertz's analysis, however, would not lead us to this conclusion. Children, and especially newly born children who have hardly entered society, or the sick and very old who have almost left it, are seen as such a small part of the organic whole that society experiences their loss much less intensely. Hertz concludes that 'death as a social phenomenon consists in a dual and painful process of mental disintegration and synthesis. It is only when this process is completed that society, its peace recovered, can triumph over death' (1960: 86).

Hertz's analysis is typically Durkheimian: the linking of different kinds of individual experiences and social actions to the collective consciousness; the stress on function without being functionalist; the use of comparative method and the focus on an aspect of social reality to make general observations about the nature of the whole. Hertz, like many of Durkheim's pupils and followers, was tragically killed in the First World War, but his brilliant essay on death is enough to indicate the extent to which the study of attitudes to death, mourning, and ritualistic mortuary practices can reveal important aspects of the nature of social solidarity and its changing forms. Thus, just as Durkheim used the study of law as an index of the change from mechanical to organic solidarity (1933), so a Durkheimian-inspired medical sociologist could usefully undertake an historical and cross-cultural study, using responses to death as an indicator of different forms of the collective conscience. A more specific study into changing attitudes to child death might achieve similar objectives, and also throw some of the current concerns about child-rearing, intervention, and child abuse into a wider perspective.

Just as Hertz's achievement was to show that death was a collective representation, or social category, one of Durkheim's major achievements in *The Elementary Forms of Religious Life* (1965) was to show that fundamental categories of human perception, such as time and space, were neither in nature waiting to be recognized, nor in minds waiting to be drawn out, but were rather products of collective social life. As forms of collective life change and develop, so new conceptual categories come into being. Thus by extension, and with specific reference to our present concern with health and medicine, it would not necessarily be inconsistent with a Durkheimian approach to conduct research which, for example, examined the relationship between changing forms of social solidarity and changing perceptions of health, disease, and medicine.

We use the cautionary phrase 'not necessarily inconsistent' for two main reasons. First, Durkheim was notoriously inconsistent in his own work, fluctuating to and fro between relativism and absolutism. For example, sometimes he conceived human nature as changeable, while at other times he implied it was essentially fixed and unchanging (Lukes 1973). Second, and more importantly, a Durkheimian approach to this issue should not be confused with a sophisticated form of subjectivism, which in medical sociology is sometimes called 'social constructionism'. This approach neither ignores disease in favour of illness, nor does it see it as a 'thing' to be explained by 'social' rather than 'biological' factors. This view holds that as all knowledge, including scientific and medical knowledge, is socially constructed, that knowledge is therefore not simply a legitimate focus of sociological enquiry, but *the* legitimate focus of enquiry.

The theoretical assumptions behind this approach are almost an exact inversion of the empiricism that informs 'scientific' medical sociology. In empiricism we observe a world of objects which we describe with (fictional) concepts. In social constructionism, which is in fact a distinct form of social relativism (Bury 1986), the world becomes intelligible to us in the way it does only because of the ideas and beliefs we have about it. In other words it is our concepts and categories or paradigms (thought) which are the realities, the subject of our investigation; for it is only through these that we derive the visions of the world that we perceive. It is for this reason that social constructivists home in on, not disease (or illness) as such, but medical knowledge and ideas. Thus in what is one of the most interesting studies in this perspective, Armstrong, examining the changing 'clinical' gaze, writes that:

> The fact that the body became legible does not imply that some invariant biological reality was finally revealed to medical enquiry. The body was only legible in that there existed in the new clinical techniques a language by which it could be read.
>
> (1983: 2)

The world of social constructionism, which owes much generally to the work of Quine (1961) and Kuhn (1970) and more specifically to that of Foucault (1972), is a world of changes, differences, and relativity. Constructionism does not make a rigid distinction between natural and social sciences, not because the latter cannot emulate the former, but because *all* knowledge is ultimately the prisoner of its paradigm. Thus medical science has not, for example, now 'discovered' that witches were 'really' mentally ill, it has merely helped to redefine problematic behaviour (Hirst and Woolley 1982).

Although Durkheim dealt with relativities and comparisons, he was not a relativist in the constructivist sense and cannot (or should not) be used in any 'justification' of social constructionism. For Durkheim, while knowledge was *socially determined*, it was not *socially constructed*. Like the constructionists, Durkheim accepted the 'independence' of knowledge but, unlike them, he believed that the (greater or lesser) validity of explanations (or systems of explanation) could be established by the empirical world behaving in certain ways – a view which, as we shall show later, got Durkheim into severe difficulties.

Thus in spite of the determined nature of knowledge, Durkheim believed there could be an objective science of society. His search for relations of invariant causality, indifference to the hermeneutic dilemma (Bauman 1978), and insistence that social facts be treated as 'things', have led most commentators to place Durkheim in the positivist tradition. We have already rejected this interpretation and, in the following section, we explain this further by examining a central issue of positivistic concern, the 'social' causes of disease.

The social origins of disease

While the idea of the social causes of disease is not new (Dubos 1959), it was given new impetus with the developments in the stress hypothesis, particularly by Wolff (1953) and Selye (1956). Over the past two decades an accumulation of research evidence has suggested that certain stressful life events – especially those involving significant change and/or loss – are associated with increased likelihood of illness (Holmes and Rahe 1967; Dohrenwend and Dohrenwend 1974; Rabkin and Struening 1976; Monroe 1983). Research has also indicated that social support, or social ties, may decrease vulnerability to illness, although there is some debate as to whether social support offers general protection (Berkman and Syme 1979; Thoits 1982), or merely acts as a 'buffer', given exposure to stressful life events (Cobb 1976; Dean and Lin 1977).

This work – which for simplicity we shall call the social support literature – has highlighted an important area of sociological interest. However, if sociology is to transcend epidemiology, or mere 'fact gathering', it must provide systematic *explanation* of these relationships, and in this respect most commentators agree that sociological explanation has been limited and fragmentary (House 1974; Morgan, Calnan, and Manning 1985; Gerhardt 1985).

Given this (acknowledged) limitation within the social support work, our first concern will be to compare the assumptions underlying the support literature with those underlying Durkheim's work. Second, we shall speculate as to whether or not Durkheim's sociology offers any potential for helping to understand the relation between society and disease. For many working in this field, the answer to this second question is obvious. Of course Durkheim's work is relevant, for the modern social support literature sees itself developing and refining his insights into social integration. In this context *Suicide* is often quoted or cited, and seen by some as *the* pioneering work on a notion of social support and its possible relation to health (Dohrenwend 1959; Berkman 1980; Williams, Ware, and Donald 1981). However, we have already suggested that such a view is mistaken. In important respects the work of the social support school and that of Durkheim belong to different sociological traditions. Therefore, *if* Durkheim's work has any relevance to the study of the social causes of diseases, its relevance has more to do with the *criticism*, rather than the *justification*, it provides for current work in this area.

There are, of course, important divergences and debates within the social support literature, but these tend to be confined to questions of data and method (Pearlin *et al.* 1981). However, at the theoretical level there is an almost consistent and unquestioning acceptance of the taken-for-granted assumptions of empiricism. It is assumed that social reality consists of existential, sensorily observed facts, or factors, and it is between these factors that invariant relations of causality are to be found, and it is about them that statements of generality are to be made (Kolakowski 1972). The introduction of more sophisticated methodological techniques such as causal modelling, or path analysis (Blalock 1972), or attempts to introduce 'meaning' as another variable (House 1974; Brown and Harris 1978), in no way alters these fundamental assumptions.

Examination of Durkheim's work on suicide shows that this was not his view of social order. As a realist the social facts with which Durkheim was concerned were sources of moral authority in society. Analysis of the relationships between suicide and, for example, religious, domestic, and political orders, were only manifestations and ways of reaching this hidden, underlying order. Similarly in his study of religion (1965), Durkheim's interest in the Arunta clans was not to describe their particular beliefs and rituals in order to compare them to other societies. Rather these religious practices were taken by Durkheim to illustrate the 'elementary forms' of all religion, as universal or general structures that characterize societies in general.

Thus a realist approach to the possible relationship between society and disease would attempt to use abstract theoretical constructs to reveal structures (meaningful or materialist) that generate observable phenomena and the relationships between them, for example between various social statuses and patterns of disease. The particular and *distinctive* Durkheimian variant of realism located the source of these causal mechanisms in various moral forces, or currents, arising from collective social life. These forces are *both* internalized by individuals and yet remain external to each of them. Durkheim called these forces collective representations. They constrain human action, first by binding individuals to socially given purposes, and second by regulating or moderating their desires and aspirations.

How then might Durkheim have attempted to explain some of the relationships between society and disease? Mestrovic and Glassner (1983) have rightly drawn attention to the central importance of a *dualistic* conception of human nature (*homo duplex*) in all Durkheim's major works. In contrast, the support literature employs a monistic, determined view of the individual and we can distinguish broadly between two versions. In the first we are simply offered an organism which is fundamentally intolerant to change. Thus House writes: 'Most [writers] see stress as occurring when an individual confronts a situation where his usual modes of behaving are insufficient and the consequences of not adapting are serious' (1974: 12). This interpretation ignores society as a complex of moral meanings. It would seem to have much more to do with the stress experienced by laboratory rats on receiving electric shocks instead of food than with those of men and women trying to make sense of changing social contexts. However, if the first version 'loses' society, the second, more sociological version, 'loses' the individual. In this (functionalist) account we find that those who are stressed are in this condition because they are 'unsocialized', or 'undersocialized', into the proper norms of society. In either case the subject is depicted as an essentially passive object, either pushed towards stress and disease by 'disruptive' factors or pulled from it by 'supportive' ones.

In the popular critical literature it is *Durkheim* who is accused of operating with a crudely deterministic view of the human subject which 'dissolves' him or her into the social group. However, for Durkheim, the individual was *both* an organism and a social being and, as such, he conceived the relationship between the individual and the group as essentially problematic and potentially volatile. While society 'exists in' and leaves its mark on people, it does not and never can 'take them over' (conquest by socialization) in the manner assumed by functionalist theory. In each person there exists both a social being and an individual being which has its roots in the organism. Each individual's life has a double centre of gravity. On the one hand there is individuality and the body on which it is based; on the other is all that expresses something other than the self (Durkheim 1973). In *The Division of Labour in Society*, for example, Durkheim argues:

> There are in each of us two consciences: one which is common to our group in its entirety, which, consequently is not ourself, but society living and acting within us; the other, on the contrary, represents that in us which is personal and distinct, that which makes us an individual.

> (1933: 29)

Within individuals then, there is a perpetual tension, or conflict, between the two consciences. From this perspective integration, rather than being simply 'support', 'regularity', or some kind of normative orientation towards society's goals, is harmony between the antagonistic poles of human existence (Mestrovic and Glassner 1983). Therefore the sources of psychological disturbance or stress come *either* from excessive repression of the individual nature by the social, *or* by the social nature being eclipsed by individual drives and appetites. From this point of view it is not a question of whether (or not) particular social situations, or given events, are necessarily stressors, but rather how we are to explain a process that upsets the balance between the individual and social components of human nature.

In a given context the relationship between the individual and social components of human nature is shaped by the collective consciousness of the social group in which the individual participates. It is useful here to look at Durkheim's theory of suicide (1952) which was, as Lukes (1973: 215) observes, 'by implication a social psychological theory about the social conditions for psychological health'. Indeed it seems reasonable to suppose that Durkheim would have been interested in expanding the scope of his theory had the stress hypothesis been available to him.

Briefly the core of Durkheim's explanation runs as follows. Individuals are constrained by moral forces in social life. There are four contradictory forms of moral force present in all societies, but they exist in various strengths in different social groups. All social life presupposes some commitment and obligation to a higher order outside the self (altruism); autonomy and individuality (egoism); predictable and inescapable limits to human action (fatalism); and uncertainty, ambiguity, possibility, and change (anomie). It is the relative strength of and balance between these forces that determine the nature of any particular collective consciousness. These meaning structures, which Durkheim saw as the essence of social reality, are not static but change generally and consistently over time, and specifically and sometimes rapidly for individuals as they move to and fro between different forms of moral authority in the course of their lives. Durkheim argued that psychological health, a sense of well-being, and, by the implication we have added here, a relatively higher protection from stress, is generated by those social orders in which there is balance between egoism and anomie (individualism) and altruism and fatalism (collectivism).

Generally modern societies, although they are not homogeneous and contain within them tightly knit structures such as highly regulated religious communities, tend to be characterized by higher levels of egoism and anomie. Individuals become increasingly aware of themselves as separate and autonomous units and social life is no longer ruled by custom and tradition. It is important to realize that, in contrast to Spencer for example, Durkheim did not argue that altruism (and fatalism) disappear in modern societies. Rather the relationship of the individual to the group changes form. The social being within individuals becomes based less on tradition, automatic conformity, and blind obedience, and more on calculation, utilitarian values, and personal interests and relationships. Marriage, for example, becomes less of a commitment to a formal institution and more an expression of a commitment to another person. The strength and duration of the marriage becomes dependent on a continuing *inter-personal* commitment.

Durkheim (1933) did not hanker after some idealized past. He welcomed utilitarianism (though not as a mode of explanation), seeing it as a potentially higher form of social order. However, he was concerned that increasing autonomy made the individual's relationship to the collectivity more problematic and tenuous and this had certain 'pathological' consequences, such as a 'forced' division of labour and rising suicide rates.

As modern societies are becoming generally more individualistic, then specific social contexts or social changes that promote altruism and help bind the individual to the group are generally beneficial to individuals. This is not because altruism, or greater altruism, necessarily and at all times promotes psychological health and well-being, but because it helps to balance increasing trends towards greater egoism and anomie. In this context the particular remedy offered by Durkheim (1952) was to organize economic life around occupational groups which would tighten the social fabric by providing individuals with more attachment and regulation.

By the same criterion, changes in the moral density of social groups, or changes in individual biographies that further dilute the 'presence' of society in individuals, aggravate general tendencies to egoism and anomie such that it upsets the social integration of the life of the individual to an extent that it becomes stressful. Durkheim expressed this as follows:

> All internal life draws its primary material from without. All we can think of is objects or our conceptions of them. We cannot reflect on our own consciousness in a purely undetermined state; in this shape it is inconceivable. Now consciousness becomes determined only when affected by something not itself. Therefore, if it individualises beyond a certain point, if it separates itself too radically from other beings, men or things, it finds itself unable to communicate with the very sources of its normal nourishment and no longer has anything to which it can apply itself. It creates nothingness within by creating it from without, and has nothing left upon which to reflect but its own wretched misery.
>
> (1952: 279)

It is into this explanatory context that Durkheim might have placed relationships between social situations or 'events' – such as divorce, bereavement, job loss – and diseases. These relationships occur not because these 'things' are necessarily stressful in themselves, but rather because they are manifestations of an underlying social psychological process which upsets the balance between the individual and social components of human nature.

The ideas sketched out above are necessarily speculative, and concentrate on the form rather than the content of a possible Durkheimian approach to the social origins of disease. However, we should now be in a position to indicate some of the most important ways in which a Durkheimian approach would be significantly different from those in the support literature.

First, a realist approach (Durkheimian or any other) would not confine the focus of its attentions to particular 'factors' from which it is then hoped explanations or theories could be induced. A realist would attempt to construct explanation from abstract theoretical models developed independently from data (Sayer 1984).

Second, a Durkheimian approach would examine the relationship between the *individual* and society, rather than reducing the former to the status of an object. It would reintroduce human agency, although not in the subjectivist sense (Mestrovic and Glassner 1983).

Third, whereas the support literature tends to see illness as pathological in itself, a Durkheimian approach would see illness as a normal and inevitable feature of a 'healthy' society. Just as crime was both normal and 'functional' in 'concentrating upright consciences', so it is only against disease that ideas of health and well-being can be realized.

Fourth, the social support work conceives of (pathological) disease caused, or rather made more likely, by specific 'traits' in society or individuals. In contrast, in a Durkheimian theory, both stress and psychological health and well-being would be seen to emanate from the same sources. Egoism, for example, is both a source of stress (in excess) and yet, balanced by altruism, it is the basis of a 'healthy' social existence. An approach geared exclusively or even predominantly towards mitigating or managing specific 'stressful factors' is unlikely to be very productive. For example the increasing individualism and autonomy, which is part of the process generating the stressful conditions of modern life, also liberated individuals from the yoke of tradition, and brought about those improvements in living standards which McKeown (1976) and others have linked with the modern rise of population.

The support literature also sometimes implies that there is some direct and consistent correspondence between social support, social stability, and relative protection from stress. From a Durkheimian point of view, this overlooks the stress that can be engendered from a collective consciousness where excessive altruism and fatalism represses even the most fundamental instincts for survival. The most stark manifestation of this process – studied amongst others by Durkheim's nephew and collaborator Mauss (1979) – is when an individual believes himself or herself bewitched and dies for that reason. The power of suggestion is so profound that it sets up a chain reaction which results in a fall in blood pressure to the low level seen in fatal wound shocks (Cannon 1941). The anthropologists studying this phenomenon tended to see it as illustrative of the unstable, child-like mind of the 'primitive' (Mauss 1979). However, a Durkheimian interpretation would locate its origins in a social milieu which produced in its constituent members a human nature where the individual was crushed by the social. The social support theorists – if they bothered to look outside the modern western world at all, which would be unusual – would simply have to add 'pointing the bone' to the list of stressful life events.

Clearly comparisons between what Durkheim might have written about health and illness and what hundreds of researchers have written about it over the past two decades cannot be pushed too far. Suffice to say that many of the technical problems of undertaking research would have interested Durkheim, who did himself make original and important contributions to the development of sociological research methods (Selvin 1965). It is also important to remember that Durkheim's own study of suicide, on which we uncritically based much of our analysis, has itself been subject to considerable critical evaluation (Douglas 1967; Atkinson 1978; Taylor 1982).

There is a final issue, perhaps the most important of all, to which attention must be drawn. Researchers working in the social support field tend to see the issue of lack of explanation as an essentially technical one, to do with more data and better methods (LaRocco, House, and French 1980; Thoits 1982). However, analysis from a Durkheimian point of view, while not disputing the importance of questions of method, would also raise a general doubt about seeking explanation through generalizations from observed empirical associations (Johnson, Dandeker, and Ashworth 1984). This 'systematic empiricism' has been subjected to such devastating attacks in 'mainstream' sociology (Willer and Willer 1973; Boudon 1974; Pawson 1978) that medical sociologists cannot remain deaf to them forever. As a result of disillusionment with empiricism, there has been a renewed interest in social realism (Harré 1978; Bhaskar 1979; Sayer 1984). In this context it is perhaps time that the social support writers started giving more attention to the real, rather than the mythological, Durkheim.

Social realism

The main source of the distinction we outlined in the previous section between Durkheim's sociology and that of the social support theorists lies in the former's social realism. In this section we look briefly at realism in sociology and its application in medical sociology.

The two main realist traditions in sociology are Marxism and struc-turalism. As the former is dealt with elsewhere in this volume, we shall confine our comments here to the observation that both Durkheim and Marxists share many of the same criticisms of positivism and subjectivism, and both search for the relationships between underly-ing structures and the empirical phenomena they generate. However, while for the Marxist this dialectical relationship is between the 'economic' and the 'non-economic', for Durkheim, as we have tried to show, it is between the 'social' and the 'representational'. For Durkheim (1933) the 'economic' was a part of the totality of the social, rather than the key to its explanation. Thus Durkheim would never have agreed with the Marxist view that the distribution of illnesses (and the nature of the medical responses to them) are system-atically generated by a given mode of production (Navarro 1974; Doyal 1979).

It is the structuralist perspective in sociology that is *closest* to the Durkheimian position, and Levi-Strauss (1968) has declared his own work to be in the Durkheimian tradition (S. Clarke 1978). While acknowledging significant differences between Durkheim and Levi-Strauss and the doubts many structuralists would have in relation to Durkheim's 'globalism', Taylor has drawn attention to the fundamen-tal similarities between Durkheimian sociology and structuralism:

> First, there is the ambition to make objective, law-like statements about a *meaningful* and essentially ideal social world.... Second, there is the ontological assumption that the explanation of observ-able phenomena involves the search for 'deep', or underlying, struc-tures which are discovered not by observation, but by the theoretical work of logic and deduction.... Third, Durkheim and the struc-turalists study social phenomena not as a mass of separable events and sequences, but in terms of general theoretical structures whose concepts express the *relations* between constituent elements.
>
> (1982: 163)

Despite the growth, development, and increasing interest in structur-alism in sociology and elsewhere (Giddens 1979), it has had little influence in medical sociology. It is true that the term 'structuralist' is often *misused* in medical sociology; for example, by Townsend and Davidson in *Inequalities in Health: The Black Report*, where they refer to a materialist 'social factors' explanation as 'structuralist' (1979: 114). However, we are referring here to the structuralist method and, for the development of this approach to the field of health and illness, it is to social psychology that we must turn.

Herzlich's work on lay perceptions of health and illness makes extensive use of the concept of social representations deriving from

Durkheim's work' (1973:v). While Herzlich's respondents saw illness as something external to the individual (and influenced by the 'un-naturalness' of urban life), health was seen as an internal quality. The distinctive feature of Herzlich's account is the way in which she attempts to show that the lay perceptions of illness she identifies, illness as 'occupation', 'destroyer', 'liberator', rather than being mere 'social constructions' are representations of the wider form of cultural life in which the individual participates. Building on aspects of Herzlich's work, Radley and Green (1985, 1987) develop a two-dimensional structural model with which to organize and classify people's adjustment to chronic illness. The first dimension, social participation retained/social participation lost, expresses the relationship between the individual and society. The second dimension, self complimentary to illness/self opposed to illness, expresses the form of the relationship between the individual and the condition.

From this framework Radley and Green develop four modes of adjustment to chronic illness. 'Accommodation' is where the illness is integrated into the person's life. 'Secondary gain' is when the inactivity brought about by the illness provides a context for other rewarding activities. 'Active denial' is the attempt to minimize the effects of the illness, and 'resignation' is where lost social activity is accompanied by a sense of being overwhelmed by the illness. The authors then provide extensive interview data to illustrate the various forms of adjustment. For the empiricist such an approach would be 'reification', as the forms identified do not 'really' exist. For the structuralist, however, it is only through these abstract models, where theory orders data rather than vice versa, that reality can be known and organized. Durkheim's sociology has far more in common with this latter form of approach than it does with the 'social factor' studies with which his work is normally associated.

Critique of Durkheim

As excellent critiques of (the real rather than the mythological) Durkheim exist elsewhere (Douglas 1967; Hirst 1975; La Capra 1985), we shall confine ourselves here to what we believe to be the central ambiguity of his sociology. We have seen that Durkheim's particular brand of social realism leads him to identify the subject matter of sociology as a collective consciousness, a group mind, which constrains individual behaviour, including illness. This leads us to ask two questions. First, how do we know this social reality? Second, what are its sources? Let us take each in turn, relating the implications of the arguments to the study of disease.

First, as the nature of social reality is not 'given' to us by experience, it is not enough merely to observe and classify relationships between diseases and social factors. All we are doing is observing various effects or manifestations of society which in no way can lead to an explanation. It is only through theoretical abstraction that we can hope to reach the underlying sources of causality, and Durkheim's *theory* of suicide provides a good illustration of how he approached this problem. There is nothing exceptional in this position. All approaches that we call rationalist do this. However, for Durkheim, social *science* must transcend rationalist argument and the logic of theory construction. It must provide empirical demonstrations which are independent from the confines of the theory. In this context Durkheim argued that the consistency of the suicide rates *proved* the 'truth' of his theory of suicide. By the same criterion, *if* he was studying the social origins of disease, he would presumably argue that specific statistical relationships between diseases and forms of social organization 'demonstrated' the theory. In his desire to transcend rational argument and deduction, Durkheim has taken us back to the empiricism he explicitly rejected at the level of theory. Rather than going beyond the limits of rationalism and empiricism, as he clearly intended to do, Durkheim vacillated between two epistemological positions he had previously identified as 'false', in the sense of being 'non-scientific'.

Our second question raises the issue of ontology. Durkheim, as we have seen, claimed that society was an irreducible reality. Therefore if Durkheim was attempting to argue that society can influence disease, what are the origins of this social reality? Here we find Durkheim is less than consistent. He was clear that it was more than material factors (positivism), or underlying material structures (Marxism). Thus Durkheim would not have seen the material environment as the *source* of 'the social causes of' disease. However, Durkheim was equally clear that society is not reducible to thought (idealism). Therefore, as we have already suggested, he would not be interested in confining sociological work to people's experiences of illness (subjectivism) or systems of knowledge *about* disease (social constructionism). Again, Durkheim had good reasons for wanting sociological explanation to avoid only being *either* materialist *or* idealist. However, if the origins of society are ultimately to be found in neither matter nor mind, and Durkheim provides no alternative, its ontological status is, to say the least, ambiguous. The irony is that we become tempted to 'read' Durkheim's concept of society as a 'fiction', a mere description of something more real. This was the very last thing he intended. In fact all his sociological work can be seen as a concerted effort to demonstrate precisely the opposite.

Is contemporary sociology justified then in allocating Durkheim an honoured, but essentially historical role? Have we now resolved the problems that Durkheim posed for us, or rendered them irrelevant? It seems that the response of modern sociology, and this is reflected by the perspectives in medical sociology, has been to retreat into schools of thought that cluster around the poles of one or other of the philosophical dilemmas that he tried to synthesize. Thus we have ontologies that are either materialist or idealist, and epistemologies that are either empiricist or rationalist. This hardly represents progress on our part. Durkheimian sociology demonstrates the severe limitation of each of them.

We conclude with a final comment on Durkheim and health. Durkheim's sociology can be seen to contradict itself, but the sources of these contradictions spring from Durkheim's consistent refusal to take the easy option. Other approaches (positivism and subjectivism, for example) have more internal consistency, but they often seem pale and dull in comparison. Thus while one can never be a committed Durkheimian, after careful reading of his work you never want to be anything else. This is a source of stress. *Durkheim* is bad for our health. His work should carry a government health warning.

References

Armstrong, D. (1983) *Political Anatomy of the Body*, Cambridge: Cambridge University Press.

Atkinson, J. (1978) *Discovering Suicide*, London: Macmillan.

Bauman, Z. (1978) *Hermeneutics and Social Science*, London: Hutchinson.

Berkman, L. (1980) 'Physical health and the social environment: a social epidemiological perspective', in L. Eisenberg and A. Kleinman (eds) *The Relevance of Social Science for Medicine*, London: Reidel.

Berkman, L. and Syme, S. (1979) 'Social networks, host resistance and mortality: a nine year follow-up study of Alameda County residents', *American Journal of Epidemiology* 109 (2): 186–204.

Bhaskar, R. (1979) *The Possibility of Naturalism*, Brighton: Harvester.

Bilton, T., Bonnett, K., Jones, P., Sheard, K., Stanworth, M., and Webster, A. (1982) *Introductory Sociology*, London: Macmillan.

Blalock, H. (1972) *Causal Models in the Social Sciences*, London: Macmillan.

Boudon, R. (1974) *The Logic of Sociological Explanation*, Harmondsworth: Penguin.

Breault, K. (1986) 'Suicide in America: a test of Durkheim's theory of religious and family integration', *American Journal of Sociology* 92 (3): 628–56

Brown, G. W. and Harris, T. (1978) *The Social Origins of Depression*, London: Tavistock.

Bury, M. (1986) 'Social constructionism and the development of medical sociology', *Sociology of Health and Illness* 8 (2): 137–69.

Cannon, W. (1942) 'Voodoo death', *American Anthropologist* 44 (2): 169–81.

Clarke, J. (1981) 'A multiple paradigm approach to the sociology of medicine, health and illness', *Sociology of Health and Illness* 3 (1): 89–103.

Clarke, S. (1978) 'The origins of Levi-Strauss's structuralism', *Sociology* 12: 405–39.

Cobb, S. (1976) 'Social support as a moderator of life stress', *Psychosomatic Medicine* 38: 300–14.

Cresswell, P. (1972) 'Interpretations of Suicide', *British Journal of Sociology* 23: 133–45.

Cuff, E., Payne, G., Francis, D., Hustler, D., and Sharrock, W. (1984) *Perspectives in Sociology*, London: Allen & Unwin (2nd edn).

Dean, A. and Lin, N. (1977) 'The stress-buffering role of social support: problems and prospects for systematic investigation', *Journal of Nervous Mental Disease* 165: 403–10.

Dilthey, W. (1976) *Selected Writings*, Cambridge: Cambridge University Press.

Dohrenwend, B. (1959) 'Egoism, altruism, anomie and fatalism: a conceptual analysis of Durkheim's types', *American Sociological Review* 24: 466–73.

Dohrenwend, B. and Dohrenwend, B. (eds) (1974) *Stressful Life Events: Their Nature and Effects*, New York: Wiley.

Douglas, J. (1967) *The Social Meanings of Suicide*, Princeton, NJ: Princeton University Press.

Doyal, L. (1979) *The Political Economy of Health*, London: Pluto.

Dubos, R. (1959) *Mirage of Health*, New York: Harper & Row.

Durkheim, E. (1933) *The Division of Labour in Society*, New York: Free Press.

—— (1952) *Suicide: A Study in Sociology*, London: Routledge & Kegan Paul.

—— (1965) *The Elementary Forms of Religious Life*, New York: Free Press.

—— (1973) 'The dualism of human nature and its social conditions', in R. Bellah (ed.) *Emile Durkheim on Morality and Society*, Chicago, Ill: University of Chicago.

Fenton, S., Reiner, R., and Hamnett, I. (1984) *Durkheim and Modern Sociology*, Cambridge: Cambridge University Press.

Foucault, M. (1972) *The Archaeology of Knowledge*, London: Tavistock.

Freidson, E. (1970) *The Profession of Medicine*, New York: Aldine.

—— (1983) 'Viewpoint: sociology and medicine: a polemic', *Sociology of Health and Illness*, 5 (2): 208–19.

Gerhardt, U. (1985) 'Stress and stigma explanations of illness', in U. Gerhardt and M. Wadsworth, *Stress and Stigma*, London: Macmillan, 161–204.

Giddens, A. (1971) *Capitalism and Modern Social Theory*, Cambridge: Cambridge University Press.

—— (1977) *Studies in Social and Political Theory*, London: Hutchinson.

—— (1979) *Central Problems in Social Theory*, London: Macmillan.

Glaser, B. and Strauss, A. (1965) *Awareness of Dying*, Chicago, Ill: Aldine.

—— (1968) *Time for Dying*, Chicago, Ill: Aldine.

Harré, R. (1979) *Social Being: A Theory for Social Psychology*, Oxford: Blackwell.

Hertz, R. (1960) *Death and the Right Hand*, Aberdeen: Cohen & West.

Herzlich, C. (1973) *Health and Illness*, London: Academic Press.

Hirst, P. (1975) *Durkheim, Bernard and Epistemology*, London: Routledge & Kegan Paul.

Hirst, P. and Woolley, P. (1982) *Social Relations and Human Attributes*, London: Tavistock.

Holmes, T. and Rahe, R. (1967) 'The social readjustment rating scale', *Journal of Psychosomatic Research* 11: 213–18.

House, J. (1974) 'Occupational stress and coronary heart disease: a review and theoretical integration', *Journal of Health and Social Behaviour* 15: 12–27.

Hynes, E. (1975) 'Suicide and homo duplex: an interpretation of Durkheim's typology of suicide', *Sociological Quarterly* 16: 87–104.

Johnson, T., Dandeker, C., and Ashworth, C. (1984) *The Structure of Social Theory*, London: Macmillan.

Keat, R and Urry, J. (1975) *Social Theory as Science*, London: Routledge & Kegan Paul.

Kolakowski, L. (1972) *Positivist Philosophy: From Hume to the Vienna Circle*, Harmondsworth: Penguin.

Kuhn, T. (1970) *The Structure of Scientific Revolutions*, Chicago, Ill: University of Chicago Press.

La Capra, D. (1985) *Emile Durkheim*, Chicago, Ill: University of Chicago Press.

LaRocco, J., House, J., and French, J. (1980) 'Social support, occupational stress and health', *Journal of Health and Social Behaviour*, 21: 202–18.

Levi-Strauss, C. (1968) *Structural Anthropology*, London: Allen Lane.

Locker, D. (1983) *Disability and Disadvantage*, London: Tavistock.

Lukes, S. (1973) *Emile Durkheim: his Life and Work*, Harmondsworth: Penguin.

McKeown, T. (1976) *The Modern Rise of Population*, London: Edward Arnold.

Mauss, M. (1979) *Sociology and Psychology*, London: Routledge & Kegan Paul.

Mestrovic, S. and Glassner, B. (1983) 'A Durkheimian hypothesis of stress', *Social Science and Medicine* 17: 1,315–27.

Monroe, S. (1983) 'Major and minor life events as predictors of psychological distress: further issues and findings', *Journal of Behavioural Medicine* 6: 189–96.

Morgan, M., Calnan, N., and Manning, N. (1985) *Sociological Approaches to Health and Medicine*, London: Croom Helm.

Navarro, V. (1974) *Medicine under Capitalism*, London: Croom Helm.

Parsons, T. (1961) *The Structure of Social Action*, New York: Free Press.

Pawson, R. (1978) 'Empiricist explanatory strategies: the case of causal modelling', *Sociological Review* 26: 613–45.

Pearlin, L., Menaghan, E., Lieberman, M., and Mullan, J. (1981) 'The stress process', *Journal of Health and Social Behaviour*, 22: 337–56.

Quine, W. (1961) *From a Logical Point of View*, Cambridge, Mass: Harvard University Press.

Rabkin, J. and Struening, E. (1976) 'Life events, stress and illness', *Science* 194: 1,013–20.
Radley, A. and Green, R. (1985) 'Styles of adjustment to coronary graft surgery', *Social Science and Medicine* 20: 461–72.
——— (1987) 'Illness as adjustment: a methodology and conceptual framework', *Sociology of Health and Illness* 9 (2): 179–207.
Sayer, A. (1984) *Method in Social Science: A Realist Approach*, London: Hutchinson.
Scambler, G. (1984) 'Perceiving and coping with stigmatizing illness', in R. Fitzpatrick, J. Hinton, S. Newman, G. Scambler, and J. Thompson, *The Experience of Illness*, London: Tavistock.
Scott, R. (1969) *The Making of Blind Men*, New York: Sage.
Selvin, H. (1965) 'Durkheim's *Suicide*: further thoughts on a methodological classic', in R. Nisbet (ed.) *Emile Durkheim*, Englewood Cliffs, NJ: Prentice-Hall.
Selye, H. (1965) *The Stress of Life*, New York: McGraw-Hill.
Sudnow, D. (1967) *Passng On: The Social Organisation of Dying*, New York: Prentice-Hall.
Taylor, S. (1982) *Durkheim and the Study of Suicide*, London: Macmillan.
Thoits, P. (1982) 'Conceptual, methodological and theoretical problems in studying social support as a buffer', *Journal of Health and Social Behaviour*, 23: 145–58.
Thompson, K. (1982) *Emile Durkheim*, London: Tavistock.
Townsend, P. and Davidson, N. (1970) *Inequalities in Health: The Black Report*, Harmondsworth: Penguin.
Willer, D. and Willer, J. (1973) *Systematic Empiricism: A Critique of a Pseudo-Science*, Englewood Cliffs, NJ: Prentice-Hall.
Williams, A., Ware, J., and Donald, C. (1981) 'A model of mental health, life events and social supports applicable to general populations', *Journal of Health and Social Behaviour* 22: 324–36.
Wolff, H. (1953) *Stress and Disease*, Springfield: Thomas.

3

Bodies of knowledge: Foucault and the problem of human anatomy

David Armstrong

Biology and sociology

As sociology struggles to establish and maintain its own disciplinary separateness the potential encroachments of biology into the social domain have been a constant threat. Indeed because of prior socialization into the biological sciences during primary and secondary education the relationship between biology and sociology can become a very real problem for elementary sociological textbooks as they try to delimit a space for their subject independent of biology.

Biology is directly concerned with living things and in so far as animal behaviour is concerned would appear to have a virtual monopoly of study and explanation. When it comes to human behaviour, and at least by implication to social phenomena, biologists have always seemed on more shaky ground but this has not prevented them from laying claims to this domain. Many biologists believe that the difference between animal and human behaviour is a quantitative rather than a qualitative one, simply a question of complexity rather than one of fundamentally different explanatory form. Such views can be seen especially in those animal ethologists who have assumed – mainly by implication – that human behaviour is not dissimilar to that of animals (Lorenz 1966; Morris 1967; Wilson 1975).

In coping with this challenge some sociological texts simply ignore the biological, others offer a more combative approach. Worsley's popular text, for example, is briefly dismissive of biological claims: 'Nor can we explain the diversity of human culture by reference to our common biological equipment.... Man, in fact, is the least biologically-determined species of all' (1977: 24–5).

Other texts, however, representing another component of sociology's relationship to biology, adopt a different strategy. They are less critical of biology because they recognize that the legitimacy of some biological explanatory accounts is an essential backdrop for the study of the social. In a relatively recent example Hirst and Woolley berate 'the dangers of a rigid demarcation between men and animals' (1982: 3) and offer several chapters on the interface between biology and sociology including brief discussions of Darwinian evolution, brain size, and genetics. Such a view finds sympathy in other texts such as Lenski and Lenski's contemporary American textbook on macrosociology: 'By ignoring or minimizing the biological foundation of human societies, [many social scientists] seemed almost to decry our animal heritage' (1982: 9).

These strategies for dealing with the problematic relationship with biology are not simply a response to some modern biological imperialism, but seem to reflect a virtually structured feature of sociology's very existence. Thus MacIver could identify the 'great dispute' with biology (1931: 313) together with an acknowledgement of the 'coequal importance' of the biological and the social as the 'ultimate determinants of everything that lives' (330). Inter-war sociology textbooks freely acknowledged the domain of biology and its relevance to society ('we must grant that self-assertion and aggression are integral elements of human nature' – Ginsberg 1934: 99) and as likely or not included, like Hirst and Woolley some half-century later, an overview of the biological context of sociological thought (Davis and Barnes 1927).

Through strategies of confrontation and accommodation sociology has fairly managed to maintain its position on the battle-front of disciplinary demarcation as the integrity of the subject attests. Equally sociology has been constantly alert to the dangers of allowing an enemy within through the importation of essentially biological theories. Organic theories which liken social organization and growth to that of biological organization and growth have always been present in sociology as a potential explanatory paradigm, but almost invariably they have been circumscribed with qualifications. Those 'sociologists' such as Spencer, whose name is virtually synonymous with organic theories, are acceptable only to the extent that organic is not exactly the same as biological. Similarly functionalism, with its biological taint, has been subjected to almost ritual denunciation by most sociological theorists. Thus just as the limits of sociology are defended by a constant programme of boundary maintenance against the external biological threat, so the examination and condemnation of organic theories and/or functionalism can be seen as an attempt to maintain the disciplinary purity of sociology from the Trojan horse of biology.

Foucault and biology

Using sociology's own 'labelling' framework it would seem that sociology as a discipline owes at least some of its success to its twin strategies of a politics of exclusion and a ritual internal purification, but that such strategies have also served to legitimize the existence of the potential enemy, namely biology. The fact that social phenomena are not to be explained in biological terms certainly circumscribes the domain of biology, but at the same time it also involves recognition of the scientific and political legitimacy of biology in its own area, namely the study and explanation of 'biological' phenomena. In other words, while biology is required to remain outside the sociological camp, sociology must in reciprocal fashion remain outside the biological. Skirmishes continue but by and large seem to succeed only in further reinforcing the impermeability of the boundary between these two broad areas of knowledge.

Yet while mechanisms of disciplinary boundary maintenance have kept biology and sociology separate there has been no explicit strategy to ward off possible incursions of, say, religion into the explanation of human behaviour. What is it about biology and sociology that locks them in conflict? Or is this the wrong question? Perhaps they are not as opposed as they might at first seem; after all, conflict at their borders merely serves to consolidate and reinforce each discipline's separate existence and formalize their points of contact. In effect, such rituals help constitute a broad map of knowledge which demarcates disciplinary spaces and points of contiguity. Religion would appear to be absent from this particular map whereas biology and sociology are present. How is it then that these two apparently opposed disciplines are so closely related within an overall structure of cognition? The answer, Foucault would argue, lies in their occupation of a common 'episteme'.

An episteme is defined by Foucault, somewhat obscurely, as the 'total set of relations that unite, at a given period, the discursive practices that give rise to epistemiological figures, sciences, and possibly formalised systems' (Foucault 1972: 191). The episteme is not a form of knowledge or type of rationality to be confused with 'the sovereign unity of a subject, a spirit or a period' (191): it basically functions as the conditions of existence of particular forms of knowledge.

In his book *The Order of Things* (1970) Foucault identifies three epistemes: one which dominated Renaissance thinking, one covering the Classical period, and the most recent which has governed the nineteenth and twentieth centuries; in each he examined the cognitive ordering of Language, Labour, and Life. How, for example, did these three epistemes see Life, that is 'living' things? In part the question is misplaced because the immanence of life in things belongs to the modern episteme. In the Renaissance animals and plants were of course recognized but perceptions of them were very different. The legends and supposed virtues of an animal or plant were as much a characteristic of its description as any morphological features. 'The strangeness of animals was a spectacle: it was featured in fairs, in tournaments, in fictitious or real combats, in the reconstitutions of legends in which the bestiary displayed its ageless fables.' (1970: 131).

The Renaissance way of seeing the natural world was transformed with the advent of the Classical episteme from the mid-seventeenth century onwards. The 'imaginary' characteristics of animals and plants were dismissed and instead living things ordered according to their perceptible physical structures. The eighteenth-century popularity of botanical gardens and zoological gardens reflected the replacement of the 'circular procession of the "show"' with the arrangement of things in a "table"' (Foucault 1970: 131). It was not that the new perception, which eliminated the cultural baggage surrounding the characteristics of living things, ushered in a better way of seeing. What changed was the underlying base of knowledge itself, 'the space in which it was possible to see [animals and plants] and from which it was possible to describe them' (Foucault 1970: 131).

In the Classical episteme the study of living things was undertaken by the discipline of natural history, perhaps best exemplified by the famous system of botanical classification derived by Linnaeus or the complex medical symptom tables of Sydenham which placed things according to their resemblances. But at the end of the eighteenth century there was another disjunction as one episteme gave way to the next in which a new science of animals and plants came into existence, namely biology. With the advent of biology the comparison of morphologies in a great taxonomic regime was replaced by a more penetrating analysis of structure and its relationship to function. Functions were invisible but marked the existence of the phenomenon of 'life', which in its turn became the principal object of the new biology.

Foucault takes issue with historians of biology who attempt to identify the subject's origins earlier than the late eighteenth century. How is it possible to write the history of biology in the eighteenth century when biology did not exist? And there was a very simple reason for the non-existence of biology, namely the non-existence of 'life' itself: 'All that existed were living beings, which were viewed through a grid of knowledge constituted by natural history' (Foucault 1970: 128).

Just as natural history was replaced by the new science of biology, the analysis of wealth gave way to economics, and the study of general grammar to linguistics. These three new knowledges were a part of a complete reorganization of knowledge in the late eighteenth century; but, more significantly, these three new sciences of Life, Labour, and Language defined a new central object for the modern episteme, namely what Foucault calls 'Man'; and with the advent of Man arose the specific studies of man in the form of the human sciences. Thus just as the historian would not find biology in the eighteenth century, so it would be equally futile to search for psychology or anthropology or sociology. Without man as an object there can be no sciences of man.

Foucault's concern with the great swathes of history governed by the episteme, together with the massive disjunctions in knowing which their change implied, was not to last as he moved on to more specific projects. Nevertheless some of the arguments of *The Order of Things* set the context for a more specific discussion of the human body in both general sociology and medical sociology. The notions of the episteme and of the 'sciences of Man' help clarify the relationship between biology and sociology. Sociology, biology, and modern medicine (and for that matter psychology) all would seem to have their grounding in a similar cognitive space. Hence it can be seen that the sociological concern with the potentially threatening frontiers of biology is not a part of a struggle between alternative knowledges but a limited jockeying for position on a stage whose limits and fundamental organization is already fixed.

Human anatomy

In 1858 a young anatomy demonstrator at St George's Hospital Medical School in London, Henry Gray, published a textbook on human anatomy. Such was the success of this book that it rapidly went to a second edition and then a third. Now over a hundred years later it is in its thirty-sixth edition and, as *Gray's Anatomy* (Warwick and Williams 1980), is one of the great classic texts of human anatomy. How are the organs ordered? What are the mechanics of the cell? How does the embryo grow? What are the tissues of the skin? These qustions all find authoritative answers in *Gray's*.

Yet human anatomy is a sub-branch of the field of biology which itself took its first faltering steps only at the end of the eighteenth century; before, it would appear that the body was seen in a different way which did not find expression in anatomical structure as revealed by the anatomical atlas. After the modern episteme it presumably will be seen as something different still.

While the study of epistemes might lead one to suspect that biology and human anatomy are not as universal and ahistoric as they might claim, there is other writing by Foucault which takes the problem of the body specifically as its remit. There are two key texts, *The Birth of the Clinic* (1973) and, later, *Discipline and Punish* (1977). Some of the arguments of the former were put into a wider framework in the latter book so their details are not of great concern here, nevertheless there are themes in *The Birth of the Clinic* which can be seen to have a direct bearing on the subsequent notion of epistemes.

The Birth of the Clinic is concerned with 'le regard' of medicine: in part this translates as the way medicine has perceived things, the way things have looked or seemed. In addition, 'le regard' is also the technique by which medicine came to have knowledge of bodies, that is came to see their interiors, organs, tissues, constancies, and variations: hence the translation, 'the gaze'. Foucault opens the book with a contemporary description of the treatment and cure of a hysteric in the eighteenth century in which 'membranous tissues like pieces of damp parchment . . . peel away with slight discomfort, and these were passed daily with the urine; the right ureter also peeled away and came out whole in the same way' (ix); this was followed by a nineteenth-century description of the anatomical detail of the brain tissues. The two clearly belong to different worlds. Neither author would be able to make sense of the other's writings; but more, neither author would be able to *see* the other's observations had they both witnessed the same event ('How can we be sure that an eighteenth-century doctor did not see what he saw': x)

Why, the modern anatomist might ask, did observers in the eighteenth century and earlier fail to see that diseases could be located to organs and tissues? Why could they not see that anatomical structure and function were intimately linked? Why did they fail to realize that death comes from disease within the body rather than as a visitation from nature outside? What is today obvious was then unknown because in the past the world was not seen according to *Gray's Anatomy*. Equally eighteenth-century studies make strange reading for modern eyes: eighteenth-century observations cannot be replicated; the humours which reportedly invested the body can be neither seen nor measured. Must we therefore explain eighteenth-century accounts of the body as fanciful or, more prosaically, as mistaken? Or, following Foucault, were they simply different and incommensurable (to use Kuhn's term) visions of the body?

While the sociology of science has mainly been interested in the classical natural sciences of physics and chemistry and their various derivatives, in recent years some studies have been made of the biological sciences (e.g. Barnes and Shapin 1979). Such investigations have tended to argue the structural continuity between social phenomena and biological theories such that, at least in part, the latter are held to derive from the former. Studies of the body itself have been fewer but these too have tended to call into question the supposed universal and 'true' character of the biological basis of the body (Wright and Treacher 1982).

However the bulk of general sociology, as argued above, has consistently failed to see biology as a problem other than in its potential encroachment into sociology. Indeed not only have the assumptions underlying biology not been called into question, but also despite resistance to biological theories *within* sociology, biological principles have been used as fundamental *bases* for sociological theorizing. Perhaps Parsons's (1949) reliance on the biological organism and its needs as one of the four most general subsystems of the system of action – all showing the influence of his physiologist mentor Henderson (1970) – needs no further discussion, especially since it is now seen as somewhat dated. Yet even one of the recent attempts at grand theory, such as Giddens's (1984) work, still discusses and acknowledges the place of a piece of walking human anatomy in the overall scheme of things. In an otherwise well-referenced text Giddens fails to mention sources for his knowledge of the biological basis of people such is his certainty of its status; by rights he should be quoting *Gray's Anatomy*.

In medical sociology things are little different: the body rules, OK. Sociologists support, criticize, collude with, and conspire against those health professionals whose claim to expertise is their sophisticated knowledge of the body – but rarely if ever to question or criticize their biological vision of that body. Sociologists study the social aspects of disease of the body – but rarely if ever to criticize that vision of the body which locates diseases therein. Is there really anything bizarre in the London medical school where the anatomists reputedly suggested the new sociologist should be located in their department because they both studied the 'whole person'?

Human anatomy has maintained its hegemony over sociology for too long. Its influence is so pervasive that its dominance has virtually been built into sociological thought. Surely it is now time to challenge the cognitive ordering of a field of knowledge held under the suzerainty of anatomy. It is time to recognize the nature of sociology's alliance with medicine and grasp the possibilities for different configurations of knowledge. 'Countless people', Foucault notes, 'have sought the origins of sociology in Montesquieu and Comte. That is a very ignorant enterprise. Sociological knowledge is formed rather in practices like those of the doctors' (Gordon 1980: 151).

In *The Order of Things* and *The Birth of the Clinic* Foucault describes the emergence of the conditions which enabled the ascendancy of anatomy and so allows a glimpse of a vision of 'how it could be otherwise'; but in *Discipline and Punish* he offers not simply a disconcerting description of alien worlds but a strategy for a new form of analysis using power as its central feature. Sociologists, general and medical, have accepted the human body as a given, as the point at which and from which they start their analyses. Following Foucault what now has to be explained is not the body as the point of commencement, but the body as the end-product of a system of force relations.

Power and the body

What is the nature of the body? Biologists answer this question by looking at it: it has tissues, cells, organs, fluids, and so on, which can all be 'seen' by the naked eye or with the aid of instrumentation. But to answer a question about the nature of the body with reference to what is seen simply sidesteps the problem because seeing is a form of perception. The body is what it is perceived to be; it could be otherwise if perception were different. The question is not therefore concerned with the nature of the body but with the perceiving process which allows the body's nature to be apprehended. What broad strategies of attention then surround the body? Foucault answers by reference to power.

Foucault identifies two systems of power. The first, sovereign power, relates to the central role of the body of the sovereign as the focus of law, justice, etc. The second, disciplinary power, arising about the close of the eighteenth century, focuses on the bodies of everyone as the points of articulation of disciplinary strategies.

Historically the supreme power of kings has tended to be reduced and constrained by a system of checks and balances, yet the body of the sovereign remained the major locus of formalized power. The sovereign was the embodiment of government. Whether or not the king was an absolute ruler, he was still required to sanction and approve all laws. Whether or not he actually held the power of life and death over his subjects, it was in his name that life was suspended and punishment meted out. It was the king who, long after he stopped leading his army in battle, remained the commander-in-chief, the king who defended the faith. In short all of the myriad functions of state focused on the body of the king. Thus the king's body was inviolate and the most heinous crime was regicide.

It is not coincidental that Foucault opens *Discipline and Punish* with an account of the punishment of an attempted regicide called Damiens. Using contemporary accounts Foucault deliberately confronts modern sensibilities and describes the brutal tortures and gory details of how Damiens' body was cut, wounded, and dismembered. True this was an extreme case but the episode symbolized an important relationship between the king and his subjects. It mattered little if the king was present in person as the magistrates, soldiers, torturers, and executioners were present as representatives of the sovereign power who had sanctioned this ritual. They each owed their positions and carried out their duties in the name of the king; their actions and their bodies were therefore extensions of the king's body.

Damiens' body which had attempted to harm the king's body was the surface on which the wrath and justice of the king was inscribed, albeit at one remove, by his officers. Damiens' body was not unusual in this respect: thieves were branded, criminals flogged, traitors tortured; the era is characterized by the scaffold and the stocks, by the instruments which marked the body. Justice involved the sovereign's body asserting its supremacy over the body of the law-breaker.

As for the crowd who watched Damiens – and indeed any crowd who watched the spectacle of the scaffold – they saw in the marking of one body by another an overt manifestation of the power of sovereignty over its subjects. Thus for the ordinary people power was glimpsed only with the concrete spectacle of the sovereign's hold over other bodies. This occurred not only in the theatre of punishment but also in the trappings of state, in the rituals and ceremonies which surrounded the king's daily life, in the processions and triumphs which marked the king's passage, the palaces and fortresses which offered physical symbols of the might of the king's body.

Foucault suggests that this system of power can be abstracted as a relationship of observation. Power existed to the extent that it was visible to those over whom it was exercised. Without the ceremonies of sovereignty, the king was as nothing. Sovereignty had to be seen – in its ostentation or in its marking of the body of the criminal – if it was to act upon the subject.

At the end of the eighteenth century a new mechanism of power emerged which Foucault calls disciplinary power. Foucault uses the Panopticon as an idealized form of this sort of power. The Panopticon was a prison designed by Bentham about the turn of the eighteenth century; it was organized as a ring-like structure with a series of cells placed around the circumference of the building and a hollow interior, at the centre of which was placed a guard tower. Each cell contained one prisoner. The outer wall of his cell was back-lit by a high window through which it was impossible to see; the inner wall of the cell on the other hand was made up of bars through which the prisoner could look to the central tower. The tower contained the guards, shielded from the view of the prisoners by a system of shutters which allowed, from their side, a full view of the cells. This description of who could see what and whom is important because, as Foucault notes, disciplinary power was predicated on 'an inversion of visibility'.

Under sovereign power the king's subjects had gazed upon the majesty of the sovereign and his symbols; in the Panopticon the gaze was from the guard to the person. It was not a simple inversion because the guard in the central tower was not a figure who represented the king. The guard was faceless, hidden behind the shutters, a sort of disembodied gaze who represented nothing more than observation and surveillance itself; indeed the guards themselves were subjected in their turn to the monitoring and surveillance of their superiors in the prison hierarchy. Thus in the Panopticon the spectacle was shifted from the body of the king to the body of the ordinary person, the king's old subject.

It is relatively easy to grasp the significance and form of sovereign power because that is the regime of power which has been formalized in the traditional analyses of power and politics: in Foucault's celebrated observation, 'we still have not cut off the head of the king' (1979: 89). We still persist in thinking and speaking in terms of power as if it emanated from a kingly person. Vestiges of the old regime exist in 'sovereign rights' or equation of the modern state with the sovereign in legal matters; but more fundamentally power is seen in political and sociological analyses as something which is seized or held, which can be usurped or overthrown, resisted or succumbed to. Power is equated with force, either physical or symbolic, which coerces, constrains, represses, blocks, or negates. But these notions, applicable to sovereign power, are quite inappropriate for disciplinary power.

Disciplinary power manifests itself through a relationship of observations; it has its effects on those who, knowing they are under surveillance, transform their actions and their identities. So how can it be overthrown? How can one seize a look? How can one get to the heart of a disembodied gaze? How can one resist surveillance when 'resistance' is one of its cardinal effects?

The presence of an omnipresent disciplinary power does not, as it would under sovereignty, imply a total society in which there is absolute 'social control' or in which 'freedom' is forever lost; as Gordon (1980) has pointed out, a disciplinary society is not the same as a disciplined one. Besides 'freedom' as it is meant today is itself a product of disciplinary power. Modern freedoms take the individual as their central focus, but it is the individual who is a product of disciplinary power. Without the individual there could no doubt be freedoms of a different sort but modern freedoms take as their object that creation of the Panopticon, Man. Bentham's brilliant invention was a prison which through self-discipline manufactured a certain form of freedom; the contemporary belief in 'the rights of man' would seem yet another facet of panopticism. Defence of the inalienable rights of man no doubt at times called for opposition to the prison but only in that it could, to those unaware of its innovative forms, symbolize the coercive power of sovereignty. Power represses and must be resisted; but this injunction only applies to the capricious power of the king. Disciplinary power on the other hand provokes and works through resistance: an up-raised hand to avert the gaze of surveillance marks the beginnings of a self-existence for the nascent individual.

Medical sociology and the patient

Just as 'the problem of the body' has been poorly theorized in general sociology, medical sociology has similarly failed to grapple with its nature and existence. There is a limited literature which has noted that something fundamental changed in medicine at the close of the eighteenth century. Historians have identified this watershed as emanating from the Parisian hospitals (Ackerknecht 1967), and some medical sociologists have fixed on this shift to explore the nature of modern medicine. Waddington (1973) suggested that it was a reorganization of social relationships within the hospital which for the first time brought masses of working-class patients under the enquiring eye of clinicians. The conditions were thus established for observant clinicians to identify localized pathology in these passive bodies and thereby inaugurate a system of pathological or bio-medicine.

Adding to Waddington's identification of the hospital as lying at the heart of the western system of medicine, Jewson (1976) took these similar events and suggested that it was not that the new doctor–patient relationship removed the constraints from observing what was 'really' hidden within the bodies of the patients, but that the new relationships produced a novel way of seeing and hence a new object. In effect, in Marxist parlance, the social/medical relations of production had created a particular clinical reality: not discovery in Waddington's sense, but rather manufacture or invention.

The different elements in Waddington and Jewson's explanations can be seen to have direct resonances with the Panopticon – passivity, observations, new knowledges, but Foucault had already reconfigured their relationships. Thus it is not a case of dominant doctor and passive patient producing knowledge, nor were they themselves structurally reproduced in medical knowledge, that is through the pathological theory of medicine. To be sure, knowledge might be said to be 'produced', but so might the passive body of the patient in that both emerged from the Panopticon: hence the central importance of the irreducible dyad of power/knowledge for Foucault.

Certainly clinical power can be likened to sovereignty, the doctor equated with the king in the control exercised over bodies. This model of power would seem to underpin much medical sociological writing. And at times such an analysis of doctor, patient, and body may be useful. Yet this focus is limited: it only examines the overt and visible majesty of the doctor and medical power; it acquiesces too easily to those situations when ceremony is reduced and concerned doctor and patient share their worlds in what Szasz and Hollender (1956) would call 'mutual co-operation'. It omits another power, more innocent and more concrete, yet abstract, even casual. Look at the lines of medical surveillance: 'What is your complaint?' 'How do you feel?' 'Please tell me your troubles.' See the routine clinical techniques: the rash displayed, the hand applied to the abdomen, the stethoscope placed gently on the chest. This is the stuff of power. Trivial perhaps but repetitive, strategies to which the whole population at times must yield. We must study power, asserts Foucault, where 'it becomes capillary', at the more extreme point of its exercise, for it is at these points that power is in immediate relationship with its field of application and where it produces its effects (Gordon 1980: 96). In which case the stethoscope is an important instrument of power. Yet who can object to its technical necessity? Who can challenge the 'value-free' nature of the whispering breath sounds it reports? Yet at each and every application it establishes, confirms, and reproduces the passivity, solidity, and individuality of the silent body it surveys. Why else would the stethoscope have become such a potent symbol of modern medicine, a self-conscious emblem to mark out the figure of the doctor.

The prisoner in the Panopticon and the patient at the end of the stethoscope, both remain silent as the techniques of surveillance sweep over them. They know they have been monitored but they remain unaware of what has been seen or what has been heard.

Medical sociology may have failed to grasp the specific significance of clinical method, such as use of the stethoscope, in a system of disciplinary power, but, it can be argued, the discipline does have a praise-worthy track record of opposing such techniques when used by medicine to treat patients as passive objects, that is as lumps of flesh to be manipulated by the doctor. However, again, such apparently noble claims rest on implicit notions of sovereign power in which the patient is somehow liberated from repressive medical techniques, or the doctor, voluntarily or involuntarily, relinquishes the power to objectify and endorses more equitable and humanist methods.

Such analyses are limited, at least in part because they imagine the body can be released from its passive status by removing objectifying techniques. But it is precisely those techniques which established the body as an object of social consciousness; without those techniques individuality would lose its embodiment. This is not to say however that the medical sociological enterprise has therefore been 'mistaken' in its promulgation of the active patient. No, rather medical sociology itself can be addressed as a component of power, a panoptic device for the transformation of medicine and for the fabrication of the autonomous 'whole' patient which it so desires to 'liberate' (Armstrong 1986).

In his later work Foucault became concerned with a new issue, what might loosely be described as 'the self'. How is it I know who I am? As usual Foucault adopts a historicist and relativist view of the problem. Perception of the self changes as does the question which might be posed about identity. In *The History of Sexuality, Vol. 1* (1979) this problem is explored through the changing self-knowledge of sexuality; Foucault argues that far from the past – in particular the nineteenth century – being a period of sexual repression, there has been a progressively increasing incitement to talk about sexuality.

The theme of sexuality of course relates to Foucault's earlier work on the body. A surveillance machinery over sexuality will focus on the most intimate bodily activities and in sexuality's wider context will bring to attention the issues of fertility and population. But there is a third element in Foucault's analysis of sexuality which has important implications for medical sociology and indeed for sociology in general. The key difference between techniques which monitor (and thereby constitute) the body and techniques which monitor (and similarly constitute) sexuality is that one is primarily a technology of seeing, the other of listening, and the latter is perhaps best exemplified by the confession.

The confession is of course a device long used in Christendom – and indeed Foucault's posthumously published further volumes in his history of sexuality go back to the Christian roots of confession and self-avowal – but it has been taken from its limited Christian setting of repentance to be meshed in with the wider context of disciplinary power. In particular the confession can be seen to have direct implications for both recent developments in medicine and for medical sociology itself. In a nutshell: if medical sociology has fought against and resisted the methods medicine uses to objectify bodies it has done this chiefly by applying the injunction: listen to the patient. Thus the confession, a technique of intimate surveillance, has been introduced under the guise of a progressive humanism.

In the last few decades the confession has been formalized in both medicine and sociology. In medicine it can be found in the shifting techniques of doctor–patient communication (Armstrong 1984) and increasing emphases on these aspects of clinical work in the medical curriculum (GMC Conference Report 1986), which in their variety help fabricate a subjective being. The confession can be found in fact in all the 'people' techniques from teaching and social work to probation and radio phone-ins. Moreover it can, especially in recent years, be found at the heart of sociology. The survey, the questionnaire, and the interview all seek to capture the essence of the confession, each methodological debate a fine tuning of the surveillance machinery.

Strategic bodies

What is the human body? It is the very core of 'embodiment'; it is the vehicle for living and experiencing; it is the enclosure of death. Within the cognitive field of the 'sciences of Man' sociology has seemed content to acknowledge the exclusive jurisdiction of anatomy and medicine in knowing this corporal component of 'person-dom'. Certainly medical sociology has at times been critical of medicalization but only in so far as medicine exceeds the (generous) limits which sociology has prescribed and invades the sociological preserve. Otherwise the alliance between medicine and sociology has worked to mutual advantage: sociology has contributed to the panoptic range of medicine while medicine has probably been one of the most important patrons of sociology in terms of jobs and research over the last decade or so.

This is not to decry the political alliance between medicine and sociology, even less to suggest killing the golden goose. The task is not to cut through the demarcation lines which separate medicine from sociology; it is not to say medicine is wrong, nor to promote alternative anatomies. Instead, what this chapter would indicate is the potential for asking strategic questions about the field of knowledge in which the medico-sociological alliance is cast.

Take some examples. How can we explain 'chronic illness'? Medicine claims it is a particular degenerative pathological process which because of the decline in acute illness has been seen more frequently in recent decades; in its turn sociology has provided the social counterfoil to medicine's biological orientation by studying the social causes and effects of chronic illness. But there are other questions on a different plane of cognition which address not only the question of chronic illness but also the explanatory forms – both medical and sociological – which surround and thereby sustain it. Thus how is it possible to speak of pathological or biological causes and effects? It is possible only since the end of the eighteenth century when, as Foucault points out, biology emerged as a distinct subject and pathology became the basis of disease. How is it possible to speak of changes in causes of morbidity and mortality? Only in the context of shifting systems of disease classification which at any moment are held to capture what really is (until the next 'revision' which 'improves' how things are to be classified). How is it possible to speak in such a way of the social causes and effects of a disease? Only since the beginning of the twentieth century when the social became an autonomous explanatory domain enmeshed with the medical (Armstrong 1983). How is it possible to speak of chronic illness? Only since the middle of the twentieth century when the focus of medical power moved from the anomaly to the most intimate aspects of life (Arney and Bergen 1983).

Or take the problem of death. What is death? What causes it? The old vision of death as a black-cloaked figure, scythe in hand, who came at the appointed hour, was replaced in pathological medicine by reference to the intra-corporal biological lesion; sociology emphasized either the social components of that cause or the social nature of dying. The alternative strategic questions would start with the pivotal place of death in pathological medicine, its seeds already held to occupy body space even at birth and acting as the key referent in the identification of what is to count as pathology (Foucault 1973). Thus it is not a question of trying to discover the factors, biological or social, which *really* cause death or surround the 'dying process' but to explore how death and these causes and effects have been operationalized (e.g. Arney and Bergen 1984; Armstrong 1986b, 1987) and hence what death actually is today.

This is not another version of the history of ideas. Ideas do not influence and generate other ideas in a never-ending procession, rather 'ideas' and knowledge are the expression of certain social practices in the way that pathological medicine is another manifestation of disciplinary power, of certain surveillance strategies and opportunities. Power, expressed as a strategic relation, is the other side of the knowledge coin.

In its frequent border disputes with psychiatry sociology appears to have been asking a different set of questions. But yet again the differences are illusory; a squabble with psychiatry, which has essentially been over control of the mind, has merely served further to reify the concept of mind. The alternative question is: how is it possible to perceive the mind as the subjective component to identity? What is the self? Again one could explore the role of the confession and its derivatives in medicine and sociology; one could investigate the historical emergence of mental differences as a means of distinguishing one person from another (Rose 1985) and the generalized problem of the neuroses which allowed for the deployment of a regime of mental hygiene across the whole population (Armstrong 1980); or document the techniques obstetricians have developed for dealing with the psychological aspects of pregnancy (Arney 1982) or the pain of childbirth (Arney and Neill 1982).

Traditional sociology, as a part of the sciences of Man, has held the banner of humanism high. But this should not preclude the asking of strategic questions about humanism, the counter-intuitive questions on its conditions of possibility. This, in part, would resonate with a strand of sociology running from Durkheim's ideas on individualism (Durkheim 1964) through Mauss's inter-war essay on the self (Mauss 1979) to a recent reassessment of the latter's work (Carrithers, Collins, and Lukes 1985).

This does not make the strategic questions anti-humanist because that would assume they existed on the same plane. Equally they are not for or against social control nor for or against power. When Bury (1986) suggests that these sorts of questions offer little guidance for action and in their implications appear gloomy for concerned social scientists, he reveals his assumption that there must be action and progesss, a non-relativist way forward that has been defined by a western tradition in the sciences of Man. The problem though is less the epistemological status of the strategic question than the framework which demands its justification. It is not sufficient to argue that these alternative sorts of questions cannot or should not be asked on a priori philosophical grounds. Quite simply they can be asked, though their answers may disturb the equilibrium of the existing cognitive field which rules on their admissibility (Rorty 1986); besides sociology has long taken a robust view of prissy philosophical objections to what is possible. The point for the moment surely is not to change *Gray's Anatomy* but to study it.

Acknowledgement

I am grateful to Sarah Nettleton for helpful comments on an earlier draft of this paper.

References

Ackerknecht, E. (1967) *Medicine at the Paris Hospital 1774–1848*, Baltimore, Md: Johns Hopkins.

Armstrong, D. (1980) 'Madness and coping', *Sociology of Health and Illness* 2: 293–316.

—— (1983) *Political Anatomy of the Body: Medical Knowledge in Britain in the 20th Century*, Cambridge: Cambridge University Press.

—— (1984) 'The patient's view', *Social Science and Medicine* 18: 737–44.

—— (1986a) 'The problem of the whole-person in holistic medicine', *Holistic Medicine* 1: 27–36.

—— (1986b) 'The invention of infant mortality', *Sociology of Health and Illness* 8: 211–32.

—— (1987) 'Silence and truth in death and dying', *Social Science and Medicine* 24: 651–7.

Arney, W. R. (1982) *Power and the Profession of Obstetrics*, Chicago, Ill: University of Chicago Press.

Arney, W. R. and Neill, J. (1982) 'The location of pain in childbirth', *Sociology of Health and Illness* 7: 109–17.

Arney, W. R. and Bergen, B. J. (1983) 'The anomaly, the chronic patient and the play of medical power', *Sociology of Health and Illness* 5: 1–24.

—— (1984) *Medicine and the Management of Living*, Chicago, Ill: University of Chicago Press.

Barnes, B. and Shapin, S. (1979) *Natural Order: Historical Studies of Scientific Culture*, Beverly Hills, Calif: Sage.

Bury, M. R. (1986) 'Social constructionism and the development of medical sociology, *Sociology of Health and Illness* 8: 137–69.

Carrithers, M., Collins, S., and Lukes, S. (eds) (1985) *The Category of the Person*, Cambridge: Cambridge University Press.

Davis, J. and Barnes, H. E. (eds) (1927) *An Introduction to Sociology*, Boston, Mass: D. C. Heath.

Durkheim, E. (1964) *The Division of Labour in Society*, New York: Free Press.

Foucault, M. (1970) *The Order of Things: An Archaeology of the Human Sciences*, London: Tavistock.

—— (1972) *The Archaeology of Knowledge*, London: Tavistock.

—— (1973) *The Birth of the Clinic: An Archaeology of Medical Perception*, London: Tavistock.

—— (1977) *Discipline and Punish: The Birth of the Prison*, London: Allen Lane.

—— (1979) *The History of Sexuality, vol. 1*, London: Allen Lane.

Giddens, A. (1984) *The Constitution of Society*, Cambridge: Polity Press.

Ginsberg, M. (1934) *Sociology*, London: Oxford University Press.

GMC Conference Report (1986) *Journal of the Royal Society of Medicine* 79: 565–80, 629–38.

Gordon, C. (ed.) (1980) *Michel Foucault: Power/Knowledge*, Brighton: Harvester.

Henderson, L. J. (1970) *On the Social System*, Chicago, Ill: University of Chicago Press.

Hirst, P. and Woolley, P. (1982) *Social Relations and Human Attributes*, London: Tavistock.

Jewson, N. D. (1976) 'The disappearance of the sick-man from medical cosmologies: 1770–1870', *Sociology* 10: 225.

Lenski, G. and Lenski, J. (1982) *Human Societies: An Introduction to Macro-sociology*, New York: McGraw-Hill.

Lorenz, K. (1966) *On Aggression*, London: Methuen.

MacIver, R. M. (1931) *Society: Its Structure and Change*, New York: Richard Smith.

Mauss, M. (1979) *Sociology and Psychology*, London: Routledge & Kegan Paul.

Morris, D. (1967) *The Naked Ape*, London: Cape.

Parsons, T. (1949) *The Structure of Social Action*, New York: Free Press.

Rorty, R. (1986) 'Foucault and epistemology', in D. C. Hoy (ed.) *Foucault: A Critical Reader*, Oxford: Blackwell.

Rose, N. (1985) *The Psychological Complex*, London: Routledge & Kegan Paul.

Szasz, T. S. and Hollender, M. H. (1956) 'A contribution to the philosophy of medicine: the basic models of the doctor–patient relationship', *Archives of Internal Medicine* 97: 585–92.

Waddington, I. (1973) 'The role of the hospital in the development of modern medicine: a sociological analysis', *Sociology* 7: 211–24.

Warwick, R. and Williams, P. (1980) *Gray's Anatomy*, London: Churchill Livingstone.

Wilson, E. O. (1975) *Sociobiology*, Cambridge: Beknap Press.

Worsley, P. (1977) *Introducing Sociology*, London: Penguin.

Wright, P. and Treacher, A. (eds) (1982) *The Problem of Medical Knowledge*, Edinburgh: Edinburgh University Press.

4

The lost subject of medical sociology

KARL FIGLIO

In this paper I will argue from both a historical and a contemporary angle that medical sociology has lost a crucial dimension from its thinking and methodologies and that this loss – of the subjective dimension – leaves it vulnerable to medical hegemony, its theories and technics contained within a perspective that alienates health and illness from the life history of the individual and of the society. To establish itself as a sociological – not a paramedical – profession, medical sociology needs to recover its lost subject.

If we look back over the past several decades of British medical sociology, we see the field standing on two legs: a methodological leg based on the social medicine of the inter-war years (Illsley 1975; Jefferys 1969; Stacey 1978); and a theoretical one built mainly on the foundations of sociology in the USA. What interests me about these two historical roots of British medical sociology is the importance of subjectivity – the actual human experience – to them both. I will press the point even further: one can trace a persistent line of thought in which 'subjective' refers not only to conscious accounts of experience, but also to the role of an unconscious and of primitive psychic processes – to psychoanalysis.

Subjectivity distinguishes a sociological approach to health and illness from an epidemiological one, and psychoanalysis offers a radical approach to the relationship of psyche to soma, and of sentient individual to social group. With that dimension apparently lost by medical sociology, its continued functioning as an ideal remains only just visible in the surge of interest in stress, life events, and other indicators of a psychological aspect of health and illness. I shall explore that subjective dimension in the two roots of medical sociology, both historically and critically, to argue that, once freed from medical hegemony, medical sociology will need to reclaim this subjectivity – and especially its unconscious dimension – in order to forge its own special character.

Social medicine and medical sociology

Social medicine tends to refer to the analysis of the illnesses of a population as aggregations of individual exposures to hazards and deprivations whose outcomes can be accumulated into statistical profiles. The social group – the community of people engaged in relationships with each other and in collective experiences and activities in relation to other groups and the environment – has not figured so much in our contemporary view of the tradition. In this section I will show that this 'psychosocial' angle has firm historical roots in British social medicine, and remains fertile for medical sociology.

Charles Webster argues that, although 'social medicine' was a term rarely used in Britain before 1942, it emerged from inter-war concerns with unemployment, malnutrition, housing, and health-care oriented towards preventive medicine (Webster 1985, 1986). The aggregated national health surveys published by the chief medical officer did not reveal the growing burden of chronic illness or the effects on health of the relentless unemployment and poverty. Webster brings out the truer picture of deteriorating health noted in local surveys, where unemployment and health could be more closely correlated and where indicators of poor health – as opposed to overt disease – appeared in figures on dental caries, height-and-weight-for-age studies of children, food expenditure by pregnant women, rickets, and maternal disablement, all of which could also be correlated with local economic and social conditions (see also M'Gonigle and Kirby 1936; McNally 1935). The (short-lived) post-war emphasis on prevention-oriented health centres, a comprehensive health service, and social medicine evolved from pressure groups, such as the Socialist Medical Association and the Committee Against Malnutrition; the patronage of an older generation of socially oriented doctors and researchers, including the neurologist, Sir Farquhar Buzzard, and Sir Arthur McNalty (former chief medical officer); and the activism of a younger generation, whose names include familiar figures, such as Richard Titmuss of the London School of Economics and Political Science, and John Ryle (the first Professor of Social Medicine, at Oxford). The convergence upon an idea of social medicine was based upon the inter-war experience with the social and economic roots of ill-health. For them, the medicine of the future would have to tackle chronic illness, whose roots lay in poverty, unemployment, bad housing, and occupational conditions.

It is easy to see that assessing the social conditions of populations in relation to their health would become a cornerstone of medical sociology. Sociology could offer to clinical medicine and to epidemiology not only an expertise in social surveys, but also the possibility of defining the nature of the social group, whose illness experience was being revealed so starkly in local studies. Writing in 1944, F. A. E. Crew, Professor of Public Health and Social Medicine at the University of Edinburgh, speaks of social medicine in words that invite the medical sociologist:

> Social medicine is medical science in relation to groups of human beings. . . . It is not merely or mainly concerned with the prevention and elimination of sickness, but is concerned also and especially with the study of all social agencies which promote or impair the fullest realization of biologically and socially valuable human capacities. It includes the application to problems of health and disease of sociological concepts and methods.
>
> (Crew 1944: 617, quoted by Webster 1986)

Crew's invitation to sociologists raises a question: what was sociological about social medicine – that convergence of concerns that grew from the stark social realities of the inter-war period? It was oriented towards the group rather than the individual, towards epidemiology, the health survey of a population, the health needs of a region; it sought a co-ordinated approach to health-care need which could easily be overlooked in piecemeal, acute, individualized medicine. In this respect the insistent uncovering of the health consequences of unemployment represented more than diagnosing additional disease: it was an attempt to make manifest chronic ill-health.

The prevalence of chronic illness – difficult as it was to pin down and politically explosive as it was – also fostered the notion of a social body. Although national authorities tried to blame the rising sickness absence rates reported by insurance companies on careless certification or on rates of sickness benefit payments (Figlio 1982; Halliday 1948; Report . . . on Insurance Medical Records 1920) the clinical vagueness of chronic ill-health shifted the attention of observers away from an infection-like causal view of illness, towards a social view in which illness could express the condition of a group as a social entity.

Sir Henry Tidy (1943) compared discharges for peptic ulcer among recruits to the British Army during the Second World War, with those for gastritis plus peptic ulcer during the First World War, and found figures of 23,574 and 709 respectively. He showed that the enormous increase represented an increase among the civilian population during the inter-war period, and not an increase during military service. Tidy's study was one among many which found a burden of non-infective chronic conditions during the inter-war years, conditions which pointed towards a pathogenicity within a population as a social group, rather than towards an increase in the more usual causal agents of disease.

J. N. Morris and Richard Titmuss – men of the younger generation of social medicine activists – also published a study of peptic ulcer covering the years 1927 to 1938, and another on rheumatic heart disease over a similar period (1944a, 1944b). The latter study showed the harmful effect on joblessness during the peak of mass unemployment, but stressed the long-term influence of poverty and bad housing that resurfaced as the depression lifted. From a social as opposed to a strictly epidemiological point of view, juvenile rheumatism could become an index of social health, and by 'such methods … Social Medicine might eventually frame a series of laws governing the manifold dynamic interactions of health with society' (1944b: 7–8).

Their other paper approaches the notion of the 'social' more closely. Here they found that peptic ulcer mortality actually fell with rising unemployment. Their conclusions take us immediately to the sociological dimension of social medicine.

> These results suggest that unemployment – or enforced leisure – led to a reduction in ulcer *mortality*: the death rate fell in those boroughs most heavily affected by unemployment. But when unemployment declined, *after pronounced depression*, mortality rose sharply. A return to work – but perhaps very insecure re-employment – meant more ulcer deaths.
>
> (1944a: 843)

> The managerial revolution, speed-up in the factory and on the road, the fungus growth of examinations, the squeezing out of the small shop-keepers all assist in making up what Ryle calls 'the mental and physical fret and stress of civilized city life'.
>
> (1944a: 845)

There is in this quotation an embryonic notion of social health and illness, of disease as an expression of the lived experience of society, rather than as an indicator of material inadequacy or uncontrolled disease agents. Illness made visible the forces at work within a population as a social group, even raised the question of what a social group was. There is a new dimension to social medicine here, which the local studies of the inter-war years, although they eroded the intended optimistic consensus on health and the individualistic clinical model of disease, only hinted at. [1]

This reconceptualization of the 'social' lay behind the coining of a new term, 'psychosocial medicine', by James Halliday in 1948. The usual term, 'social medicine', he argued, had been co-opted into usages such as state medicine or preventive medicine, and stripped of its essential social meaning. His notion was more cultural, in the sense of a social group organized and (self-)experienced in both material and symbolic aspects. One of the pioneering studies of this cultural approach was C. P. Donnison's *Civilization and Disease* (1937).

Donnison surveyed studies of the health of native populations, including groups whose traditional living and working had been disrupted by western economies. He found that diseases such as heart disease and cancer were pretty much non-existent unless there had been an intrusion of capitalist economy (see also Eyer and Stirling 1977).

In the cultural approach, a cluster of illnesses common to modern western culture, but not to cultures seen to be unchanging and traditional, becomes a symptom of the pathology of civilization; the advance of civilization is registered as much in its epidemiology as in its trade figures. To be civilized is to be stressed and vulnerable to stress diseases. It is to be destabilized as a society, nervous with the 'mental and physical fret and stress of civilized city life'. The literature reports on discontent, manifested in sickness absence rates and in claims for compensation. Strident demands for time and money to make good an injury showed to these medical observers and policy-makers a disruption of traditional work and community life parallel to the disruption of organismic stability in the case of physical illness – disorientation and discontent expressed in the alien language of disease (Figlio 1982). Early discussions of the Medical Sociology Group of the British Medical Association (1926) were concerned with monotony at work and with the spread of disaffection within the workforce. Neurasthenia, a kind of malaise with multiple vague symptoms, had become an important medical category in the early part of the century, and so had neurosis.

Neurosis traditionally referred to a disorder of the nervous system or to functional illness: conditions with no apparent organic pathology. But in the twentieth century neurosis has come to mean a disturbed psychological state, a condition of the psyche and not of the body. Freud invented the term 'psychoneurosis' around 1895 to establish a classification and aetiology of neurosis in wholly psychological terms, distinct from 'actual neurosis', whose origin might lie in disturbed nerve action, and from 'traumatic neurosis', resulting from physical shock. And as psychoneurosis also figured increasingly in routine compensation law (Figlio 1982), though less in the strict sense of Freud's concern with hysteria and obsessions than in the general acceptance of a class of wholly psychological illness, it found a way into popular consciousness in the early part of the twentieth century.

The First World War also pushed the notion of psychological trauma and psychoneurosis into public consciousness through the massive problem of 'shell shock' or 'war neurosis' (Figlio 1986a; Stone 1985). Here was a condition suffered by men who showed no physical injury, but who were incapacitated by paralyses; anxiety states;

phobias; loss of confidence, concentration, and attention; terrifying dreams. An elaborate network of hospitals and treatment centres was set up in Britain, many of them using standard techniques for nervous disorders: electricity, massage, baths, manual labour, rest and quiet, plus a firm but sympathetic host. But one, the Maghull Military Hospital near Liverpool, established a centre for the study of nervous conditions and for treatment along psychoanalytic lines; indeed it became a training centre for psychotherapy, and remained the only psychotherapy clinic in Britain at the close of the war.

Even during the war, writers on shell shock were looking ahead to the problems of psychoneurosis in the civilian population. Grafton Elliot Smith and Thomas Pears's popular book, *Shell Shock and its Lessons* (1917), addressed the future civilian problem of neurosis. The Cassel Hospital in London, still a pioneering centre for in-patient psychoanalytic treatment today, was established by T. A. Ross just after the war, with the explicit aim of making use of the wartime experience with psychoneurosis. Ross himself was an important popularizer of psychoanalysis during the inter-war years. The Tavistock Clinic was set up at this time with a similar aim (Dicks 1970).

The work of the Industrial Fatigue (later 'Health') Research Board started during the First World War with studies on munitions workers, and continued over many years, looking at sickness absence and nervous conditions as well as at more traditional areas, such as ventilation. The Medical Research Council also became interested in such areas, particularly through the work of their Miners' Nystagmus Committee, which produced three reports on this epidemic condition of coal-miners during the 1930s. Both in terms of personnel – with men such as the Cambridge anthropologist and psychologist, W. H. R. Rivers, who helped to establish the centre at Maghull, and Milais Culpin, a major writer on psychoneurosis with respect to public and occupational health in the inter-war period – and in terms of the understanding of miners' nystagmus expounded by the committee, psychoneurosis was a leading concept. This committee was an epitome of inter-war thinking on psychoneurosis: an indicator of general consciousness, and a vehicle for the development of expertise (Figlio 1982). Through the work of this committee, one can see the joint concerns of social medicine for material and psychosocial aspects of life brought to a focus.

Psychoneurosis underlay the notion of psychosocial; psychoanalysis was at the heart of the notion of psychoneurosis. Although psychoanalysis had a direct impact in Britain only after the Second World War, with an important channel being provided by the child guidance movement (Yelloly 1980), it was very important in indirect ways, and this becomes clear in the two themes above: the experience of shell

shock and the studies of psychoneurotic aspects of occupational illness. The currents leading into psychoneurosis were also the currents
through which psychoanalysis flowed into professional thinking in
Britain: the centre at Maghull, organized on psychoanalytic lines; the
Cassel Hospital; the Tavistock Clinic; writings flowing from these
experiences, such as those of Elliot Smith and Pears; T. A. Ross;
Milais Culpin; W. H. R. Rivers; the Oxford psychologist, William
Brown; C. G. Seligmann, later to be head of the Royal Anthropologi-
cal Society; and the surgeon, Wilfred Trotter, who was also Ernest
Jones's brother-in-law. Although psychoanalysis had made few
inroads into psychiatry before the First World War, shortly after the
close of the war the prominent neurologist, Farquhar Buzzard, could
address the Royal Society of Medicine about the necessity of psychoanalysis in psychiatry.

To speak in this period of psychoneurosis was to enter psychoanalytic discourse. This means that the understanding of causes,
whether individual or social, was mediated by it; albeit a form of
psychoanalysis filtered through writers such as Rivers, Brown, Ross,
and Bernard Hart, psychiatrist at University College, London. Using
psychoanalytic techniques, Rivers on the British side and Simmel on
the German side resolved aspects of the aetiology of shell shock into
the relationships among the ranks of men in the army. [2] And when the
same way of thinking was later turned on the symptoms of the inter-
war civilian population, psychoneurotic symptoms became lenses
through which individual and social life, often submitted to the
intense pressures of the restructuring of working practices, to high
unemployment and poverty, and to breakdown of traditional
communities, could be brought to a focus: the virtual made visible
(Figlio 1982).

I will exemplify this approach, using the work of James Halliday (J.
A. C. Brown 1961: 97–100; Figlio 1982). James Halliday was a
regional medical officer for the Department of Health for Scotland.
He also worked as a medical referee for national health insurance, and
in this capacity he took a special interest in the diagnosis given to
people certified 'incapable of work' (Halliday 1943). There had been a
large increase in sickness absence claims in the inter-war period, leading to questions about vague diagnostic labels on certificates, such as
'debility'. An inter-departmental committee (Report ... on Insurance
Medical Records 1920) had already tried to deal with the problem of
diagnostic categories in 1920, and before that another committee
(Report ... on Sickness Benefit Claims 1914–16) had investigated the
problem of so-called 'excess claiming' shortly after the introduction
of national health insurance in 1911 had brought out the new actuarial
experience of women workers, who were for the first time systematic-

ally insured. Then, too, government officials complained about labels like 'debility', while women's representatives argued that they expressed forms of ill-health not properly seen and understood before. Analysing many thousands of cases referred to him as a medical referee, Halliday rebuffed official scepticism in similar terms: the vague diagnostic categories on sickness certificates documented the gap between the presentation of ill-health and the medical understanding of that ill-health. Doctors saw unhealthy people in ever-growing numbers, no matter how optimistic national reports on the health of the nation might have been, and they used the best – albeit inadequate – diagnoses that their antiquated physicalist medical model offered them, in the face of the mass ill-health presented to them.

Halliday took a sample of his cases as referee, and found that a large proportion (running from 39 per cent to 77 per cent) of cases listed, for example, as gastritis, neurasthenia, debility, anaemia, and rheumatism, could be labelled 'psychoneurotic'. He went on to argue that a whole cluster of cardiovascular, respiratory, gastro-intestinal, genitourinary, endocrine, nervous, and locomotor illnesses could better be understood as forming an aetiological category of their own, regardless of the system of the body in which they were found. He formulated the 'concept of a psychosomatic affection', which gave weight to emotion as a precipitating factor, and to a range of factors that cut across the normal nosological categories. He said that controlled investigation of the onset or recurrence of many conditions, including asthma, peptic ulcer, hypertension, mucous colitis, exophthalmic goitre, and rheumatoid arthritis followed upon an emotionally upsetting event or a period of abnormal stress (Halliday 1948: 45ff). And he proposed and employed a diagnostic methodology based on what he called 'fields of medical observation and discourse', centred on 'the field of the person', 'the field of the environment', and 'the field of the mechanism', leading to the questions, 'What kind of person was this [who fell ill]?'; 'Why did he become ill when he did?' and 'Why did he become ill in the manner that he did?' (Halliday 1948: 29–31; for an earlier formulation, applied in detail to rheumatoid arthritis, see Halliday 1937).

I shall return to Halliday later, to take up the theme of psychosomatic aetiology as a lens for bringing to a focus the epidemiological character of a social group, rather than that of an aggregate of individuals settled in the same environment and exposed to the same dangers. For now, I would like to bring this section to a close, noting that the concepts of psychosomatic illness and psychosomatic epidemiology took root in the same period as studies of the health of local populations brought out clear relationships between the material aspects of the life of a community and its ill-health. Here is an embryonic psychosocial medicine and alternative model for medical sociology.

Medical sociology and its theory: the Chicago School and Parsons

In the previous section I argued that psychoneurosis and a psychosomatic conception of illness pushed for a reintegration of the subjective side. This push came both from the population, through its mass presentation of incomprehensible symptoms, and from sectors of the medical profession, in the conceptualization of psychosomatic affections. I have also said that psychoanalysis, both directly and through its diffusion into the general popular culture, set out a framework which fostered the articulation of this new perspective. Medical sociology contains a similar potential in its theoretical traditions, as well as in the orientation it has inherited from social medicine, and psychoanalysis has been important here as well. The subjective side, psychoanalytically speaking, is essential to a theory of social processes and, therefore, to the nature of sociological enquiry itself. The reintegration of the subjective side shifts the emphasis from groups as aggregates to groups as communities.

Two salient features of medical sociological theory in Britain will advance this case: (1) it has relied heavily on importation from the USA; (2) sociology there – especially Parsonian medical sociology – has been deeply influenced by psychoanalysis. The first point has been made by Stacey (1978) in her review of the state of medical sociology. One need only consider the provenance of the major areas of thinking in the field to come to a similar conclusion: think of the impact of the oft-cited Chapter 10 of Parsons's *The Social System* (1951: Social structure and dynamic process: the case of modern medical practice); add to it the whole areas of doctor–patient interaction, based on symbolic interactionism and ethnomethodology; or labelling theory, owing so much to Goffman; or deviancy studies, indebted as they are to the tradition of participant observation methods developed at the University of Chicago.

I will put the second point – the case for the impact of psychoanalysis on US sociology – in three forms: (1) the evidence for its rapid acceptance; (2) then the way it underpins Parsons's thinking thoroughly, particularly Chapter 10 of *The Social System*; (3) finally, in the historical context of analysing society as a social system.

The reception of psychoanalysis

Freud's work was translated into English in the USA almost as fast as it appeared in German, thanks to the efforts of the psychiatrist, A. A.

Brill. Psychoanalysis was also discussed by sociologists from an early date. *The American Journal of Sociology* published a large number of articles before 1936, in spite of the hostility of the editor, E. Faris (see Jones 1974 for a bibliography). A change of editorship in 1936 was followed by a peak year for psychoanalytic publications dealing with contemporary topics around social and psychological disorganization (Jones 1974: 30–1). The journal acted as a psychoanalytic forum long before sociologists themselves wrote substantially on psychoanalytic topics. Before 1940 nearly two-thirds of such papers were written by non-sociologists, whereas after 1940 the proportion had dropped to less than a quarter. The themes of early papers include general discussions, such as Ernest Groves on 'Sociology and psycho-analytic psychology' (1917) and more specific ones, such as Thomas Eliot on 'A psychoanalytic interpretation of group formation and behaviour' (1920). The prominent sociologist of the Chicago School, Ernest Burgess (1940), saw a reluctance among sociologists to accept psychoanalysis before 1919, but considered it to have made valuable contributions in establishing the role of unconscious factors in behaviour (see also Sebald 1982); in emphasizing wish-fulfilment and in the analysis of dynamic traits and patterns in personality. Another figure from the Chicago School, Harold Lasswell, trained as a psycho-analyst and applied psychoanalytic ideas to understanding criminal deviance. He also wrote on 'insight interviews' in sociology, which he attributed to psychoanalytic thinking (1940, and see also p. 88).

I mention the Chicago School because it was the most influential centre for sociology in the USA in the period before Parsons began to publish, and because it ran the most prestigious journal in the field, the *American Journal of Sociology*. Other journals came into the field, such as *Social Forces* in 1922, and the *American Sociological Review* (1936), but in the period of Freud's lifetime it was the University of Chicago and the *American Journal of Sociology* leading the field. Martin Bulmer (1984), in his study of the Chicago School, doesn't put special weight on psychoanalytic currents within Chicago sociology; he calls it an important example of the interdisciplinary spirit so characteristic of the centre, but none the less a minor tributary. Against this conclusion, however, it is important to point out that the men within Chicago sociology who, in his view, showed significant interest in psychiatry (Harold Lasswell, Edward Sapir, John Dollard, and William Thomas) also took a specific interest in psychoanalysis. Bulmer refers to John Dollard's statement in an interview that 'analysis was up for discussion all the time', and that he was himself deeply interested in psychoanalysis. He recalled a discussion group in the medical school, which included Lasswell, Frank Knight, and Philip Miller, and the visiting professor, Franz Alexander, who was later to be one of the many psychoanalysts who went to the USA and gave massive impetus to post-war psychoanalysis there. Alexander 'indeed gave his chief course in sociology, believe it or not. So the discussion of psychoanalysis was raging all the time' (quoted by Bulmer 1984: 200). Bulmer also points out that the principal exponent of psychoanalysis was actually Willian Ogburn (Dollard's supervisor), who is mainly known for quantitative work. Ogburn had already published two papers in the 1920s on psychoanalytic themes, one on irrational factors in economic activity (1919), the other on the importance of the psychoanalytic understanding of motive in order to control bias in research into areas with a large subjective component (1922). He published many more under the heading of 'social psychology', whose psychoanalytic content I have not assessed; in addition he was president of the Chicago Psychoanalytic Society.

There are also indications of a less immediate infusion of psychoanalytic ideas at Chicago. One finds, for example, a small but regular stream of student course papers and dissertations concerned with psychoanalysis. Already in 1917 there were papers of this sort: 'The Case of H—— B——, a study on pathology of mental attitude from the standpoint of psychoanalysis'; another which set out 'to show what types of neurosis are most plainly evident from the above statements [of a case study].... According to Freud neuroses may be divided into two main classes – psycho-neuroses and actual neuroses'; another case study, showing the problems of a family with a German wife and an English husband, with a marginal note, 'Oedipus Complex'. These papers are part of a series of student case studies of families for a course in which 'identification' seems also to have been one of the set themes: a clear indication of the use of psychoanalytic concepts in sociology teaching (University of Chicago B 173 f9).

Students were also required to write autobiographical accounts, presumably to prepare them for case studies of families. (Autobiography was important in the Chicago School, and was also associated with psychoanalysis: see p. 101.) These case studies were like clinical interviews, and indeed one member of the department, Louis Wirth, wrote on the notion of 'clinical sociology'. He wanted to secure a place for the sociologist among the professionals who dealt with social problems, and especially to ward off the encroachment of psychiatry into areas such as juvenile delinquency, which was a part of the growing child guidance movement (itself a main route of psychoanalytic influence into broader social areas in both Britain and the USA; see Yelloly 1980). Wirth questioned the typical hierarchical division of labour that made the social worker subservient to the psychiatrist, saying that

it is difficult, for instance, for social workers who have an acquaint-
ance with sociology and social psychology to understand why the
treatment of the patient has to be administered by the psychiatrist,
while the treatment of the members of the patient's family and the
members of his social groups can safely be entrusted to the social
worker.

(1931–2: 56)

He went further, and qustioned the psychiatrist's control of individual
psychotherapy, in a way that brought out the importance of psychoanalysis: 'In most textbooks on psychiatry one searches in vain for as
objective and concrete a description of the psychiatrist's technique as
the psychoanalysts have given of their method of procedure' (57).

Wirth went on to advocate a social understanding of the nature of
the individual and of delinquency, what was called 'the cultural
approach'. His paper was in part a defence of the professional status of
social workers within the child guidance movement, but it highlights
the idea of a clinical sociology – of clinical casework and treatment, for
which psychoanalysis stood as a model of scientific method. And
Harold Lasswell (1940) described the 'insight interview', a prolonged
and complex, intensive rather than extensive, interview, ideally ending
in a clear and sustained avowal by the subject of his impulses. This
kind of interview, which he contrasted with the variety of sociological
methods of obtaining information from subjects, he based firmly on
psychoanalysis.[3]

The notion of a 'mosaic of Chicago School Social Science' (Perry
1964) seems an apt depiction. The organized research interests,
methods, and spirit of Chicago social sciences (Bulmer 1985) nucle-
ated new ways of working well beyond the university. Harry Stack
Sullivan, co-founder of the William Alanson White Psychiatric
Foundation and of the associated Washington School of Psychiatry,
set up to bring psychiatric and social investigation together, organized
two colloquia on 'Personality Investigation' with a contingent of
Chicago social scientists in 1928 and 1929, 'forging a new unit for
study for the whole of social science and psychiatry – *the interpersonal
event or relationship*' (Perry 1964: xix). Sullivan, a psychoanalytic
psychiatrist, developed the now classic method of participant observation, based on his theory of interpersonal relations, itself based on
clinical work. Participant observation required the social researcher to
use his or her own responses to events as an involved group member:
'This participation in the data cannot be avoided if one is to do more
than count noses or other crude indices of human existence and
functional activity' (Sullivan 1936–7/1964: 15). The model is psychoanalysis, and indeed Sullivan advocated psychoanalytic-style training
for social research, so that the researcher could become a tool of

investigation, actively engaged yet relatively free of bias from collusion with group pressures (28–9).

The offspring of this marriage of psychoanalysis and sociology, seen in the foundation of the Washington School of Psychiatry and the elaboration of a clinical-type methodology, are evident in contemporary medical sociology, from the classic studies of the socialization of medical students (Becker 1961) to recent work in the interactionist mode. But I will leave the history of this infusion of the field by psychoanalytically informed sociology, and turn to the contribution of the single most influential theoretical sociologist in medical sociology, Talcott Parsons.

Parsons and psychoanalysis

Parsons sketched the development of his work in medical sociology in a retrospective overview in 1964. His roots, he explained, were in economics and, in particular, in grappling with the notion of self-interest as the principal characteristic of modern industrial society within Marxist theory. The professions seemed to him to stand outside any easy categorization because of the more traditionalist nature of their service relationship with a client. Medicine presented particular difficulties, because in one respect – that of the application of science to practical affairs – it was a rational, universal, value-neutral activity of the sort that typified modern society; while in another respect – the sensitivity of patients to their doctors' emotional attitudes – medicine did not fit the model of rationality that one would expect from the sociological typifications of modern versus traditional society, as in Tonnies's distinction between *Gesellschaft* and *Gemeinschaft* or Weber on rationality.

He intended to do an empirical study of doctors, but they seemed insensitive to the deeper level of the doctor–patient relationship that he wanted to explore. L. J. Henderson, a physiologist known for his work on the equilibrium between blood gases and the atmosphere, became his principal consultant. Elton Mayo, who had taken part in the Chicago School 'Personality Investigation' colloquia in 1928–9 and who studied disharmonies in industrial settings, led him towards the psychological – and particularly psychoanalytical – aspects of the problem. Henderson had just published his paper on the 'Physician and patient as a social system' (1935), and Mayo urged him to read Freud, which Parsons did extensively. (He was later to undergo an analysis. On Parsons and psychoanalysis see Gerhardt 1977.)

The other main input into his thinking at this time was psycho-somatic medicine, which brought home the importance of the doctor's attitude – as opposed to his science – to the recovery of the patient, and undercut any clear distinction between physical and mental illness. For Parsons these ideas meant that all illness had a motivational aspect (and was, therefore, also a form of deviance) and that the doctor had somehow to combine both the universality of science, with its attention only to the illness and not to the person, and the emotionally charged engagement with the patient's unconscious wish to be ill and dependent, entailing pressure on the doctor to collude. It also meant that doctoring continuously served the social role of therapeutically controlling this form of deviance. Indeed he argued elsewhere that modern western society channelled deviance into illness which it then controlled therapeutically, rather than with direct suppression (Parsons 1958).

In the general sense psychoanalysis must have reinforced his interest in the unconscious; he certainly spoke of his fascination with psychoanalysis – but particularly with the heart of psychoanalysis: transference and counter-transference and the development of procedures in therapy that made use of them. In the transference the patient's earlier, and now internalized, relationships to his or her parents were invested in the doctor; in the counter-transference, the doctor's similar relationships were invested in the patient; together they invite a collusion for both to remain in forms of parent–child relating. But the training and the processes of psychoanalysis, Parsons argued, could both protect the doctor from this collusive pressure and foster the beneficial aspects of the patient's sensitivity to the emotional attitude of the doctor, which Parsons saw acting powerfully when psychosomatic aspects of illness were considered. Psychoanalysis gave him a model that squared the circle of his understanding of medicine, as both a rational and a professional pursuit, as self-interest and collectivity-oriented practice: the doctor, through understanding transference and counter-transference, and through attending to the process of recovery rather than the application of science alone, could remain affectively neutral with respect to the universalistic and functionally specific aspect of his work, yet able to engage in and benignly foster the essentially emotional and relational aspects of illness and recovery (compare Sullivan's 'participant observation').

At first Parsons sought the unconscious emotional dimension of the doctor's work. He had begun, after all, with an interest in economics, centring on the notion of self-interest and the apparent inadequacy of that notion to comprehend professions. Only much later did he think of the patient's role, complementary to the doctor's (though the unconscious aspects of illness, treatment, and recovery were in his mind all along). Now he thought of doctor and patient together as a 'minimal collectivity' with self-disinterest – a collectivity-orientation – applying to both doctor and patient roles (1964: 338). The systemic character of a small society characterized by a small set of system variables comes to the fore. This orientation connects Parsons's work with a major current of social thinking in both Britain and the USA in the late nineteenth and early twentieth centuries, in which the ideas of system, equilibrium, and organic hierarchy represented, in social theory, the liberal ascendancy in politics. These were the days of 'New Liberalism' in Britain and the 'Progressive Era', including the 'New Deal', in the USA (Freeden 1978; Russett 1966).

His early economic and political interests had found their clearest expression in the doctor–patient relationship through his analysis of self-interest. Now his systemic theorizing also found its clearest expression in the social dimension of that same relationship, developed in *The Social System* (1951) and that immensely fertile Chapter 10, which laid out the reciprocal nature of the doctor and patient roles and placed them squarely in the social setting, where the main issue was the expression of motivated withdrawal from society – deviance – in the form of illness; and the social response in the benign traducing of the deviant by the doctor.

It is curious that medical sociology has fed so long from Parsons, while largely ignoring these two centrepieces of his thinking: the unconscious in its psychoanalytic sense; and the social – as opposed to individual – dimension, for which the individual doctor–patient relationship served as the epitome and object of fascination, but never stood on its own (discussed by Gerhardt 1977). What it seems mainly to have taken up is a catechismic depiction of the sick role, in the form of lists of rights and obligations, with the unconscious left out; and a micro-empirical preoccupation with interactions (Murcott discussed this limited view of Parsons – 1977).

We can see the importance of psychoanalysis to Parsons in the number of his publications dealing with it from the 1930s onwards, and even more clearly in the shift in perspective he gives to sociological problems, such as 'social control'. For Parsons social control is realized as self-control rather than external oppression – a notion well known among theorists of the family, who see the family as the site at which compliance is induced in the next generation (Poster 1978). For Parsons, social control is an aspect of the identification of the child with the parents (Parsons 1952). He takes the concept of identification from Freud, who introduced it in 'Mourning and melancholia' (1917). In many writings on the Oedipus complex, Freud goes on to say that the child resolves the struggle to love his/her contrasexual parent without fear of injury by the other parent by giving up his intense need for them, with a later willingness to tranfer these feelings and invest them in other people, and by managing the loss of the parents of his childhood dependency through taking aspects – images

– of them into himself and identifying with them. That process, the 'Dissolution of the Oedipus complex' (1924), becomes the central theme of maturation, and the model of dealing with loss. With it, Freud also built his structural theory of the psyche, the tripartite division into id, ego, and super-ego. The introjection and identification with parents forces a split in the ego with aspects of parental introjects residing outside the ego, as an observing, criticizing faculty. The cluster of these not wholly assimilated aspects of parental images he called the super-ego, which now carried on an internal relationship with the ego – all based on the early object hunger of the child and the capacity to internalize and identify with threatened objects of affection.

For Parsons, this model provided the basis of social control, with super-ego properties extending beyond the parents to external values. It also meant that the basis of social control lay not in learning, but in identification. This mutual assimilation of self and other implied an irreducible attribute of subject in relation to object. Such a relationship entailed an essentially system character for society, which could not be resolved atomistically into an aggregation of simpler events. This is the 'object relational' aspect of psychoanalysis, as opposed to its early concern with the management of drives, which had routinely affected – both positively and negatively – the acceptance of psychoanalysis by social theorists (Burgess 1940; Sebald 1982).

Psychoanalysis was crucial, therefore, not only to Parsons's notion of a profession, caught between modern and traditional positions in western society, but also to his elaboration of a social theory of the system nature of society. The individualistic dimension, say of the sick role, resonated immediately with the social dimension, and there was an irreducible relational foundation to the individual in society, one that could not be atomized into the play of individual self-interest.

System thinking

This system nature of society will carry us to the final section of this paper. But first I will ground it in its historical context. I have already alluded to the ideological character of system thinking – the liberal ascendancy. Barry Richards (1986a) has described the social democratic nature of psychology at this time, by which he means the attempt to represent social and political processes in terms of the consensus of individuals and the mitigation of conflict. If society is an aggregate of individuals seeking areas of harmony, then irreducible sectional disjunctions in the society – class, but also perhaps race and gender – are swept aside as the self-consciousness of its citizens is reconstituted as an ever-reforming consensus of individuals in the aggregate. The irreducible sectional interests are included within the greater whole which society represents for each section, often using organic metaphors, in which the parts work in harmony for the good of the whole.

For Richards, psychology could articulate such a self-consciousness powerfully because it theorized the self itself. If the model of the self were harmonious, organic, and hierarchical, then the individual in society naturally carries these same features. Even more: the growth of psychological services in the early twentieth century could care for the psychologically injured individuals, thereby reconstituting socially and politically structured contradictions of self-in-society as personal distress; by providing caring services, the distressed individual came even more to depend on the parental care-giver. Such a relationship of dependency was fostered both in the provision of services and in the theories of self that were based on harmonious dependency of parts to the whole, with the parts drawn into relationship with each other. Here again, we have a object relational analysis of the service relationship and of the traduction it entails: but where Parsons saw the irreducible nub of the collectivity and the point at which benign influence could actuate recovery, Richards sees a destructive and addictive relationship, which also becomes a model of the relationship of citizens to society and the state.

Historical scholarship of this period supports Richards. I mentioned the New Liberalism in Britain and the Progressive Era in the USA, movements that sought to combine the ideology of free market competition with one of social solidarity. The imagery of the period abounds in organismic metaphors from nineteenth-century social Darwinism which draw individuals into the social organism but retain the social struggle for existence, perhaps, by externalizing the struggle into competition between nations (Semmel 1960).

The New Liberalism, with thinkers such as the sociologists J. A. Hobson and L. T. Hobhouse, stressed the mutuality of individual and society, and the surmounting of the sense of contradiction in society. The liberal programme called for an active state which, like the mind in relation to the body, would draw the social organism together and consciously direct its energy – a 'practical' socialism (Freeden 1978: 42). It spoke of community and of co-operation: biological, sociological, physical, ethical. This theme infused planning issues, including progressive legislation, such as minimum wages, unemployment insurance, health insurance, and pensions. Although liberal thinking focused on an ethical reordering of social relations, it stayed within the belief that social problems lay in the distribution of wealth, rather than in the capitalist organization of production. The solution lay in improving efficiency in order to increase wealth, and investment in welfare could be packaged as an investment in productive capacity, an argument made explicit by the then Liberal Party adviser, Herbert Samuel (1902; Freeden 1978).

The emphasis on efficiency converts social relations into system components, and professionals become the engineers of the social machinery. This notion of the value-neutral status of science and of the politically neutral professional expert is rooted in the reduction of social relations to productive efficiency, of contradiction to conflict and conflict management, of social structure to the aggregation of individuals.

Medical sociologists would probably say that Parsons was a consensus thinker, in the tradition I called the liberal ascendency. In contrast, many would also say that social medicine – although its class analysis of wealth and illness do not of themselves break with the liberal tradition – has pushed in the direction of working-class advocacy, so that this root of medical sociology diverges from the Parsonian root.

I have argued for an enriched view of both social medicine and of Parsons: of social medicine, because inter-war social observation of health and illness opened up the areas of psychoneuroses, psychosomatic illness, and psychosocial aspects of medicine; of Parsons, because his notion of a social system was built on irreducibly relational ideas rooted in psychoanalysis: the motive, including the urge to be deviant, is always there; it is no theory of co-option, but one of struggle towards cohesion, just as the child struggles through the Oedipal stage before introjecting his or her parents into now muted internal relationships.

From a psychoanalytic viewpoint, I would say that all monistic or unilateral theses, whether of conflict or of consensus, must fail. Moreover, construing Parsonian theory as consensus-based, in contrast to contradiction-based, partakes of the same monistic bias, in ignoring the psychoanalytic roots that would elude any such interpretation. Similarly the psychoneuroses articulated a distress – gave a voice to it – just as surely as they opened new territory for medical, and therefore state, hegemony. (On the analysis of medical progress as hegemony, and a reply, see Armstrong 1986; Figlio 1986b.) Parsons formulated the inescapable unconscious urge to deviate, to refuse 'mature' responsibility, and the way modern society channels such urges into forms to be handled by experts rather than policemen. To see these two currents as only co-option is to lose track of both a Marxist and a psychoanalytic premise: that the moment is always dialectical. The ego strives for synthesis within a sea of contradictory needs whose nature can be well exemplified in the Oedipal struggle, in which having both mother and father, being both male and female, child and adult, form the nuclear and unresolved core experience of maturation.

Conclusion: making medical sociology social

I have argued that the psychosomatic side of social medicine contains an essential social moment, and the systemic side of Parsons contains a structure-breaking dynamic moment. Recent psychoanalysis offers medical sociology an enriched view of 'social', one which includes the individual and the social in one field and one which holds the sectoral, oppositional, and factional groupings of society in a dynamic relational matrix.

Without such a holistic view, medical sociology gives unwitting support to a 'medical model' that conceives of illness as a form of accident (Figlio 1985), even when that model includes a notion of psychosomatic. Without a notion of the unconscious and of unconscious defence, and faced with the dualistic choice of disease as either accident or wilful misconduct in the trivial and malicious attribution of 'choosing' to be ill, medical sociology of course opts for the former, and either avoids the whole issue by sticking with studies of health-seeking behaviour, based on models of rational decision-making, and 'lay' interpretations of (pre-existent) illness; or it tries to graft an accident model on to a belief in the personal and social significance of illness, as in the studies of life events; or it joins with traditional social medicine to produce epidemiologies of material deprivation and health.

But if medical sociology could develop its own concepts and methods, what internal platform could it stand upon? What notion of health and illness might it build upon – what would be essentially sociological? To my mind, it must examine the roots of the essential alienation by which society is reconstituted as an aggregate of individuals (the liberal ascendancy), and the illnesses people suffer occur as accidental misfortune, individual events that take shape in the aggregate (the accident model) (Figlio 1985).

From a psychoanalytic perspective on social life, the alignments and oppositions of sectors, whether of internal psychic life or of social groupings, can be treated as unconscious defences against anxiety; defences which require 'others', whether internal or external, into which endangering feelings can be projected. Such a view makes it impossible to consider any individual or sector in isolation, because of the unconscious relationship that is established by these projections.

I will give an example of the position in which medical sociology often finds itself, and of a psychoanalytically informed recasting of the problem, using a post-war experience of illness well known to medical sociologists: the overwhelming of medical services by so-called 'trivia'. But first I will have to go outside medical sociology, in order to expand on the notion of the social relations as defences against anxiety. It shows the shift from schismatic and rationalistic thinking to a holistic formulation, and the notion of unconscious defence, in which political groups reveal their deep interrelatedness.

Barry Richards (1986b) has shown such a shift in the understanding of war and military defence in the period on either side of the Second World War. War has often been thought about as a final bursting forth of instinctive aggression, and since the Second World War, the peace has supposedly been kept by a balance of terror: the model is one of forcing one's opponents to see the folly of attack; one which adds this spur to being reasonable to the 'enemy's' flagging control of its own barbaric impulses. From this position cynics say that war is inevitable and politicians praise the strength they have mustered against the threatened eruption of enemy impulses.

Richards has documented the emergence from the 1930s of a psychoanalytic understanding, according to which war erupts from the unconscious and anxiety-arousing character of psychic defences themselves, rather than from innate aggressiveness. The belligerents are locked into a mutual projection system in which each unburdens its own sense of internal 'badness' by projection into the enemy. Projection thus both constitutes the enemy (as the object which receives and absorbs these projections), and relieves anxiety, arising from unassimilated internal badness (see also Segal 1987). The apparent political opportunism of using foreign policy to upstage domestic troubles might be looked at profitably in this way; the manoeuvring to displace attention on to foreign problems literally displaces outwards the experienced source of anxiety, which now focuses on other places beyond one's individual and, by identification, collective, internal space. Whatever conscious use politicians may make of such distractions of public attention, the mechanism has unconscious roots and engulfs everyone: each side grows in self-righteousness as its internal badness is projected; both sides experience a relief of anxiety because the problem now lies distant, in foreign territory where 'good' acts can be directed against it. The situation may become dangerous, but the danger has been externalized, and is no longer felt as an unnameable internal dread.

The mutual projection systems at work in such a situation bind groups into larger units, because they need each other to receive projections. They have therefore a systemic character. But, as Richards's (1986b) and Segal's (1987) arguments suggest, they are also inherently unstable, and must increase in instability: if the projection-recipient (constituted as enemy) contains one's own projected badness, including omnipotent phantasies of annihilating the sources of aggression, then the more a nation arms itself, the more the enemy becomes menacing. To arm is also to project unconscious aggressive – even exterminating – impulses into the enemy, and thereby to increase its threat. More armament seems necessary for protection against the conscious experience of danger from outside, which is really a projection of internal threat. And so the cycle of projection and incremental defence must spiral upwards, its unconscious roots unrecognized, while conscious policy feeds a sense of either euphoria in one's own power (despair if one does not identify with it), or perplexity at the craziness of a policy which, held within conscious terms of reference, none the less makes a kind of sense.

With the notion of defence in mind, let us return to the problem of 'trivia'. The liberal economists have their account: demand can be controlled only by price; the medics have theirs: the secularization of society has left them to deal with many problems as if they were medical; medical sociologists have theirs: the (accurate) discovery of a mass of unrecognized illness, a tip of a clinical iceberg.

Cartwright (1967: 44–51; 1980: 53–8) took what was, in effect, a systemic tack on the problem by asking what kinds of doctors complain of trivia, and she found that they saw medicine mainly as the application of science and that they lacked engagement in medical advance, compared with their more tolerant colleagues. The complaining doctor was also less satisfied with his or her own practice. She also showed that doctors could 'train' their patients: doctors who complained actually carried a lower case-load of repeat-visits than those who didn't complain. Here is a social system, but it lacks the essential core that Parsons builds upon: the unconscious. Do we have in the trivia met by complaining doctors a social defence system, and if so, what are doctors and patients doing to each other?

If, as in the case of defence policy, each group is projecting internal 'badness', then each can externalize and control it through actions against the other. The patient can repeatedly attack the doctor's competence by displaying his or her failure; the doctor can attack the patient's knowledge or integrity: the sense of internal helplessness can be aggressively disowned. In an interesting study that suggests the unconscious aggression that can build up, Melville (1980) chose a small number of dangerous drugs which had been well publicized in normal medical channels, and compared their prescribing rates among general practitioners (GPs), grouped according to criteria like Cartwright used. Distressingly, but not surprisingly, the dissatisfied GPs were prescribing such drugs to patients (the externalized, projected source of their anxiety and sense of helplessness?) significantly more often than their more satisfied colleagues. One can only speculate on what their patients enacted, perhaps repeatedly assaulting their GPs with unmitigated symptoms. Doctor and patient were locked into a system together.

The unconscious dimension is not explored in these two studies.

They attempt to grasp what kind of doctor the repeating (out-of-role) patient has, but they slip towards an essentialism, in trying to pin down characteristics such as 'frustration' as the doctor's property. This view implicitly rests on a notion of society as an aggregate of individuals or social sectors who carry their own properties, which they contribute to a functioning social system; the overall stability of the system is conceived as an assembly of actions and interactions, the resultant of individual wills in a market-place society. The underlying matrix: the system as a process; on-going object relations constituted from dependency; the urge to establish an internal life with internal objects undamaged by aggression; and the need to control anxiety, often by primitive techniques for evacuating it into others; all this remains unrecognized but active underneath mechanistic, systemic accounts.

A systemic analysis need not fall into a dualistic cleavage of individual from social; or subjective from objective; nor need it imply a rigid functionalism. But it tends to do just that, and in that case, medical sociology becomes either paramedical or subjective and individualistic in orientation. That is the dilemma in forging an inherently sociological identity for medical sociology – where to stand, if not with the objective methodology of medicine or with the documentation of opinion and feeling of patients and practitioners as subjects? In my view, one resolution lies with the psychoanalytic matrix which medical sociology has always carried.

To document my case in the jointly historical and critical terms of this paper, I want to return to the work of James Halliday. Halliday represents the psychoanalytic current in social medicine: but where the names of John Ryle, Richard Titmuss, and the Peckham Health Centre are common currency, James Halliday is scarcely known today.[4] And yet he wrote prolifically and from deep personal experience with local health problems, especially of coal-miners, and with the running of national health insurance. His early published work includes a study of the psychological aspects of rheumatoid arthritis, in which he describes in detail the reorientation in diagnosis and recording that a psychosomatic aetiology promotes (1937). We can see a forerunner of 'life event' studies in his work; but more than that: it is biographical, it embeds illnesses within the life story of the patient, and rejects the illness-as-accident model. Disease as a pathological moment is reconstituted as an aspect of a lived life, that is part of history.

Halliday's main work, *Psychosocial Medicine: A Study of the Sick Society*, was published in 1948 and reprinted a year later. This is where he coined the term 'psychosocial'. The subtitle indicates that he applies his biographical thinking to the health of society as well. Falling ill means a disintegration, and the mode of enquiry is the same as for a person: one must ask, 'What kind of social group is this, that is what group characteristics are relevant and causal?'; 'Why did the community become sick when it did, that is what are the causal environmental factors?'; and 'Why did the community take ill in the manner it did?' (1948: 152).

For Halliday, a healthy group attracts members and is integrated; a sick society repulses them and disintegrates. Psychological bonds are either robust or weakened, whether by internal or by external factors, and the contributions of smaller groups to the larger group reflect the same integrated quality or its disintegrating, uncohering quality. A society, therefore, has patterns that make it a social system, with groups functioning within a larger 'containing community' (1948: 146, 149).

Disease spreading through a society seems to support mechanical models of causation, but really unmasks a low group immunity. Low group immunity signifies low morale, which provokes the search for a new leader who will realize for the group one of the two virtually present currents within its phychosocial processes: either to act upon the disintegrative forces or to embody reintegrative urges; to intensify either the sense of cross-purposes or that of common purpose. Illness, but also other mass phenomena, such as unemployment, sickness benefit rates, falling birth-rate, social fragmentation (for example in regional nationalism and emigration), and several other phenomena that he finds in modern Britain, indicate a loss of morale and of social coherence.[5]

Healthy societies, he argues, 'extrude' problem members: it is a sign of ill health when a group retains them and they become foci of 'social fragmentation', splitting society into smaller, factional groups. Fragmented groups move in either a disintegrating or a reintegrating direction through the leaders they choose. Halliday speaks of both 'inner' and 'outer' objects of destructiveness, that is objects in which the cause of deterioration is located. A disintegrating society always contains inner destructive tendencies, but it will look for them outside and try to destroy them there. The primary purpose of war, he says, is to try to externalize this destructiveness and to establish new internal relations freed of destructive tendencies. But they return to the internal objects when the war ends, unless reintegrative processes have been set in motion (1948: 160–1).

Halliday's emphasis on internal disintegration, focused upon internal destructive objects and the group's choice of a leader who will embody either the wish to project the internal 'badness' and fight it 'outside' (Bion's 'fight or flight basic assumption group' – 1961), or one who will embody reintegrative urges (reparative urges, in Kleinian terms) presages the 'social defence' orientation, so characteristic of the

British school of psychoanalysis.[6] So does his analysis of party politics, according to which the aggression felt towards the state for its obsessional stifling of creativity can be split off and relocated in one of the two parties. His is a rich depiction of the tendency of groups towards disintegration because of internal 'badness', that is the sense of being internally damaged by internal destructiveness; and of the drive to externalize the cause of this disintegration, but also to repair internal damage.

Halliday conceptualizes social groups in terms of their 'sociodynamic' aspects, even where there are material accounts of the same phenomena. The family is a psychosocial unit for him, not just an economic unit. The falling birth-rate in Britain since the 1870s signals neither a response to economic hardship nor an individual voluntary choice, but a 'national infertility' (1948: 137); an index of 'communal psychological or social health', along with suicide, chronic sickness, and occupational incapacity rates. The Royal Commission on Population was about to report on the declining birth-rate, and would agree with Halliday that it reflected primarily behavioural regulation (Mitchison 1977: 23–38). Halliday correlated these phenomena with the increasing incidence of psychosomatic affections, and with the threat to the obsessional control of events, which having children entailed (1948: 131). Similarly, when looking at occupational mortality rates, Halliday compared wives (rather than male workers), in order to assess the social aspect of social-class-linked epidemiological measures.[7] He found that the wives of skilled miners and textile workers had a 40 per cent and 24 per cent respectively higher mortality rate than wives of unskilled miners and textile workers, while the excess mortality of the latter two groups was only 8 per cent and 9 per cent respectively higher than for unskilled groups generally. The skilled groups, he said, also suffered a higher death-rate from hypertensive and cardiovascular illness and had a more remarkable fall in birth-rate; here, too, he referred to 'a class more likely to contain more obsessional personalities than their unskilled counterparts' (1948: 188–9).

Halliday's approach has a distinctly contemporary character. Epidemiology and medical sociology are increasingly looking at psychosocial factors in illness. (For overviews, see Marmot 1981; Parkes 1971; Totman 1979.) Some of the early work came from the Tavistock (Parkes on bereavement – 1972). Areas of intense interest include the failure of the coronary risk factors to account for much of the variation in coronary heart disease in the population and the 'life event' approach to illness susceptibility. What marks the latter off from Halliday's approach, however, is their quasi-medical, that is their non-sociological character. Illsley (1975) argued that medical sociology now had the chance to develop its own concepts, methods, and goals. To my mind, a major area of medical hegemony that could be open to sociological reformulation is on the nature of the social group in relation to illness.

We have little to go on in this new territory, beyond the obscured roots of medical sociological tradition that this paper has dwelt upon. The quest for a sociological model would have to take an independent view of the main line of medical research in this area, with its emphasis on quantifying illness susceptibility as episodes of failed coping or of 'stress'. A biographical approach to the individual and a historical approach to his or her society is needed – rather, a psychobiographical and psychohistorical approach. Only in the telling of a story – especially in its intrapsychic and external aspects together – do the 'facts' and their meaning come together. The conditions to which individuals and groups are submitted, their attempts to form their lives within these 'factual' constraints and their coherence individually and collectively form a historical account that integrates fact, meaning, and purposiveness.

In other words the subjective side of life needs to be reintegrated into a properly sociological epidemiology. My argument rests on the belief that any such project will have to be based on a psychoanalytical understanding, in the sense of the broader current of thinking and practice rooted in the notion of a dynamic unconscious. At an unconscious level, the language of mind and body converge, as do motive and cause, fact and meaning. Analytical methods also concentrate upon a life story, on the process of development rather than on abstraction of pathogenic moments.

The need for a sociological epidemiology takes us back to the Chicago School and to inter-war social medicine, then forward through social defence analysis into a possibility for holding together a view of illness as part of a life history, as well as physical and mental damage. Those sociologists did not study illness, but they did study deviance of all sorts other than illness, as case histories and as extended ethnographies based on participant observation. Psychoanalysis contributed to a method in which unconscious aspects of group life were probed by 'insight interviews', in which the achievement of insight during the interview was used as a validation of hypotheses, as it is in psychoanalysis, and in which the extended in-depth process of interviewing replaced survey methods. Autobiography was also used, producing classics like Clifford Shaw's *The Jack Roller* (see the discussion by Burgess 1930), and the idea that an autobiography of a delinquent, like the autobiography of a patient in analysis, could be curative (Wirth 1931–2: 65). In social medicine Halliday proposed a biographical method of questioning and record-keeping, and his attempt to delineate the nature of the classification, 'Psychosomatic affections', became a historical exercise.

The particular psychoanalytical-sociological models for such an approach are yet to be devised, but there may be a lead in the social defence view of social dynamics, in which social structures relieve anxiety through projection of internal conflict, yet only temporarily and in a way that requires repeated defensive reinforcement. The ill population provides opportunities for organized caring for others – an external relationship in place of an internal one, in which nameless dread is replaced by palpable definable disease spatially delimited and containable in both the physical and the social body. Parsons (1958) said that modern western society channelled deviance through illness, which could then be restored through medical services. In a Durkheimian view, the deviant is needed to delineate the normal and inform the sense of collective coherence. In a more psychoanalytic view – as expressed by Parsons – the deviant community doesn't just fall away from normality; it is motivated, so the restoration of deviants to normality required the restoration of normal motivation: first the collective anxiety about chaos is projected into a 'wilfully' deviant community – safely externalized – and then mitigated in that externalized form.

Parsons implicitly enlarges this model beyond illness behaviour as a form of deviance; he says; in line with his psychoanalytic thinking, that all illness has a psychosomatic core. So his model extends to the production of illness, when seen as a social phenomenon.

The mutual reinforcements between internal and social alienation, whereby 'objective' conditions replace unnameable intrapsychic pain, are unknown. Nor do I want to press this crude model beyond illustrating a line of thinking (see Bakan 1968 for a fascinating analysis of illness as alienation).

I offer this rough model to tie together the social defence orientation, which I have traced through Halliday's social medicine and into contemporary British psychoanalysis, with Parsonian medical sociology, which remains one of the pillars of British medical sociology. The conceptual and institutional framework of medical sociology must shift away from medical hegemony, in order to develop its autonomy. I have argued that a psychoanalytically informed sociology lies nascent in the tradition of medical sociology and offers a place to stand.[8]

Acknowledgements

I should like to thank Joan Busfield, Nicky Hart, Ludmilla Jordanova, Barry Richards, and Graham Scambler for their help.

Notes

1 Webster (1986) notes a significant and rapid change in terminology in the late 1930s, with 'social medicine' replacing 'public health'.

Perhaps this change signals an attempt to reconceptualize the nature of health in properly social terms.

2 Psychoanalytic psychotherapy of shell-shocked soldiers brought to light repressed rage at the officers because of the wounding of self-esteem inflicted on enlisted men. The external danger, noise, and relentless pressure from shelling overwhelmed the soldier, in part, because of barely controlled violence between ranks of personnel – an on-going feature of military social relations. See Ferenczi *et al.* 1921; Figlio 1986a; Rivers 1920; Stone 1985).

3 The 'insight interview' was a method of collecting information and verifying informants' reports by offering interpretations of their accounts. If interpretations led informants to a clearer grasp of their own life stories, this insight gave weight to the statements and their meaning. This methodology, in contrast to precise formulation and inter-observer reliability with respect to items on a questionnaire, is modelled on the psychoanalytic process.

4 Ryle's personal collection of offprints, from the Institute of Social Medicine, Oxford, contains several of Halliday's publications, so it is likely that he knew of Halliday's work. Halliday's papers also appeared in the standard medical press. The offprint collection of the Institute is deposited at the Wellcome Unit for the History of Medicine, University of Oxford, whom I should like to thank for the opportunity to use this collection.

5 The identification of social health and individual health, of society with a person, is similar to the 'culture personality' orientation of psychoanalytically informed anthropology in the USA in the 1930s and 1940s (Mead, Benedict, Erickson, and others). Like the structural-functionalism of Parsons, this line of thinking invites criticism for emphasizing social homogeneity in notions like coherence and health. I would put two points against too easy an adoption of this criticism: (1) any social formation apprehended as a social sector, no matter how much its existence expresses a momentary fixing or congealing of social processes or a resolution of social forces (see E. P. Thompson 1968), must none the less have some group character, as a dynamic moment, and therefore some coherence. The difficulty of joining historical, social, and political studies with notions of group identity is no argument against it; (2) psychoanalytic views of group structure are fundamentally dynamic and relational, built on the resolution of conflict and the disposal of disintegrating forces, such as anxiety. Homogeneity or coherence thus emerges from the dynamic situation, which is actively maintained, and not from essentialist notions such as a classless society. The latter view would, in psychoanalytic terms, be a partial and defensive position. For a criticism of the culture-personality school, see Lindesmith and Strauss (1950).

6 The classics of this analysis of group defences against anxiety include Bion 1961; Menzies 1970. The inter-war work on psycho-neuroses as a social phenomenon found an important post-war institutional realization in the Tavistock Institute of Human Relations, with its social defence orientation (indeed one of its classic studies, Trist and Bamforth's on coal-mining, cited Halliday as one of its few antecedents – 1951).

7 This procedure had already been established in epidemiology as a way of teasing out social influences on illness, but Halliday used it to elaborate a specifically psychosocial aetiology. Recent literature has criticized this method (Fox and Adelstein 1978), but this criticism affects neither the historical issue – Halliday as an example of a psychosocial orientation with roots in the inter-war period – nor the difficulty in understanding unexpected relationships between social class and illness or unaccounted-for class-related factors.

8 A psychoanalytically informed medical sociology will have to develop both methodologies and theories, so it is worth bringing work of a joint sociological-psychoanalytical sort, or of a sort that leans in that direction to the reader's attention. (On the latter: Antonovsky 1986; Blaxter 1983; Freund 1982; Williams 1983.)

Of the former sort, and because it demonstrates the possibility of a workable methodology, I'd like to draw special attention to the work of Brede and Zeul (1986) on the social relations of work. These researchers, one a psychoanalyst, the other a sociologist, combine psychoanalytic and sociological interviews of factory workers, and analyse the mutual formation of intrapsychic and social aspects of work life, especially with respect to conflict. In a similar vein, Klaus Horn (1975), a medical sociologist and psychoanalyst, uses psychoanalytic interviews to analyse unconscious conflict in symptom presentation. He argues that primitive intrapsychic conflict, as it is channelled through early socialization in the family, lays the groundwork for macrosociological features of a society. Conversely social relations can organize collective internal life, especially when primitive intrapsychic conflicts remain unresolved because of, for example, changes in family structure leading to erosion of paternal authority.

The work of Brede and Zeul and Horn, and of course Halliday, directs us towards an understanding of the individual in the social group as a dynamic relationship. The individual uses the group as a vehicle for the expression and resolution of primitive conflict at the same time as the group channels and even structures the form that conflict can take. From such a perspective, the usual epidemiological and sociological correlation of social factors in illness seems accidental, perhaps only tangentially related to the inherent conditions of health and illness.

We should also look well outside medical sociology for models and methodologies, to fields like social history, oral history, anthropology, and biography that try to comprehend the individual within the group. Recent oral history methodology seeks to reconstruct the histories of communities, in which the convergence of conscious and unconscious aspects of life is registered (P. Thompson 1978). Ronald Fraser (1984) has recently written an autobiography of his childhood, which treats it as a project in oral history and psychoanalysis at the same time. Some medical sociologists do use ethnographic methods and ways of thinking, for example in studying lay conceptions of illness and the way community behaviour can build around conversations about illness (Blaxter 1983).

References

Antonovsky, A. (1986) 'Social inequalities in health: a complementary perspective', paper presented to the third European Science Foundation Workshop on Inequalities in Health, London.

Armstrong, D. (1986) 'The problem of the whole person in holistic medicine', *Holistic Medicine* 1 (1): 27–36.

Bakan, D. (1968) *Disease, Pain and Sacrifice: Toward a Psychology of Suffering*, Chicago, Ill. and London: University of Chicago Press.

Becker, H. S. (1961) *Boys in White; Student Culture in a Medical School*, Chicago, Ill: University of Chicago Press.

Bion, W. R. (1961) *Experiences in Groups and Other Papers*, London: Tavistock.

Blaxter, M. (1983) 'The cause of disease: women talking', *Social Science and Medicine* 17: 59–69.

Brede, K. and Zeul, M. (1986) 'Psychoanalyse und qualitative Sozialforschung', *Fragmente: Schriftenreihe zur Psychoanalyse* 19: 117–36.

Brill, A. A. (1940) 'The introduction and development of Freud's work in the United States', *American Journal of Sociology* 45: 318–25

British Medical Association (1926) 'Report on a meeting of the Medical Sociology Group,' *British Medical Journal* ii: 201.

Brown, J. A. C. (1961) *Freud and the Post-Freudians*, Harmondsworth: Penguin.

Bulmer, M. (1984) *The Chicago School of Sociology: Institutionalization, Diversity, and the Rise of Sociological Research*, Chicago, Ill. and London: University of Chicago Press.

—— (1985) 'The Chicago School of Sociology: what made it a "School"?', *History of Sociology* 5 (2): 61–77.

Burgess, E. W. (1930) Discussion of 'The Jack Roller', in C. R. Shaw (1930) *The Jack Roller*, Chicago, Ill: University of Chicago Press; repr. (1973) in *On Community, Family and Delinquency*, University of Chicago Press.

—— (1940) 'The influence of Sigmund Freud upon sociology in the United States', *American Journal of Sociology* 45: 356–74.

Cartwright, A. (1967) *Patients and their Doctors; A Study of General Practice*, London: Routledge & Kegan Paul.

—— (1980) *General Practice Revisited*, London: Routledge & Kegan Paul.
Crew, F. A. E. (1944) 'Social medicine: an academic discipline and an instrument of social policy', *Lancet* ii: 617–19.
Dicks, H. V. (1970) *Fifty Years of the Tavistock Clinic*, London: Routledge & Kegan Paul.
Donnison, C. P. (1937) *Civilization and Disease*, London: Baillière.
Eliot, T. (1920) 'A psychoanalytic interpretation of group formation and behaviour', *American Journal of Sociology* 26: 333–52.
Eyer, J. and Sterling, P. (1977) 'Stress-related mortality and social organization', *Review of Radical Political Economics* 9 (1): 1–44.
Ferenczi, S. *et al.* (1921) *Psychoanalyes and the War Neuroses*, London: International Psycho-Analytical Press.
Figlio, K. (1982) 'How does illness mediate social relations? Workmen's compensation and medico-legal practices, 1890–1940', in P. Wright and A. Treacher (eds) *The Problem of Medical Knowledge; Examining the Social Construction of Medicine*, Edinburgh: University of Edinburgh Press.
—— (1985) 'What is an accident?', in P. Weindling (ed.) *The Social History of Occupational Health*, London: Croom Helm.
—— (1986a) 'Psychoanalytic psychotherapy and the experience of the First World War', paper presented in the seminar 'Psychoanalysis and War' in the series 'Psychoanalysis and History', Conway Hall, London, sponsored by the History Workshop Centre for Social History, Oxford.
—— (1986b) 'For the social history of medicine: a reply to David Armstrong', *Holistic Medicine* 1 (2): 135–43.
Fox, A. J. and Adelstein, A. M. (1978) 'Occupational mortality: work or way of life?', *Journal of Epidemiology and Community Health* 32: 73–8.
Fraser, R. (1984) *In Search of a Past: The Manor House, Amnersfield, 1933–1945*, London: Verso Editions and New Left Books.
Freeden, M. (1978) *The New Liberalism: An Ideology of Social Reform*, Oxford: Oxford University Press.
Freud, S. (1896) 'Heredity and the aetiology of the neuroses', *Standard Edition of the Complete Psychological Works of Sigmund Freud*, London: Hogarth 3: 141–56.
—— (1917) 'Mourning and melancholia', *Standard Edition* 4: 237–58.
—— (1924) 'The dissolution of the Oedipus complex', *Standard Edition* 19: 173–82.
Freund, P. E. S., with Fisher, M. (1982) *The Civilized Body: Social Domination, Control, and Health*, Philadelpia, Pa: Temple University Press.
Gerhardt, U. (1977) 'The Parsonian paradigm and the identity of medical sociology', paper presented to the British Sociological Association, Medical Sociology Conference.
Groves, E. R. (1917) 'Sociology and psycho-analytic psychology: an interpretation of the Freudian hypothesis', *American Journal of Sociology* 23: 107–16.
Halliday, J. L. (1937) 'Psychological factors in rheumatism', *British Medical Journal* i: 213–17, 264–9.
—— (1943) 'Dangerous occupations: psychosomatic illness and morale', *Psychosomatic Medicine* 5: 71–84.

—— (1948) *Psychosocial Medicine: A Study of the Sick Society*, New York: Norton; London: Heinemann (1949 edn).

Henderson, L. J. (1935) 'Physician and patient as a social system', *New England Journal of Medicine* 212: 819–23.

Horn, K. (1975) 'Die Bedentung des psychoanalytischen Krankheitsbegriffs für die Medizin und die Sozialwissenschafften', *Psychiatrische Praxis* 2: 139–49.

Illsley, R. (1975) 'Promotion to observer status', *Social Science and Medicine* 9: 63–7.

Jefferys, M. (1969) 'Sociology and medicine: separation or symbiosis?', *Lancet* 7 June: 1: 111–16.

Jones, R. A. (1974) 'Freud and American Sociology, 1909–1949', *Journal of the History of Behavioural Sciences* 10: 21–39; includes a comprehensive bibliography of relevant articles appearing in the *American Journal of Sociology* and the *American Sociological Review*.

Lasswell, H. D. (1940) 'The contribution of Freud's insight-interview to the social sciences', *American Journal of Sociology* 45: 375–90.

Lindesmith, A. R. and Strauss, A. L. (1950) 'A critique of culture-personality writings', *American Sociological Review* 15 (8): 587–600.

M'Gonigle, G. C. M. and Kirby, J. (1936) *Poverty and Public Health*, London: Victor Gollancz.

McNally, C. E. (1935) *Public Ill Health*, London: Victor Gollancz.

Marmot, M. (1981) 'Culture and illness: epidemiological evidence', in M. J. Christie, and P. G. Mellett (eds) *Foundations of Psychosomatics*, London: John Wiley.

Mathews, F. H. (1967) 'The Americanization of Sigmund Freud: adaptations of psychoanalysis before 1917', *Journal of American Studies* 1 (1): 39–62.

Melville, A. (1980) 'Job satisfaction in general practice: implications for prescribing', *Social Science and Medicine* 14A: 495–9.

Menzies, I. (1970) *The functioning of Social Systems as a Defence Against Anxiety*, London: Tavistock Institute of Human Relations.

Mitchison, R. (1977) *British Population Change Since 1860*, London: Macmillan.

Morris, J. and Titmuss, R. (1944a) 'Epidemiology of peptic ulcer: vital statistics', *Lancet* ii: 841–5.

—— (1944b) 'Health and social change: I – The recent history of rheumatic heart disease', *Medical Officer* 1–8.

Murcott, A. (1977) 'Blind alleys and blinkers: the scope of medical sociology', *Scottish Journal of Sociology* 1 (2): 155–71.

Ogburn, W. F. (1919) 'The psychological basis for the economic interpretation of history', *American Economic Review* 9, supplement: 291–308.

—— (1922) 'Bias, psychoanalysis and the subjective in relation to the social sciences', *Publications of the American Sociological Society* 17: 62–74; repr. in O. Duncan (ed.) (1964) *William F. Ogburn on Culture and Social Change*, Chicago, Ill: University of Chicago Press.

Parkes, C. M. (1971) 'Psycho-social transitions: a field for study', *Social Science and Medicine* 5: 101–15.

—— (1972) *Bereavement: Studies of Grief in Adult Life*, London: Tavistock; Harmondsworth: Penguin (1975 edn).

Parsons, T. (1951) *The Social System*, London: Routledge & Kegan Paul.

—— (1952) 'The superego and the theory of social systems', in T. Parsons (1964) *Social Structure and Personality*, London: Collier Macmillan (Free Press of Glencoe): 17–33.

—— (1958) 'Definitions of health and illness in the light of American values and social structure', in T. Parsons (1964) *Social Structure and Personality*, London: Collier Macmillan (Free Press of Glencoe): 257–91.

—— (1964) 'Some theoretical considerations bearing on the field of medical sociology', in T. Parsons (1964) *Social Structure and Personality*, London: Collier Macmillan (Free Press of Glencoe): 325–58.

Perry, H. S. (1964) 'Introduction', in H. S. Sullivan (1964) *The Fusion of Psychiatry and Social Science*, New York: W. W. Norton.

Poster, M. (1978) *Critical Theory of the Family*, New York: Seabury Press; London: Pluto Press.

Report of the Departmental Committee on Sickness Benefit Claims (1914–16), *Parliamentary Papers* xxx: 1ff; xxxi: 429ff.

Report of the Interdepartmental Committee on Insurance Medical Records (1920), *Parliamentary Papers* xxii: 19–48, Cmd 836.

Richards, B. (1986a) 'Psychological practice and social democracy', *Free Associations: Psychoanalysis, Groups, Politics, Culture* 5: 105–36.

—— (1986b) 'Military mobilizations of the unconscious', *Free Associations: Psychoanalysis, Groups, Politics, Culture* 7: 11–26.

Rivers, W. H. R. (1920) *Instinct and the Unconscious: A Contribution to a Biological Theory of the Psychoneuroses*, Cambridge: Cambridge University Press.

Russett, C. (1966) *The Concept of Equilibrium in American Social Thought*, New Haven, Conn: Yale University Press.

Samuel, H. (1902) *Liberalism: An Attempt to State the Principles and Proposals of Contemporary Liberalism in England*, London: Grant Richards.

Sebald, H. (1982) 'Freud: instinctivist or behaviorist? The mirages of American sociology', *Journal of the History of Sociology* 4 (1): 64–89.

Segal, H. (1987) 'Silence is real crime', *International Review of Psycho-Analysis* 14: 3–12.

Semmel, B. (1960) *Imperialism and Social Reform: English Social-Imperial Thought, 1895–1941*, London: Allen & Unwin.

Smith, G. E. and Pears, T. (1917) *Shell Shock and its Lessons*, Manchester: Manchester University Press.

Stacey, M. with Homans, H. (1978) 'The sociology of health and illness: its present state, future prospects and potential for health research', *Sociology* 12 (2): 281–307.

Stone, M. (1985) 'Shellshock and the psychologists', in W. F. Bynum, R. Porter, and M. Shepherd (eds) *The Anatomy of Madness: Essays in the History of Psychiatry*, 2 vols, London and New York: Tavistock, vol. 2: 242–71.

Sullivan, H. (1936–7) *The Fusion of Psychiatry and Social Science*, New York: Norton (1964 edn).

Thompson, E. P. (1968) *The Making of the English Working Class*, revised edn., Harmondsworth: Penguin.

Thompson, P. (1978) *The Voice of the Past: Oral History*, Oxford: Oxford University Press.

Tidy, Sir H. (1943) 'Peptic ulcer and dyspepsia in the army', *British Medical Journal* ii: 471–7.

Totman, R. (1979) *Social Causes of Illness*, London: Souvenir Press (E & A).

Trist, E. L. and Bamforth, K. W. (1951) 'Some social and psychological consequences of the longwall method of coal-cutting', *Human Relations* 4: 3–38.

University of Chicago, Department of Special Collections, file B173f9.

Webster, C. (1982) 'Healthy or hungry thirties?', *History Workshop Journal* 13: 110–29.

—— (1985) 'Experiments in social medicine'. Versions of this paper have been presented in various settings, including the autumn conference of the Society for the Social History of Medicine, London; for an abstracted version see C. Webster (1986) 'The origins of social medicine in Britain', *Bulletin of the Society for the Social History of Medicine* 38: 52–5.

Williams, R. (1983) 'Concepts of health: an analysis of lay logic', *Sociology* 17 (2): 185–205.

Wirth, L. (1931–2) 'Clinical sociology', *American Journal of Sociology* 27: 49–66.

Yelloly, M. (1980) *Social Work Theory and Psychoanalysis*, New York/London: van Nostrand.

5

Parsons, role theory, and health interaction

UTA GERHARDT

Talcott Parsons has wrongly been criticized for not preaching what, in fact, he often practises. Role theory in medical sociology has argued that Parsons's conceptualization of the sick role – first explicated in Chapter 10 of *The Social System* (1951a) – has two faults: first, it supposedly fails to account for the variability of normative expectations in the health field as well as the variety of subjects' illness behaviour; second, it supposedly fails to account for chronic illness which, to be sure, concerns an increasing proportion of the population and has developed into a major cause of death in modern society. Both criticisms, however, may be refuted if Parsons's conceptual stance is taken into account in its full original version.

The two criticisms aim at what, in an earlier publication, I have termed the incapacity paradigm of health and illness in Parsons's work (Gerhardt 1979). Parsons's second paradigm, focusing on what he calls the 'positive achievement' side of health and illness (1951a: 438), namely that of deviance, is not even made the target of ill-placed criticism. The deviance paradigm which draws upon psychoanalytic thinking is more or less completely disregarded in the secondary literature. Nor do those who redesign Parsonian categories take notice of the fact that the notion of social control which belongs to this perspective elucidates the way in which 'unconscious psychotherapy' may be said to prevail in health interactions.

This paper aims in a quasi-archaeological manner to re-establish some of the roots of modern medical sociology's concepts. The purpose of this undertaking is not to advocate that theory in medical sociology return to Parsons's ideas of social systems. Nor should it forgo what valid criticism has been raised over the last four and a half decades. Rather, it appears to me that if a Parsonian approach in medical-sociological thinking is to be found faulty, and should be overcome, this should be done through convincing refutations based on the knowledge of the whole of Parsonian thought. Partial criticism based on incorrect understandings of the contents and purpose of Parsons's work should not be found acceptable.

If the question regarding the adequate theoretical framework in medical sociology is still that of 'How much Parsons?' (Gerhardt 1977), the answer should not be given on the basis of personal preferences for other theories, nor insufficient knowledge of Parsons's writings. Hasty and sometimes ill-informed rejection of his ideas, or their acceptance and use through distorted or reinvented concepts, have led to the paradoxical situation that Parsonian thinking is often adopted by authors who claim to have critically overcome it. Frequently psychoanalytic notions are introduced to close a gap which Parsons seemingly left open while, in fact, his deviance approach is heavily based on psychoanalytic imagery. The idea of reciprocity is held against him with emphatic reference to symbolic interactionism while, in fact, reciprocity is the core of the social-systems model. Thus it appears that the question of how much Parsonian thinking is needed in medical-sociological theory can be answered only if the full scope of his ideas in this field is acknowledged.

Uses of the sick-role concept

Between 1951 and 1958 Parsons developed the notion of sick role in three major steps. In the same year as Chapter 10, an article appeared in the *American Journal of Orthopsychiatry* focusing upon 'illness and the role of the physician' (1951b) while, one year later, together with Renée Fox, he edited an issue of the *Journal of Social Issues* specializing in the sociological analysis of illness and medical care (1952a, 1952b). In the years 1953–6 he developed the L-I-G-A-scheme idea of social control with occasional references to the sick person's experience when undergoing medical treatment. In 1958 in a contribution to Jaco's (1972) reader *Patients, Physicians and Illness*, he added the organism as a fourth system to the hierarchy of culture, society, and personality, and he placed illness as a socially legitimate form of withdrawal in the wider framework of cultural definitions of health and illness.

At this stage, when the major outline of his sick-role conception was developed, the critical reaction set in which charged his approach with inaccuracy as well as irrelevancy. In 1958 Dahrendorf launched his devastating attack on Parsons's work which likened consensus and integration within the social system to the acrimonious harmony of Aldous Huxley's 'brave new world'. Two years later, in 1960, Mechanic and Volkart (1960) held that Parsons's sick role was too vague to account for what was termed illness behaviour, namely the attitudes, beliefs, and layers of symptom perception which make a person actively seek medical care for a complaint. This line of criticism was continued throughout the 1960s and most of the 1970s. When at the 1974 Toronto Conference of the International Sociological Association Twaddle organized a session in honour of Parsons, the concept of sick role was hailed by many contributors as what it had been widely perceived to be since the early 1960s, namely an empirical conceptualization of the norms which regulate social action with regard to illness as deviance. At the end of the 1970s, however, it was pointed out, if only with faint effect, that the sick-role concept was originally meant as a sociological rather than a social-psychological tool of analysis. Arluke, Kennedy, and Kessler (1979) emphasized the strictly normative frame of reference on a social-system level of thought, and my own refutation (Gerhardt 1979) of Margaret Gold's criticism made it clear that the identity of medical sociology was more endangered by misinterpretations of Parsons's genuinely sociological endeavour than by his seeming allegiance to the 'medical model'. One year earlier, Parsons had again delineated his standpoint in what became his last book, *Action Theory and the Human Condition* (1978). It ventured an even more comprehensive view of health and illness than the texts from the early 1950s, but his view on the sick role remained unchanged. Unfortunately neither this last text nor an earlier one undertook to come to terms with the many misrepresentations which the sick-role concept had suffered for nearly two decades.

In 1961 Wrong held that Parsons's was an 'oversocialized conception of man' which led to normative determinism and an unduly mechanistic explanation of social life. This view that Parsons proposed a normative-determinism stance of sociological explanation also became prevalent in the literature focusing on the sick role. A considerable number of studies undertook to show, as Twaddle and Hessler (1979: 118) summarize, that

1 its theoretical domain was too narrow,
2 it applied only to a limited range of sickness,
3 its formulation suffered from a management bias, giving undue weight to professional definitions,
4 that although it could be thought a reasonable description for society taken as a whole, little was revealed about known variability within societies.

Such variability was to be documented through empirical research, especially during the 1960s. Gordon (1966), in a study of New York residents, found that although the different diseases and illnesses on his list were by and large expected by his respondents to be treated along the lines of a perceived sick role, much subcultural variability in sick-role expectations, as well as a distinction between sick role and impaired role, were not represented in Parsons's formulations. In an earlier study Mechanic (1959) had proved that the obligation to get well was lacking in the case of the chronically ill and disabled, which made theirs a different type of sick role or a role more or less distinct from that of the sick. Kassebaum and Baumann (1965) found that conceptions of illness and sociocultural patterns of help-seeking varied between different ethnic groups. Twaddle (1969) checked on the correspondence of each right and obligation taken from Parsons's model with the expectation held in the population, and he found that from the standpoint of conformity and nonconformity at least seven different patterns existed. Pflantz and Rohde (1970), under the impression that incumbency of the sick role is widespread in western societies, undertook to question the deviance connotation it carries. They argue that since a large proportion of the population fails to consider itself healthy, it is conformity involved here, and Parsons erred when he assumed that illness was the exception rather than the rule in modern society.

A major line of counter-arguments concentrated on the issue of responsibility, especially with reference to psychiatric disturbances. Erikson (1957) pointed out that if a mentally ill person fulfils the expectation to get well, that is seeks professional help, the act of help-seeking exposes him to the dilemma that it also unleashes the prospect of lifelong stigmatization. In the mid-1960s two often-quoted teams of a doctor and a social worker, Sobel and Ingalis (1964) and Bursten and d'Esopo (1965), argued that the expectation to get well might be replaced in psychiatric cases by an obligation to remain sick which is established for the patient by his relatives or significant others. The same argument was made by Petroni (1969), who suspected here a 'much neglected sick role contingency'. This suggests a partial non-applicability of Parsons's notion for mental illness. Denzin and Spitzer (1966) show that psychiatric patient role behaviour cannot be predicted using a Parsonian sick-role model, and Blackwell (1967) concludes that, at least for the upper-middle class, a Parsonian-like role notion of sickness applies to physical but not to psychiatric illness.

The reason that such differentiation is presumed valid is that a difference is perceived between somatic and mental incapacity regarding the right or expectation that a person be not deemed responsible for his illness. As Segall explains in a retrospective, ten years later: 'In the case of a physical condition, the situation is relatively clear. ... However, when the condition also has psychological connotations, the question of personal responsibilities arises' (1976: 164).

This question governs Freidson's (1970) laborious endeavour to distinguish between six types of sick-role incumbency along the lines of alleged responsibility for one's condition, as well as the degree of exemption from normal duties and the expectation to achieve full recovery. All this, as Levine and Kozloff (1978) rightly state (but wrongly phrase as criticism against Parsons), epitomizes sick-role expectations as normative determinants of patient role behaviour. That is empirical variations of the latter (usually elicited through variations of expressed expectations regarding appropriate behaviour) are meant to find no adequate representation in Parsons's all pervasive sick-role model.

At the outset of most of the cited research, it is explicitly or implicitly stated that Parsons located the sick role much too closely to the doctor's role, and such propinquity to 'professional dominance' in modern medicine should be avoided. Even Gallagher, who otherwise refrains from many of the usual misinterpretations, criticizes Parsons for this alleged shortcoming. At the 1974 World Congress of Sociology he presented the first secondary analysis to recognize the *duality* of explanatory models used by Parsons. Distinguishing between an adaption model which he proposes to retain, and a deviancy model which he suggests be discarded, Gallagher means to advocate a useful change towards an unbiased recognition of Parsons's illness explanation. That he perceives the Parsonian framework as 'medico-centric', and comments that 'the flaw in the theory is that it overestimates the therapeutic impact of the physician and medical institutions' (Gallagher 1976: 213), may be indicative of the sad fact that the practice of misunderstanding Parsons's ideas may have been adopted even by those who engage in reading the original texts before evaluating them. Possibly the impact of the continuous misreading of Parsons's theory has become stronger over the last twenty-five years than the impact of the authentic contents of the original works.

The notion of sick role and physician's role as a social system

In 1935 the physiologist Lawrence J. Henderson, who also chaired a circle of scholars discussing the contribution of Vilfredo Pareto on modern social thought, published an article entitled 'Physician and patient as a social system'. Talcott Parsons, who temporarily participated in the Pareto Circle, kept a lifelong admiration for his mentor and friend to whom he owed the adoption of the notion of 'social system'. The book epitomizing this perspective in sociology acknowledges in its preface this intellectual debt. It may therefore not be by chance that the only chapter of The Social System (1951a) which aims at demonstrating the analytical grip of the elaborated taxonomy deals with medicine and illness. Chapter 10, entitled 'Social structure and dynamic process: the case of modern medical practice' attempts to illustrate, through an analysis of the doctor–patient relationship as a social system, what the analytical perspective outlined in the book may accomplish. Thus from the outset in Chapter 10, the sick role is regarded as a complementary counterpart to the practitioner's role, and both are introduced as concatenated elements of the social system of medical practice.

It is true that Parsons himself frequently describes the two-rights-two-obligations structure of the sick role (1951a: 436f; 1951b: 613f; 1978: 76–7). But as far as the physician's role is concerned, he fails to describe in matching clarity and detail the corresponding structure of exemptions and obligations. It is evident, however, that the physician's role – governed by the same value orientations (defined along 'pattern variables') as the sick role – functions as a counterpart to the latter.

The two rights on the patient's side are based on exemptions. First, the normal mechanism of being rewarded for fulfilment and punished for non-fulment of one's duties in the family, at work, and so on, is conditionally set aside. Second, the blame of being held responsible for one's failure or incapacity is held back and, instead, the person is spared the respective negative sanctions. Instead the sick have a right to receive, at least to a certain degree or for a certain time, a 'regular' income and others' 'regular' support (esteem) without 'earning' or 'deserving' them. They may plead irresponsibility for their present state without being sanctioned like anybody normally would who proves unfit to take responsibility for his own actions (or failures to act).

The two duties, on the other hand, safeguard the conditional nature of the two rights' being granted. First, the obligation to get well ensures that those who enter the sick role pledge themselves to leave it speedily, not at their own discretion but at that of their significant non-sick environment. It is the latter that dictates the conditions of sick-role incumbency. This dependency on others' definition of the situation is enhanced by the second obligation. The injunction to seek competent help from a physician and follow his advice, that is partici-pate in the treatment to the best of one's ability, urges the patient to relinquish his adult rights to mastery and manipulation of others until, in turn, these rights are reappropriated through relinquishing the sick status.

For the sake of symmetry, the two-rights-two-duties structure of the physician's role ought to be depicted in similar terms. Since Parsons does not explicitly describe it in sufficient clarity, I venture to piece its outline together from evidence taken from Chapter 10. This yields a conceptualization showing in what way the sick and the physician's roles are complementary.

The patient's duty to seek competent help may find its counterpart in the doctor's obligations to be solely guided by the welfare of the patient (1951a: 438, 477). Likewise, as counterpart of the patient's obligation to get well, Parsons's frequent reference to the need that the doctor must apply the highest possible standards of technical competence and scientific knowledge may indicate a role obligation (1951a: 437f). Thus the two duties making up the doctor's role are those to serve but the patient's welfare, and to ensure that this is done with the utmost professional competence.

It is more difficult, however, to determine the two *rights* of the doctor. If they are to be symmetrical to those of the sick they are also to mean exemptions. First, I find that Parsons's extended argument on the physician's unavoidably being compelled to injure a patient's body and to gain access to confidential information on a patient's private life indicates a right as well as an exemption. The right which is granted to the physician is that to 'enter' every sphere of a person's body or life story, and the exemption is that from being sanctioned by the patient, his significant others or the public for intruding into forbidden territory. Thus, one of the doctor's rights *qua role* is his 'free' access to highly guarded taboo spheres. Parsons stresses that 'Some of these may not otherwise be accessible to others in any ordinary situation, others only in the context of specifically intimate and personal relationships' (1951a: 453).

The doctor's other right is presumably to exclusiveness of trust and contact. Parsons emphasizes the special non-business nature of the doctor–patient relationship by pointing out how odd it would be if a car buyer were expected to approach 'the Chevrolet dealer only through the Ford dealer' (1951a: 439). The doctor has the right to expect the patient to entrust him exclusively with treatment and, if a 'second opinion' is sought, to co-operate rather than compete with his colleague. While Parsons describes only what I consider the counterpart of the doctor's right to exclusive care, namely that the patient is not supposed to 'shop around', it is the doctor's role which is the origin of such expectations. The respective exemption is double. First, the claim to exclusiveness of care relieves the doctor from the threat and worry that he might lose the patient through unpleasant or painful therapy. Second, it also means being exempted from the 'third-party-control' of other physicians or a concerned lay public who otherwise might judge every step of an ongoing treatment and possibly interfere with what they consider unnecessary surgery or medication. In fact the exemption from being taken to justice for violating others' bodily integrity is the necessary counterpart of the doctor's right to administer controlled '"injury" of the body' (1951a: 452). A similar argument may be made for the psychiatrist administering drug treatment or ECT, which alter the patient's bodily state, and even the psychoanalyst, who by reviving a patient's traumata may trigger auto-aggressive reactions. In such cases the doctor is protected against responsibility for the patient's suffering or even death if the rules defining proper therapeutic conduct are fulfilled. Thus the principle of normal reciprocity does not apply under the auspices of an ongoing diagnostic or therapeutic relationship. This 'reciprocity moratorium' concerns some of the most vigorous cultural conditions of self-preservation. That is the principle of revenge, or punishment, is normally retaliation for injury such that justice be restored. This general principle of 'an eye for an eye, a tooth for a tooth' in the face of bodily harm is set aside (the latter, of course, nowadays being miti-gated by the practice that justice is restored by a sentence of a criminal court). If the doctor were not protected in his role performance by this exemption, he would be utterly incapable of applying the most effec-tive and competent therapy in accordance with the best technical and scientific standards, which are compulsory to him under the aegis of modern medical care.

This symmetrical two-rights-two-duties structure of the practitioner parallel to the sick role is related to their identical 'pattern variable' normative orientations. The picture is that of two concomitant realiz-ations of one and the same basic pattern: *universalism* in the sick role means that it is according to generalized rather than personalized criteria that it is decided how sick one is, while universalism in the physician's role relates to the generalized rather than personalized standards of professional competence (as realized through technical procedures). *Achievement orientation* in the sick role ensures that, in Parsons's words, 'it is a contingent role into which anyone, regardless of his status in other respects, may come. It is, furthermore, in the type case temporary' (1951a: 438). Achievement orientation in the doctor's role, however, refers to the fact that through intensity of training high standards of excellence are achieved, and the position of physician is not open to inheritance, and so on. *Affective neutrality* in the patient role relates to the fact that getting well is to be tackled as a general problem, says Parsons, rather than one connected with the emotional value of specific people. It should be mentioned, however, that this does not rule out the emotional needs of the patient introduced into treatment: the patient's desire for dependency and being loved is a vital ingredient of the therapeutic relationship (see p. 126). Affective neutrality in the doctor's role is the necessary corollary of the fact that medical practice is applied science. The common feature between the scientific and the practical here is objectivity, as Parsons explains:

> The physician is expected to treat an objective problem in objective, scientifically justifiable terms. For example, whether he likes or dislikes the particular patient as a person is supposed to be irrele-

vant, as indeed it is to most purely objective problems of how to handle a particular disease.

(1951a: 435).

Functional specificity in the sick role is the same as that in the doctor's role, since all goings-on are strictly confined to the achievement of high technical competence. For the patient, it entails that he does not use his doctor as a bona-fide marriage counsellor or a remedy against loneliness.

Lastly, both the sick role and the physician's role follow a *collectivity orientation*. For the former, it ensures that getting well is seen as accomplishing a common task in co-operation with the doctor. That is collectivity here refers to the dyad where treatment and recovery are located in society's organization. For the latter (that is the doctor), collectivity orientation above all means a ban on the profit motive for all diagnostic and therapeutic action. Here, collectivity refers also to the values embedded in a 'code of honour' of the profession, that is the strict 'don't' placed on competition with other doctors and on exploiting the patient's helplessness or ignorance (lay perspective). It is with regard to such collectivity orientation as opposed to self-orientation that the professions in modern society – above all the medical profession – have developed into a realm distinct from the capitalist-business organization of industry (Parsons 1939).

Thus a parallel two-rights-two-duties structure and a joint, albeit two-sided, salience of the value orientations of universalism, achievement, affective neutrality, functional specificity, and collectivity spirit, make the sick role and the practitioner's role into a *social system*. As such, medical practice has a functional significance for the society as a whole (which, again, is conceptualized as a social system). It is within the framework relevant for modern industrial society that medical practice safeguards one of the most basic values in this society, namely *health*.

Parsons's strong endorsement of health as a most important concern in a democratic social structure which relies on equal opportunities in the educational and labour markets has often been overlooked by medical sociology. It frequently surmises that he concentrates on illness and its confinement to the sick role. But, in fact, the theme of sickness is tackled only because that of health appears crucial when equal chances of developing and using one's capacities within an 'achieving society' are in question. In the language of *The Social System*, health is named a prerequisite of the society's functioning:

The problem of health is intimately involved in the functional prerequisites of the social system. ... Certainly by almost any definition health is included in the functional needs of the individual member of the society so that from the point of view of the functioning of the social system, too low a general level of health, too high an incidence of illness, is dysfunctional.

(1951a: 430)

In 1978 Parsons introduces the term 'teleonymy' to account for a 'healing power of nature . . . , a property of living systems . . . by virtue of which such systems have a capacity to cope, often without outside intervention' (1978: 67). Such 'teleonymy' accounts for a *vis medicatrix naturae*, and the breakdown of teleonomic capacities, namely illness, only needs the *vis medicatrix* where nature does not provide appropriate remedies. That this is *not* geared towards so-called somatic illness alone but, rather, towards psychological and psychiatric disturbance is due to the fact that the normal social roles which the sick individual becomes unable to fulfil are primarily dependent upon mental accomplishments safeguarding interactive reciprocity within the family and work-place. It is here that medical sociology has its prime subject matter, maintains Parsons:

> Since it is at the level of role structure that the principal direct interpenetration of social systems and personalities comes to focus, it is as an incapacity to meet the expectations of social roles, that mental illness becomes a problem in social relationships and that criteria of its presence or absence should be formulated.
>
> (1958: 258)

The sick role is thus conceptualized as a social 'niche' where the incapacitated have a chance to recover from their weakness(es), and overcome their urge to withdraw from rather than actively tackle the vicissitudes of the capitalist labour market (Gerhardt 1979). The doctor's role in this is to provide the legitimation to enter the sick status as well as to spur the urge to leave it. It is in this way that reciprocity between patient and doctor in their sick role and physician's role make for the former's return to normal rights and duties as a full-fledged member of the work-force and other areas of daily concern.

It ought to be mentioned briefly that only too literal a reading of Parsons's text could ever have produced the misunderstanding that his was a notion which applies only to acute illness. In the 1974 contribution to the Toronto session, he finally made it clear beyond doubt that the sick-role concept could be applied to chronic illness. The issue is one of approximation rather than accomplishment of the goal of recovery, and permanently being exempted from a partial range of one's duties rather than temporarily being exempted from more or less the total range of one's duties, and so on. In fact, Parsons uses the example of his own then mild diabetes to illustrate how the sick role in chronic illness stays the same as a role and appears differently in individual cases.

In the social-system idea regarding the doctor–patient dyad, the reciprocity between their roles is pictured with a view to economic exchange, as between producer and consumer. While the doctor is not only a producer of care but also a consumer of the patient's willingness to be treated, the patient emerges as a producer of the health service by the very token of consuming it (1964b; 338). However, where health is involved, the modern doctor is vastly more competent to treat than the lay person. This motivates Parsons to insist on a basically unequal structure of the two-role system. The recent trend towards more democratization in the doctor–patient relationship, epitomized as a *fiduciary* element, appears ill-placed where health matters are at stake:

> The fiduciary responsibility ... should be regarded as shared by sick persons. ... I fail, however, to see how it is at all possible to eliminate the element of inequality. To get too far in attempting to do so would surely jeopardize the therapeutic benefits of the vast accumulation of medical knowledge and competence which our culture has painfully built up over a very long period.
>
> (1975: 267, 272)

Thus the social-system perspective detects in the sick-role–physician-role structure of medical practice a predominant concern with health as a prerequisite of (mental) capacity in an equal-opportunity society. Derived therefrom is a concern with illness as a loss of this capacity. The latter is to be regained when occupying a 'sick status' where the normal conformity–gratification/failure–sanction association is waived temporarily.

Health interaction and the power of the doctors

When in 1951 Parsons stated that the sick status was a 'negatively achieved' role, he assured his reader that 'of course, positive motivations also operate, which by that very token must be motivations to deviance' (1951a: 438). The idea of unconscious motivation behind deviance, ranging from sin to criminality and particularly illness, was promulgated in our century by psychoanalysis. Parsons himself was a trained analyst, and he reports in his autobiographical account of how his theoretical views in medical sociology developed that it was Elton Mayo who, possibly in the late 1930s, urged him to read Sigmund Freud's works:

> I was particularly fascinated by Freud's account of the psychoanalytic procedure including his discovery of the phenomenon of transference [remembers Parsons, adding] It was, I think, a little later that psychoanalysts came to be much concerned with countertransference and thus were able to fill out the paradigm to which I referred of a 'subtle emotional interplay' between doctor and patient.
>
> (1964b: 331)

However, already during the 1950s and with increasing vigour during the 1960s, an analytical perspective gained momentum where a reference to an unconscious motivation to fall ill, and psychoanalytically inspired reference to 'subtle emotional interplay' between doctor and patient, could only be viewed as cynically taking the side of established authorities against what could be considered the justifiedly or understandably deviant conduct of a patient or criminal. That the labelling approach was from early on directed against the Parsonian view that unconscious motivation be involved in becoming deviant – be it marijuana use, homosexuality, mental illness, or hustling – is made clear by Howard Becker's emphatically insisting on turning around the sequence of what is cause and effect. Namely, motivation is to come after behaviour:

> The sociological view ... ask[s] who breaks rules, and ... search[es] for the factors in their personalities and life situations that might account for the infractions. ... Such an assumption seems to me to ignore the central fact about deviance: social groups create deviance by making the rules whose infraction constitutes deviance, and by applying those rules to particular people and labelling them as outsiders. From this point of view, deviance is *not* a quality of the act the person commits, but rather a consequence of the application by others of rules and sanctions to an 'offender'. The deviant is one to whom that label has successfully been applied; deviant behavior is behavior that people so label.
>
> (1963: 8–9)

In this vein, the doctor is no longer to be seen as the agent of transference renouncing at countertransference in 'subtle emotional inter-play' which leads the patient back to recovery. Rather the doctor is now the agent of a much coarser and more coercive type of social control. In 1966 Scheff's study *Becoming Mentally Ill* identified the doctor as the one who inadvertently applies the lifelong stigmatizing label which forever spoils the patient's identity and life chances. In 1968 Scheff found that not only the 'public crisis' caused by the to-be-hospitalized mentally ill, but also every doctor–patient encounter contained a 'hidden agenda' of labelling and camouflaged force.

In 1970 Freidson's *major opus* brought together the topic of the special status of the professions in modern society with that of social control exercised by the doctor. Freidson's main insight is that the medical profession's social power derives from its control over the definition of illness, not only treatment. That is an element of labelling is recognized already in the diagnostic categories which are basic to the doctor's work. Thus the cognitive grid of medicine itself is understood as the locus of control from where the dominance of the medical profession in modern society emanates.

This view was elaborated further during the following decade by various authors, the trend being set by Kosa (1970) and Zola (1972, 1975). They point out that medicine as an institution of social control has become a predominant influence in the whole society, and its power is overtaking that of religion and the law. This view, which has been promulgated by Talcott Parsons at least from 1958 onwards, if in a less angry tone, is never credited to him but often voiced in resentment against his seemingly opposite standpoint. Barbara and John Ehrenreich's (1974) essay on health care and social control acknowledges the apparently contradictory views of Freidson and Parsons in this debate but makes them separate sides of the same problem. On the one hand, there is a type of medical dominance which they call disciplinary control and derive from Parsons's ideas (although overlooking his psychoanalytical leanings) and, on the other hand, they perceive another type which they call co-optative control and trace to Freidson's writings (although disregarding the latter's intellectual debt to Parsons). Thus professional dominance is at once understood to be exclusionary and expansionist social control. Exclusionary control supposedly is directed towards the hitherto under-doctored poor who are drawn into an upper-class system of medical care. Expansionist control avowedly is directed towards the affluent middle classes whose insurance-provided entitlement to care is expanded without limits to incorporate more and more aspects of life-style into medical management.

Eventually in the mid-1980s this perspective has gained so much momentum, that Parsons, who was ironically the first to link social control and medicine, is generally heavily criticized. For instance, Hart's *The Sociology of Health and Medicine* (1985), which strikes the reader as theoretically informed while based on a wide array of empirical findings, refers to Parsons in two connections: first, she cites Szasz and Hollender's (1956) three types of therapeutic relationship (activity/passivity, guidance/co-operation, mutual participation) to get beyond the unavoidability of control and endorse a model of health interaction where 'the asymmetry which Parsons saw as paramount to the social control function of medicine will be absent' (1985: 103–4). Second, Hart identifies professional privilege as the outcome of political action of capitalist-minded medical associations backed by the modern state; therefore she advocates that the target of health policy should be to transform professional power into expertise by putting into worldwide practice what so far is but the political credo of the NHS:

> There is an important sense in which organized medicine serves as a preservative of social solidarity, but it is not the one which Parsons had in mind. Since the war, the NHS has been the primary symbol

of citizenship in Britain. By promising to treat everyone in an equal fashion, it stands as a testimony to the idea of social equality in a democratic society.

(1985: 130).

In a way, this does not do justice to Parsons. Such a stance taken against his thoughts suggests that he has less to offer than Szasz and Hollender's three-type taxonomy, or the founder ideology of the NHS. It might even be argued that Parsons more likely than not could agree with the claim that ready access to health care should be a citizenship right, if only because he makes health the cornerstone of equal opportunity in the capitalist ('achievement') society.

If his ideas on social control are recapitulated in their original depth, it becomes clear that he perceives the nature of medical work, namely to diagnose and to cure and care, as limiting the scope of what is to be incorporated into the realm of medical jurisdiction. Likewise, if Parsons's ideas on political power are reviewed, it becomes clear that he advocated a rather impersonal notion of political influence which owes more to Max Weber's distinction between rational and traditional authority than to adapted Marxism, where politics are but an outflow of personalized power and privilege. Ultimately the question in this sector of medical sociology may be that of 'How much Marxism?' It ought to be kept in mind, though, that the ideology of resentment and overpowering which currently figures as Marxist in the literature on medical dominance has little to do even with the original theories of Karl Marx. But this is a different topic altogether.

Parsons's notion of social control: 'unconscious psychotherapy' and the modern rise of medicine

The positive motivation to deviance which Parsons identifies as the origin of illness is conceptualized in obviously psychoanalytical terms. When, in the early 1940s, psychoanalytically inclined social scientists attempted to make sense in social-pathology terms of the murderous anti-Semitism prevailing in Nazi Germany, Parsons (1942) contributed an analysis which he concluded by suggesting that only the psychoanalytically trained psychiatrist might possibly attempt to re-educate Nazi followers among the German population with any hope of success. In this vein, a theme with a long tradition in American social science received a new variation, namely that social pathology (comprising such diverse areas of deviance as blindness, political radicalism, or stuttering) was to be understood, predominantly, under a psychoanalytically informed perspective. While, in 1951, Lemert produced a book on social pathology which continued the tradition of 'social pathologists' previously sharply criticized by C. Wright Mills

(1943), Parsons made a definite attempt to deviate from this then well-entrenched view.

When, in the same year as *The Social System*, he published the article entitled 'Illness and the role of the physician', his aim was 'to discuss certain features of the phenomenon of illness, and of the processes of therapy and the role of the therapist, as aspects of the general social equilibrium of modern Western society' (1951b: 609). The unconscious motivation behind illness, as well as its being overcome under the auspices of the 'subtle emotional interplay' of the doctor–patient relationship, was conceived as a mechanism within modern society to deal with anti-social tendencies in a maximum-feasible humane way. Parsons, who was himself critical of modern medicine's preoccupation with what he termed a 'bacterio-technological perspective on illness' (1952a: 2), advocated a shift of attention from the somatic to what he called the psychical factors in illness. In 1978 he summed up that illness could result from three 'combinations of factors', namely,

> some failure to cope with the exigencies of the physical environ-
> ment, as in the case of invasion by agents of bacterial infection ... ,
> malorganization of the relations of organic and action level sub-
> systems of the more general human condition or from internal
> pathological processes such as a malignant tumor.
>
> (1978: 69–70)

For the sociologist who investigates the conditions under which the social order functions, the second of these factor combinations is of most interest. The breakdown of one's capacity to perform in inter-action, lacking the chance to remedy one's deficiencies or defaults by 'pulling oneself together', is what he understands as the sociologically relevant aspect of illness. It is here that the sociologist's contribution to medicine is in place. This is emphasized at the outset of Chapter 10:

> At one time most medical opinion inclined to the 'reduction' of *all*
> illness to a physiological and biological level in both the sense that
> etiology was always to be found on that level, and that only through
> such channels was effective therapy possible. This is certainly not
> the predominant medical view today. If it ever becomes possible to
> remove the hyphen from the term 'psycho-somatic' and subsume all
> of 'medical science' under a single conceptual scheme, it can be
> regarded as certain that it will not be the conceptual scheme of the
> biological science of the late nineteenth and early twentieth cen-
> turies. It is also certain that this conceptual scheme will prove
> applicable to a great deal of the range of social action in areas which
> extend well beyond what has conventionally been defined as the
> sphere of medical interests.
>
> (1951a: 431)

The basic notion pertaining to this view is that the child's socialization, that is his/her experience of learning the roles of adult performance at work and in the family, is achieved through repression of the needs for dependency, passivity, and irresponsibility, acquiring instead need-dispositions for independence, activity, and responsibility for one's own conduct and socio-economic status. It is such adult attitudes underlying need-fulfilment which are seen to break down when illness strikes. Parsons epitomizes the withdrawal component of illness under the sociologist's perspective that the social order would cease to function if everbody would freely take advantage of the liberties (exemptions) from normal obligations and constraints (and from the concomitant repression of unconscious wishes) which family and occupational life entail. The pattern is of special importance for industrial society since it relies more than its historical predecessors on 'compulsive independence' as a mental prerequisite of normalcy among its competing individual members:

> The alienation involved in the motivation to illness may then be interpreted to involve alienation from a set of expectations which put particular stress on independent achievement. Because of this complex, the importance of the passivity component of the deviance expressed in illness is particularly great, because the ambivalent motivational structure about the dependency-independence problem is particularly prominent. ... In this light the motivation to illness may, with only apparent paradox, be characterized as a case of 'compulsive independence from the requirement to be independent'. It is a kind of 'to hell with it all' pattern of withdrawal.
>
> (1958: 286)

From this it follows that therapy has to fulfil two functions: first, it has to restore the person's behavioural controls which have broken down. This is achieved through therapy's arousing and assisting the person's own endeavour to re-repress his dependency needs and readopt his independence need-disposition. Second, by this other-oriented work which is based on intrinsically interactive virtues, namely transference (especially with renunciation at countertransference) and competence in the interest of another rather than oneself (with strict prohibition of exploitation), therapy has to stress collectivity-orientedness as a social virtue in modern society where self-orientation prevails. It is thus within the deviancy paradigm of illness and its cure or care that the societal function of the medical profession comes to light most clearly. Parsons, under this paradigm, outlines the stages of social control which describe the course of medical treatment, and he reflects about the role of medicine as safeguard against the all-pervasive seductions of social life into the amenities of withdrawal from one's duties.

However, since the doctor–patient relationship is viewed as a social system, it is clear that the four stages of social control characterize the doctor's work as well as the patient's compliance (which is also called work). From the doctor's perspective, the succession of stages is described as follows:

> In the first place, there must be *permissiveness*: allowing, even encouraging the patient to express deviant ideas, wishes, and fantasies. ... The second ... is ... *support*: a more holistic kind of acceptance. ... This ... consists in valuing the sick actor ... as a bona fide member. ... It becomes doubly necessary that the permissive-supportive aspects of the therapeutic process should not stand alone. ... The therapist must frustrate ... desires by refusing the looked-for reciprocation. ... Concomitantly or increasingly the therapist *introduces conditional rewards* ... for the patient's good work in the therapeutic situation. ... Ideally speaking, the patient gradually gives up his deviant orientation and comes to embrace maturity in its stead.
>
> (1952b: 40–1)

From the patient's view, or rather from the doctor's view with a stance of 'taking-the-role-of-the-other', the same reads somewhat differently:

> The permissive and supportive treatment of the sick person, by giving him what he wants, undercuts the alienative component of the motivational structure of the illness. He finds it much more difficult to feel alienated towards objects who treat him with kindness and consideration than he would otherwise be disposed to feel. ... At the same time the element of dependency, through 'transference', is a basis of a strong attachment to therapeutic personnel, which can then be used as a basis of leverage to motivate the therapeutic 'work' which eventually should result in overcoming the dependency itself. ... Building on this, then, the active work of therapy, adapting to the fundamental conditions of the biological and psychological states of the patient, can take hold and operate to propel toward recovery.
>
> (1958: 287–8)

The idea of reciprocal four-stage social control is stressed in all publications after *The Social System*, focusing on medical practice as a topic or as an example for system processes (1951b: 615; 1953: 242, etc.; see also Gallagher 1976: 208). It is still present in Parsons's last work on the health–illness issue. In his paper discussing the teleonymy proposition (1978), he gives the following description: permissiveness of the physician presupposes that he acts under the affective–neutrality pattern; his support attitude resembles the 'parental concern for the welfare of young children who have not yet attained the capacities for autonomous performance in many areas'; denial of re-ciprocity 'takes the form of refusing to respond to various kinds of overtures that patients make towards the therapist . . . as love object or as target of inappropriate hostility and aggression'; and manipulation of rewards means 'to reinforce the patient's own attainment of insight into his condition and the motivational background manifested in such insight' (1978: 77–8).

The similarity with psychotherapy needs no more pointing out. It is obvious that Parsons perceives all medical care – albeit idealized such that the sociologically relevant 'unconscious motivation to deviance' is treated – as more or less identical with what Freud called the 'psycho-analytic cure'. In *The Social System* the view is held against a 'militantly organic' type of modern medicine with 'anti-psychiatric' leanings that 'unconscious psychotherapy' is an ingredient of medical care as such (1951a: 462). In 'Illness and the role of the physician' (written in the same year), he stresses his leanings towards Franz Alexander's special-ized psychosomatic medicine (1932, 1952) and explains why it is that the sociologically relevant side of medical practice is what psycho-analysis has recently come to represent. Parsons writes:

> It is highly probable that, whether or not the physician knows it or wishes it, in practicing medicine skillfully he is always exerting a psychotherapeutic effect on his patients. Furthermore there is every reason to believe that, even though the cases are not explicitly 'mental' cases, this is necessary. This is, first, because a psychic factor is present in a very large proportion of ostensibly somatic cases, and, secondly, apart from any psychic factor in the etiology, because illness is always to some degree a situation of strain to the patient, and mechanisms for coping with his reactions to the strain are hence necessary, if the strain is not to have psychopathological consequences.
> (1951b: 616)

This beneficial although mildly repressive way of dealing with the antisocial forces of deviance is hailed by Parsons as modern society's ever-expanding version of social control. In fact, he surmises, treat-ment rather than punishment has become more and more the preva-lent paradigm of how the ongoing social order in a democratic society is to be reconciled with the liberal values of freedom and equality. This, to be sure, finds a rationale, on the one hand, in the modern type of health problems, namely problems leading to psychological with-drawal from effective role functioning rather than problems due to infections or physical incapacities. Thus the first reason for medicine's dominance lies in the changed prevalence patterns of illness, as stated in a sweeping characterization:

With the development of industrialization, urbanism, high technology, mass communications and many other features of our
society, there has been a general *upgrading* to higher levels of
responsibility. Life has necessarily become more complex and has
made greater demands on the typical individual, though different
ones at different levels. The sheer problem of capacity to meet these
demands has, therefore, become more urgent. The motivation to
retreat into ill-health through mental or psychosomatic channels,
has become accentuated and with it the importance of effective
mechanisms for coping with those who do so retreat.

(1958: 281)

It is understood that the non-coercive forms of treating rather than
punishing deviance have a covert but powerful reverse side. A common element of value orientation is the commitment towards effectiveness for the doctor who treats and for the patient who restores his
capacity. It is the second rationale for the medical profession's dominance over the legal profession, the church, and social work in industrial society that modern tendencies towards instrumental activism are
best represented in the values of medical practice. Parsons states in his
personal account of how he came to be interested in the field of
medical sociology that the doctor and patient alike are, through their
roles, striving towards effectiveness and integrity; he continues

As I see it the pattern of this value-complex has not changed in the
relevant time-period, but the *content* has become more inclusive and
more generalized, so that those committed to the value-pattern, and
so situated in the social system that they must take an important
share of responsibility for its implementation, must consider a wider
range of conditions to fall within their sphere than before, and must
be open to the relevance of a wider range and higher level of
facilities, notably knowledge and skill, than before.

(1964b: 354)

If Parsons's critics were right, the doctor's reciprocity-bound control
over the patient (invoking that of the patient over the doctor as its
informal corollary) would be but an ideological offshoot of the control exerted by the medical profession over the populace which is its
clientele. Parsons (1963), in an article focusing on the conservative
politics of the American Medical Association, argues that a discrepancy of influence exists between few big-city practitioners who have a
dominant say in professional politics, and the mass of practitioners in
relatively underpriviledged positions. The dilemma making such discrepancy possible is that between the 'art of medicine' and scientific
medicine. Indeed, the values of the industrial society have only partly
been adopted by the AMA, says Parsons, since it represents the

interests of the traditionally single-handed small-entrepreneur practitioners while the bulk of medical work nowadays is state and insurance financed. From this vantage point, he finds the charges against
the medical profession's seeming self-interestedness understandable
but unwarranted; he argues

> Medical ideology from far back has credulously, and to a large
> extent rightly, stressed the physician's putting the welfare of his
> patients above any personal self-interest. In these terms, a sharp
> contrast could be drawn between the 'disinterested' or 'collectivity-
> orientated' outlook of the professional and the 'self-interested' ori-
> entation of business and commerce. The fact remained, however,
> that the physician was placed as much as any businessman in the
> position of pricing his own services; his assessment of a fee on a
> patient was a 'vote' to put the money into his own pocket, a
> consideration particularly prominent in the case of large surgical
> fees from well-to-do patients. Thus, whatever the moral attitude in-
> volved, assertion of the rightness of the pattern of individual prac-
> tice had, for structural reasons, to include insistence on the physician's
> right to determine what his financial remuneration ought to be. It
> was not a very long step from here to the idea, prevalent among
> unfriendly critics of the profession, that the physician was just like
> any other businessman, primarily concerned with 'feathering his
> own nest'. Personally I do not think for a moment that the critical
> institutional difference between business and the profession with
> respect to the profit motive has been eliminated. What I do argue is
> that insistence by the official spokesmen of 'organized medicine'
> that the individual fee-for-service mode of organization is the
> morally ideal one lays the profession wide open to the charge that
> they have abandoned their ancient and honorable devotion to the
> welfare of the patient.

(1963: 29)

The political side of professional dominance, then, becomes an issue
of the politics of the main professional association. As such, it is open
to criticism, and Parsons points at what he considers a major mistake
in professional politics. The AMA's short-sighted opposition against
state-funded health maintenance programmes, Parsons says, spoils the
image of the profession without guaranteeing its independence in the
long run. This, it appears, indicates a more sophisticated analysis of
the political side of organized medicine than some of Parsons's critics
have so far been willing to see. In fact the *idealized* reciprocity pattern
may hold more politically compelling truth in the name of liberal
democracy than the AMA's policy which sticks too literally to the
interests of the traditional 'small-entrepreneur' physician. Certainly

the Ehrenreichs' conjectures about class conflict in the surgery due to unanticipated consequences of state-funded health programmes do not provide the answer to this intriguing problem. It would be vital before inequality in any context of society is generally equated with illegitimate power that the difference be seen between a relationship where both interacting sides *accept* what happens, and one where action is imposed by one side upon another. The issue concerned is that of legitimation. Deriving his thoughts from a Weberian theorem which explicitly distinguishes between authority and force (where the latter is the 'last resort' of the former), Parsons (1964a) recognizes four types of such last-resort force in social-control relationships. Medicine, from this perspective, must be based neither on inducement nor on coercion or persuasion but, rather, on activation of commitments to reach its chosen goals. Regarding the latter, indicating rational authority in Weber's terms, neither power nor force can be legitimized. It is essential that there is two-way rule-governed acceptance of the one side's claim to dominance, and the other side's willingness to comply (Weber says, obey). The reason lies in the fact that the one side's claim to dominance (in the doctor's case, expertise and competence) is met by the other side's belief in the legitimacy of such a claim (Parsons explicitly discusses 'trust' as a condition *sine qua non* of any healing relationship). This non-violent type of supremacy in social life Parsons characterizes with the succinct statement: 'Appeal to "conscience" is the prototypical case' (1964a: 39). In this respect it is consequential of the Ehrenreichs to propose to undermine an ongoing relationship of trust between a doctor and a patient by the latter's displaying cynicism rather than gratitude (1974: 37). However, whether this solves the problem of the seeming disequilibrium of influence in the doctor–patient relationship without jeopardizing the patient's capacity to recover ought to remain an unanswered question.

Concluding remark

It may have become clear from the arguments I have raised that Parsons's thinking is often more intellectual than his critics would like to grant. In an astonishing way, Parsons's ideas became simplified, were recognized in not more than a truncated version, or were essentially disregarded when they became the target of criticism. On the other hand, it often happens that what is overlooked is then diagnosed as missing, and what is distorted is then castigated as badly thought out. The question therefore arises of what medical sociology owes to Parsons. It is likely that only if the exact lines of Parsons's works are reconstructed can their contribution towards our own conceptualizations in medical sociology be fully appreciated. Only then may they be judged on their own merit in a fair and constructive way.

References

Alexander, F. (1932) *The Medical Value of Psychoanalysis*, London: Allen & Unwin.
—— (1952) *Psychosomatic Medicine: Its Principles and Applications*, London: Allen & Unwin.
Arluke, A., Kennedy, L., and Kessler, R. (1979)'Re-examining the sick-role concept: an empirical assessment', *Journal of Health and Social Behavior* 20: 30–6.
Becker, H. (1963) *Outsiders: Studies in the Sociology of Deviance*, New York: Free Press.
—— (1967) 'Whose side are we on?', *Social Problems* 14: 239–47.
Blackwell, B. L. (1967) 'Upper-middle-class adult expectations about entering the sick role for physical and psychiatric dysfunctions', *Journal of Health and Social Behavior* 8: 83–95.
Bursten, B. and d'Esopo, R. (1965) 'The obligation to remain sick', *Archives of General Psychiatry* 12 (April): 402–7.
Dahrendorf, R. (1958) 'Out of Utopia', *American Journal of Sociology* 64 (1): 115–27.
Denzin, N. and Spitzer, S. (1966) 'Paths to the mental hospital and staff predictions of patient role behavior', *Journal of Health and Human Behavior*, 7: 265–71.
Ehrenreich, B. and Ehrenreich, J. (1974) 'Health care and social control', *Social Policy* 5 (1): 26–40.
Erikson, K. (1957) 'Patient role and uncertainty: a dilemma of the mentally ill', *Psychiatry* 20: 263–74.
Freidson, E. (1970) *Profession of Medicine*, New York: Dodd, Mead.
Gallagher, E. (1976) 'Lines of reconstruction and extension in the Parsonian sociology of illness', *Social Science and Medicine* 10: 207–18.
Gerhardt, U. (1977) 'How much Parsons?', paper presented to the British Sociological Association's Medical Sociology Group Conference (unpublished).
—— (1979) 'The Parsonian paradigm and the identity of medical sociology', *Sociological Review* 27 (2): 229–51.
Gold, M. (1977) 'A crisis of identity: the case of medical sociology', *Journal of Health and Social Behavior* 18: 160–8.
Gordon, G. (1966) *Role Theory and Illness: A Sociological Perspective*, New Haven, Conn: College and University Press.
Hart, N. (1985) *The Sociology of Health and Medicine*, Ormskirk, Lancs: Causeway.
Henderson, L. J. (1935) 'Physician and patient as a social system', *New England Journal of Medicine* 212: 819–23.
Huxley, A. (1932) *Brave New World: A Novel*, London: Chatto & Windus.
Jaco, E.(ed.) (1972) *Patients, Physicians and Illness*, New York: Free Press (2nd edn).
Kassebaum, G. G. and Baumann, B. O. (1965) 'Dimensions of the sick role in chronic illness', *Journal of Health and Human Behavior*, 6: 16–27.
Kosa, J. (1970) 'Entrepreneurship and charisma in the medical profession', *Social Science and Medicine* 4: 25–40.

Lemert, E. (1951) *Social Pathology*, New York: McGraw-Hill.

Levine, S. and Kozloff, M. A. (1978) 'The sick role: assessment and over-view', *Annual Review of Sociology* 4: 317–43.

Mechanic, D. (1959) 'Illness and social disability: some problems of analysis', *Pacific Sociological Review* 2: 37–41.

Mechanic D. and Volkart, E. (1960) 'Illness behavior and medical diagnosis', *Journal of Health and Human Behavior* 1: 86–94.

Mills, C. W. (1943) 'The professional ideology of social pathologists', *American Journal of Sociology* 49 (September): 165–80.

Parsons, T. (1939) 'The professions and social structure', *Social Forces* 17 (4); repr. *Essays in Sociological Theory Pure and Applied* (1949), Glencoe/Ill: Free Press.

—— (1942) 'The sociology of modern anti-Semitism',in I. Graeber and S. H. Britt (eds), *Jews in a Gentile World: The Problem of Anti-Semitism*, New York: Macmillan.

—— (1951a) *The Social System*, Glencoe: Free Press.

—— (1951b) 'Illness and the role of the physician', *American Journal of Orthopsychiatry*, 21: 452–60; repr. C. Kluckhohn and H. A. Murray (eds) (1964) *Personality in Nature, Society and Culture*, New York: Knopf: 609–17 (2nd edn).

—— (1952a) (with Fox, R.) 'Introduction', *Journal of Social Issues* 8 (4): 2–3.

—— (1952b) (with Fox, R.) 'Illness, therapy and the modern urban American family', *Journal of Social Issues* 8 (4): 31–44.

—— (1953) (with Bales, R. A. and Shils, E. A.) *Working Papers in the Theory of Action*, New York: Free Press.

—— (1956) (with Smelser, N. J.) *Economy and Society*, London: Routledge & Kegan Paul.

—— (1958) 'Definitions of health and illness in the light of American values and social structure', in T. Parsons (1964) *Social Structure and Personality*, New York: Free Press.

—— (1963) 'Social change and medical organization in the United States: a sociological perspective', *Annals of the American Academy of Political and Social Sciences* 346: 21–33.

—— (1964a) 'Some reflections on the place of force in social process', in H. Eckstein (ed.) *Internal War: Basic Problems and Approaches*, New York: Free Press.

—— (1964b) 'Some theoretical considerations bearing on the field of medical sociology', in T. Parsons (1964) *Social Structure and Personality*, New York: Free Press.

—— (1975) 'The sick role and the role of the physician reconsidered', *Health and Society* 53 (3): 257–78.

—— (1978) 'Health and disease: a sociological and action perspective', in T. Parsons, *Action Theory and the Human Condition*, London: Macmillan.

Petroni, F. A. (1969) 'Significant others and illness behavior: a much neglected sick role contingency', *Sociological Quarterly* 10: 32–41.

Pflantz, M. and Rohde, J. (1970) 'Illness: deviant behavior or conformity?', *Social Science and Medicine* 4: 645–53.

Scheff, T. (1966) *Becoming Mentally Ill: A Sociological Perspective*, Chicago, Ill: Aldine

—— (1968) 'Negotiating reality: notes on power in the assessment of responsibility', *Social Problems* 16 (summer): 3–17.

Segall, A. (1976) 'The sick role concept: understanding illness behavior', *Journal of Health and Social Behavior* 17 (June): 163–70.

Sobel, R. and Ingalis, A. (1964) 'Resistance to treatment: explorations of the patient's sick role', *American Journal of Psychotherapy* 18: 562–73.

Szasz, T. and Hollender, W. (1956) 'A contribution to the philosophy of medicine: the basic model of doctor–patient relationship', *Archives of Internal Medicine* 97: 585–92.

Twaddle, A. G. (1969) 'Health decisions and sick role variations: an exploration', *Journal of Health and Social Behavior* 10: 105–15.

Twaddle, A. G. and Hessler, R. H. (1977) *A Sociology of Health*, St Louis: Mosby.

Wrong, D. H. (1961) 'The oversocialized conception of man in modern sociology', *American Sociological Review* 26: 183–93.

Zola, I. (1972) 'Medicine as an institution of social control', *Sociological Review* 20: 487–503.

—— (1975) 'In the name of health and illness: on some socio-political consequences of medical influence', *Social Science and Medicine* 9: 83–7.

6

Goffman, interactionism, and the management of stigma in everyday life

SIMON WILLIAMS

Introduction

In this chapter I shall consider the importance of Erving Goffman's analysis of stigma both for his mainstream sociological concerns and for the field of medical sociology. The chapter falls into three main sections. In the first, I examine Goffman's analysis of stigma, delineating some of the important conceptual distinctions and analytical insights and attempt to highlight how this analysis feeds into his general sociological concerns. It should be said at the outset that the focus is less on the *process* of labelling an act or attribute as stigmatizing than it is on the *consequences* of such a process for the person so labelled and on the management of stigma in everyday life, although both aspects will be dealt with. The second section goes on to explore and highlight the importance of stigma and Goffman's analysis of this phenomena for medical sociology at both an analytical and empirical level. Finally, in the last section I consider some of the ways in which Goffman's analysis has implications for health care policy and practice. First, however, a word about Goffman's sociology more generally may prove useful as a background to what follows.

A digression: Goffman and sociological theory

According to Dawe (1971), there are two sociologies, both of which emerged from a reaction to the Enlightenment. One takes as its problem the establishment of *order* and asserts the ontological primacy of social systems over social actors. To the extent that individual intention is theorized it is said to derive from the central societal value system. The second is premised on the notion of 'autonomous man' and takes as its problem the libertarian question of how humankind can achieve *control* over the institutions that it creates. Thus a vocabulary of social action, will, and agency follow: society is the creation of its members.

Where does Goffman fit into this schema? It seems that his socio-logical perspective derives from the latter social action paradigm. Goffman, in his lifetime, was the major exponent of the dramaturgical perspective premised upon the metaphor of the stage in which actors in everyday life seek to foster and control the impression of self that others have of them. Goffman studied at the University of Chicago with its distinctive version of symbolic interactionism and was con-siderably influenced by scholars such as Mead, Durkheim, and Simmel. As Manning (1973, 1976) has noted, he stands at the nexus of two different levels of sociological analysis. His work attempts to bridge 'situations' and 'structures'. The fluidity and dynamics of humanly defined situations are linked up to rules in relation to social structure. Goffman's essentially moral stance, his defence of that little ritually sacred god the 'self in society' – leading him at times to introduce existential concerns most associated with Sartre (Lofland 1980) – is juxtaposed with his concern for the formal properties of face-to-face interaction derived from Simmel. Moreover, Goffman interjects a Durkheimian concern for ritual which feeds into an analysis of the functional rules of social order as maintained in that little social system, the 'encounter', and seems to owe much to the work of Radcliffe-Brown.

Symbolic interactionisms began to re-emerge in the 1960s with the decline of functionalism. Goffman was instrumental in this interac-tionist resurgence with such classics as *The Presentation of Self in Everyday Life* (1969), *Asylums* (1968a), and *Stigma* (1968b), all of which have had a profound and lasting impact upon the sociological mind. Furthermore, Goffman's contribution to medical sociology is quite considerable. Although it would have been easy to focus on his analysis of mental illness and total institutions, and the ramifications this has had for psychiatric practice and institutional care, I have chosen to concentrate on a less-well-recognized and explored aspect of his work: the analysis of stigma and its management in everyday life.

The analysis of stigma

The etymon of stigma and its types

The Greeks originated the term *stigma* to refer to bodily signs, cut or burnt into the body, which were designed to expose the bearer as a slave, a criminal, or social outcast, someone 'ritually polluted' who was to be avoided, especially in public places. However, today the term is applied more widely to any condition, attribute, trait, or behaviour that symbolically marks the bearer off as 'culturally unacceptable' or 'inferior' and has as its subjective referent the notion of shame or disgrace. Goffman distinguishes three different types of stigma: there are stigmas of the body (blemishes or deformities): of character (the mentally ill, the homosexual, or criminal for example) and of social collectivities (racial or tribal); all of these are subject to historical and cultural variability. For example in Tibet, Burma, and Turkey crippled and maimed people are ostracized as 'lesser human beings', yet in other societies, for instance Korea and Afghanistan, they are considered to possess 'unusual' culturally valued abilities and are assigned a special superior status (Scott 1970).

Why is stigma of interest to Goffman and how does it relate to his central sociological concerns? Some very general answers to these questions may provide a useful framework within which to view his analysis of stigma.

Some linkages

As Lofland (1980) has ably documented, the early Goffman's sociology focuses upon two central issues: the *encounter*, which Goffman (1961) has defined as a focused interaction in which both parties agree to sustain a single focus of cognitive and visual attention; and the *self in society*.

Goffman poses the 'Hobbesian problem of order', but he is not, as is traditional within sociology, concerned with macro social order but with how sustained social interaction is possible. Like Garfinkel, Goffman approaches this question from the opposite pole. Instead of focusing on social order and its maintenance, he displays a keen interest in analysing the ways in which sustained social interaction can or does break down, the sources and consequences of such interactional tension and the manner in which such malaise is managed (Lofland 1980). This method serves to highlight the taken-for-granted rules and rituals embedded in the social encounter, which function to keep the wheels of interaction well oiled and maintain a single definition of the situation. Two major threats to the stability of the encounter revolve around (1) a discrepancy between a participant's actual focus of cognitive attention and the officially relevant one, and (2) various 'discrepant facts' which throw doubt upon the current definition of the situation being sustained (Lofland 1980). Obviously a stigmatizing attribute is one such source of tension introduced into encounters involving '"mixed contacts" – the moments when stigmatized and normal are in the same "social situation"' (Goffman 1968b: 23). This 'primal sociological scene' is an important concern in Goffman's analysis of stigma.

However, Goffman's major interest is in the vicissitudes of that sacred little object, the self; 'the self is in part a ceremonial thing, a sacred object, which must be treated with proper ritual care' (Goffman 1972: 91). This leads him to focus upon another problem. As Lofland states, this revolves around the question 'what are the conditions of being able to perform and sustain a given official self? Stated in reverse, what are the things that disrupt the maintenance of a given official self?' (Lofland 1980: 41). Again, stigma and its management – especially 'passing' and 'covering' – are important here, 'providing the student with a special application of the arts of impression management, the arts basic to social life through which the individual exerts strategic control over the image of himself and his products that others glean from him' (Goffman 1968b: 155).

A final point is that Goffman's sociology is profoundly moral in character, 'marked by a passionate defence of the self against society' (Freidson 1983: 359). His work in general, and his analysis of stigma in particular, displays an existentialist concern with the human condition and with matters of mood, feeling and passion (Manning 1973). *Stigma* deals, both sensitively and compassionately, with some of the most fundamentally painful human experiences and we can see these humanistic concerns pulsing through Goffman's analysis (Lofland 1980). Moreover, as Schudson has noted, 'Goffman's sociology is anchored in the assumption that embarrassment is of fundamental social and moral significance' (Schudson 1984: 633).

Goffman's conceptualization of stigma in everyday life

Some of the early Goffman's work links up with the sociology of deviance, especially the labelling perspective as first espoused by Becker, Erikson, and Kitsuse, which draws on the earlier work of Tannenbaum and Lemert. This perspective rocked the foundations of deviance theory by turning the tables and focusing not upon the 'deviant act' so much as the 'societal reaction' to such behaviour. The basic idea is that social deviations from some normative framework represent stigmatized roles stemming from a 'process' involving 'primary deviation' (the original infraction), societal reaction, and 'secondary deviation' (which involves the person's response to the negative societal reaction). Labelling and the symbolic assignment of the normative rule breaker to a deviant/stigmatizing role status, often involving some sort of 'degradation ceremony', are thought to have important consequences for subsequent deviation on the individual's part, and lead to deviant identity formation through an internalization of the externally imputed stereotypical role. The individual's stigma can come to dominate both ego and alter's perceptions, and influence in a negative fashion the treatment accorded the 'deviant' individual: it becomes a *'master-status'* or 'total identity' and one which is extremely difficult to disavow.

In this context Scott (1972) has proposed a framework for analysing deviance as a property of social order. Scott follows Erikson and others in defining deviance as 'a property that is conferred upon a person by others' (Scott 1972: 12). For Scott

> This property is conferred upon an individual whenever others detect in his behaviour, appearance, or simply his existence, a significant transgression of the *symbolic universe* by which the inherent disorder of human existence is made to appear orderly and meaningful. More simply, the property of deviance is conferred on things that are perceived as being anomalous when viewed from the perspective of the symbolic universe.
>
> (1972: 22)

The term 'symbolic universe' is drawn from the work of Berger and Luckmann (1967) and refers to an all-embracing frame of reference in a society that forges for its members a sense of order and solid seeming social reality. Thus deviance is a relative concept. A phenomenon is only deviant relative to the 'symbolic universe' of a particular, historically situated, society.

There have been some important critiques of the labelling perspective (Gove 1980; Fox Piven 1981, amongst others). However, it is not my intention here to review all the criticisms and counter-criticisms surrounding the labelling perspective; Plummer (1979) has a fine account of such issues. Goffman's most explicit application of this perspective is to be found in *Asylums* where, in the 'moral career of the mental patient', he documents with both sensitivity and compassion the contingencies that transform an individual into the stigmatized role status of mental patient, and the mortifications to the self which follow under the heavy machinery of the mental hospital. However, it is Goffman's book *Stigma*, which leads us back into everyday life and away from the 'total institution', that I wish to focus upon as it deals explicitly with stigma and the contingencies surrounding its management in routine social interaction. As Freidson has put it, *'stigma* is "The Presentation of *Discredited* Self in Everyday Life"' (Freidson 1983: 359). *Stigma* highlights the force a stigmatizing label and the attendant stereotypical beliefs and attitudes can have upon an individual's sense of identity and being, and Scott's framework will be useful to keep in mind when considering Goffman's analysis.

Goffman's sociological definition of stigma turns on a distinction between what he refers to as *'virtual social identity'* – the stereotyped imputations of the attributes and social category of another we make in routine social interaction, which are transformed into 'normative expectations' as to what the individual *ought* to be; and '*actual social identity*' – the category and attributes the individual actually possesses. The stigmatized are those who have a deeply discrediting discrepancy between virtual and actual social identity. Those who do not depart negatively from the particular expectations at issue, Goffman terms 'normals'. As he states:

> While the stranger is present before us, evidence can arise of his possessing an attribute that makes him different from others in the category of persons available for him to be, and of a less desirable kind. ... He is thus reduced in our minds from a whole and usual person to a tainted, discounted one. Such an attribute is a stigma, especially when its discrediting effect is very extensive; sometimes it is called a failing, a shortcoming, a handicap. It constitutes a special discrepancy between virtual and actual social identity.
>
> (1968b: 12–13)

A stigma, then, 'is really a special kind of relationship between attribute and stereotype' (Goffman 1968b: 14). That is to say, it is a meaning imposed upon an attribute via images, stereotypes, and attitudes which potentially discredits members of a particular social category. Goffman seems to concur with the labelling theorists when he notes that the attribution of a stigma stems from the definitional workings of society, for before a difference can matter much it must first be conceptualized by society as a whole. Stigma is a societal reaction that 'spoils' normal identity, it is a perspective generated in social situations by virtue of unrealized norms that impinge upon the encounter. But what norms are involved? Goffman states:

> The norms dealt with in this essay concern identity or being ... failure or success at maintaining such norms has a very direct effect on the psychological integrity of the individual. At the same time, mere desire to abide by the norm – mere good will – is not enough, for in many cases the individual has no immediate control over his level of sustaining the norm. It is a question of the individual's condition, not his will; it is a question of conformance not compliance.
>
> (1968b: 1, 952–3)

A permanent spoilage of identity is involved, or as Lemert has put it concerning secondary deviance, 'others' categorizations 'become central facts of existence for those experiencing them, altering psychic structure producing specialized organization of social roles and self-regarding attitudes' (Lemert 1967: 41). Scott (1972) has outlined some of the major features of a deviant label and two are pertinent here. First, it carries negative moral connotations, the bearer of the deviant label usually being viewed as being 'morally inferior'; and second, deviant labels are 'essentializing labels' in that they carry 'certain implications about character that extend to all areas of personality' (Scott 1972: 15). The unhappy consequence of this is that when a deviant label is applied to an individual he is often demarcated off from the rest of the group and moved to its margins. This fits into Goffman's conception of stigma when he notes that:

> By definition ... we believe the person with a stigma is not quite human ... we construct a stigma theory, an ideology to explain his inferiority ... [and] ... we tend to impute a wide range of imperfections on the basis of the original one. ... Further, we may perceive his defensive response to his situation as a direct expression of his defect.
>
> (1968b: 15–16)

Moreover, stigmas 'spread out in waves' from the stigmatized person to his or her close connections, something Goffman terms a 'courtesy stigma'.

However, stigmatized individuals tend to adhere to the same normative beliefs about identity as others do and have a deep-seated sense of being 'normal' human beings. Yet because of their adherence to such identity beliefs they are aware of what others regard as their stigma, and at times are likely to agree that they do indeed fall short of what they 'ought' to be. For Goffman 'shame' becomes a central possibility and the central feature of the stigmatized individual's life situation revolves around:

> a question of ... 'acceptance'. Those who have dealings with him fail to accord him the respect and regard which the un-contaminated aspects of his social identity have led them to anticipate extending and have led him to anticipate receiving; he echoes this denial by finding that some of own attributes warrant it.
>
> (Goffman 1968b: 19)

Persons with a particular stigma have similar learning experiences concerning their 'plight' and similar changes in their self-conception. Goffman terms this a 'moral career', and I shall be touching on certain aspects of it within the course of this chapter.

Yet the stigmatized are a quite heterogeneous population of people. One crucial factor is the issue of visibility (or 'evidentness'), namely how well or how badly the stigma functions as a means of communicating the individual's possession of it. Obviously the level of visibility of different conditions varies considerably and is, to a very large degree, context-dependent. For example the notched teeth of someone displaying one of Hutchinson's signs connected with congenital syphilis may pass unnoticed by those with little knowledge of the condition. Goffman further distinguishes between this aspect of a stigma and its 'known-about-ness', referring to the extent to which others know about the attribute; its 'obtrusiveness', meaning the extent to which it actually interferes with the flow of interaction – for example a business man confined to a wheelchair bears a stigma which is relatively unobtrusive around a conference table, yet a man with a stammer finds that he continually violates the tacit code of communication etiquette in spoken encounters; and its 'perceived focus', which refers to the conception others have, not necessarily objective, as to what spheres of life-activity the stigma disqualifies the individual from – a facial disfigurement may impair acceptance in face-to-face encounters while diabetes may disqualify an individual from certain occupations. These conceptual distinctions are useful because they serve to highlight the contextual dependency of stigmatization (or secondary deviation).

The discredited and discreditable

The issue of the 'evidentness' or 'known-about-ness' of a stigmatizing condition is of crucial importance to the distinction Goffman draws between the 'discredited' and the 'discreditable'. The discrepancy between an individual's actual and virtual social identity may be known about before interaction proceeds, or it may become evident as the individual presents him or herself before others. Such individuals are referred to by Goffman as discredited persons. He suggests that a major problem confronting a discredited person is that of 'managing tension' generated during social interaction, and hence the need to manage the impression others have of him or her: a management of a spoiled identity. Such individuals have special reasons for feeling that mixed contacts will lead to anxious 'unanchored interaction'. For Goffman, the ambiguity and potential for social disruption surrounding such encounters can result in avoidance, rejection or withdrawal by either party. The commonest response when confronted by a discredited person is for the normal

> to give no open recognition to what is discrediting of him, and while this work of careful disattention is being done, the situation can become tense, uncertain, and ambiguous for all participants, especially the stigmatized one.

> (1968b: 57)

Referring back to the earlier discussion, we can see here Goffman's concern for things that can threaten interactional order. Goffman has elsewhere dealt with the 'pathology of interaction-uneasiness' (1972) and with the methods used to blend embarrassing matters smoothly into the encounter (1961), some of which will become apparent in the course of this chapter.

So far I have dealt with the discredited person. However, when an individual's 'differentness' is not immediately apparent and is not known about beforehand, Goffman refers to him or her as a discreditable person, and a different set of contingencies rear their head. The issue

> is not that of managing tension generated during social contacts, but rather that of managing information about his failing. To display or not to display; to tell or not to tell; to let on or not to let on; to lie or not to lie; and in each case, to whom, how, when, and where.
>
> (1968b: 57)

The information an individual has to manage is of two main kinds. First, there is 'social information', which is reflexive and embodied, meaning that it is conveyed by the very person it is about via bodily expression in the presence of others. Pertinent here are 'stigma symbols', which are signs drawing attention to a 'debasing identity discrepancy' reducing our evaluation of the individual. For instance, the wrist markings that disclose attempted suicide or the pock-marks on a drug addict's arms which individuals may attempt to conceal are good examples of such symbols. Also visibility, as discussed above, is an important baseline from which the individual works in stigma management. The other main type of information pertains to the issue of 'personal identity', in the criminological not psychological sense of the word. This refers to 'positive marks' or 'identity pegs' and the unique combination of biographical facts that come to be attached to a person, enabling us to make a personal identification and to know something about the individual.

It is the plight of the discreditable – those with a stigmatizing attribute as part of their life history, part of their personal identity – and the question of 'information control', just how much of one's personal identity it is safe or advisable to reveal, that Goffman is most interested in. In short, the problem and consequences of avoiding the stigmatized role by managing undisclosed, discrediting information, or in Goffman's terminology the problem of 'passing' as normal.

Passing and covering

Passing and *covering* are interactional adaptive strategies concerned with the management of information and tension. Goffman argues that because of the great rewards in being treated as 'normal' almost all individuals who are in a position to pass will do so, occasionally at least. Even those with a visible stigma may find themselves sometimes passing quite inadvertently, as when blind or facially disfigured people are not recognized as such in fleeting encounters or darkened rooms. I referred earlier to the concept of the 'moral career' of the stigmatized. Two phases of this for Goffman consist of the learning of the normal's point of view regarding the stigma and the learning that he or she is disqualified according to it. The next phase consists of learning how to cope with the way others 'treat the kind of person he can be shown to be' (Goffman 1968b: 101). A later phase concerns learning how to pass as normal, 'where a differentness is relatively unapparent, the individual must learn that in fact he can trust himself to secrecy' (1968b: 101).

However, contingencies attach to such passing as the individual must lead a 'double life' with his or her world divided up into those who know of the 'shameful difference' and those who do not. For example it is possible for a discrediting to occur because of what becomes apparent about the person in social interaction, threatening the individual's virtual identity and leading to an 'embarrassing incident'. An extreme example would be the case of the person with epilepsy suffering a *grand mal* seizure before others previously 'kept in the dark'. A basic contingency in passing is that the individual will be discovered by those who can personally identify him or her and who 'include in their biographical record of him unapparent facts that are incompatible with present claims' (1968b: 95). Blackmail is also a possibility. Close relationships may be compromised by a deficiency in shared information, and the individual who passes may also be called to a 'showdown' by others who later learn of the discrediting facts and confront the person with having been false. The price paid for passing may be a high level of anxiety in living a life that can be collapsed at any moment, and the individual consequently has to be 'alive to aspects of the situation which others treat as uncalculated and unattended. What are unthinking routines for normals can become management problems for the discreditable' (Goffman 1968b: 110). Furthermore, the individual who passes leaves open the possibility of learning what others 'really think of his kind'. Of course, in order to forgo such problems individuals may voluntarily disclose discrediting information, thus transforming themselves into discredited persons with uneasy social situations to manage.

If passing represents one possibility open to the stigmatized individual, 'covering' represents another. As Goffman puts it, 'it is a fact that persons who are ready to admit possession of a stigma ... may nonetheless make a great effort to keep the stigma from looming large'

(1968b: 125). Here we are back to the problem of reducing tension, a central issue in Goffman's sociology; 'The individual's object is to reduce tension that is, to make it easier for himself and the others to withdraw covert attention from the stigma, and to sustain spontaneous involvement in the official content of the interaction. ... This process will be referred to as *covering*' (1968b 125–6). Covering is important because obtrusiveness increases the difficulty of maintaining easeful inattention regarding the stigma. Thus concerning the blind, dark glasses may be worn not only to convey the fact of blindness but at the same time to cover evidence of defacement, 'a case of revealing unsightedness while concealing unsightliness' (1968b: 126). A related type of covering attempts to restrict the display of those failings most centrally identified with the stigma.

Covering is important for Goffman because individuals have to learn about the structure of interaction. Thus one can learn from their efforts about the taken-for-granted features of interaction. For instance one learns about the code regarding 'attention cues' through which spoken interaction is organized by observing how the blind sometimes learn to look directly at the speaker in order not to violate the tacit code of eye contact in face-to-face interaction (see Scott – 1969 – discussed later on this point).

Ego identity and the 'normal deviant'

The concept of identity is central to Goffman: social identity facilitates an understanding of stigmatization and personal identity relates to the problem of information control. Both, however, are part of other people's concerns and definitions regarding the individual. Goffman thus introduces a third subtype of identity, 'ego identity', allowing him to consider what the individual subjectively feels about his or her stigma and its management; 'the subjective sense of his own situation and his continuity of character that an individual comes to obtain as a result of various social experiences' (1968b: 129). Particularly important here are the 'out-group' of normals and the 'in-group' of fellow sufferers in prescribing how an individual should 'be' and view him or herself. As is characteristic of much of Goffman's work his stance here is not cool or cynical, it is compassionate and sensitive, even, at times, one of moral outrage at the way such individuals are treated.

Goffman sensitively discusses the 'identity ambivalence' regarding self, 'those oscillations of identification and association' the individual exhibits toward his fellow stigmatized, that the stigmatized individual experiences. The sight of the person's 'own kind' may at times repel since the individual still supports the norms of the wider society:

but his social and psychological identification with these offenders holds him to what repels him, transforming repulsion into shame, and then transforming ashamedness into something of which he is ashamed ... he can neither embrace his group nor let it go.

(1968b: 131–2)

The stigmatized individual may be able to hide the discrediting attribute from others but cannot do so from him or herself. While such persons may regard themselves as ordinary human beings, others do not. The stigmatized must attempt to resolve this dilemma and professional experts may help to hammer out a code, a 'philosophy of life', a 'recipe of being', an 'ego identity', which attempts to mitigate the problem. The individual's 'own group' may inform the code of conduct that professionals advocate for him or her and those who share a similar stigma Goffman terms one's 'own'. Those who are 'normal' but privy to the life of the stigmatized and sympathetic to their plight he terms the 'wise'. Goffman states, 'the character these spokesmen allow the individual is generated by the relation he has to those of his kind. If he turns to his group, he is loyal and authentic; if he turns away, he is a craven fool' (1968b: 137). They may advocate a militant line, encouraging stigmatized individuals to identify with their 'difference' and to challenge the normals' treatment of them: a form of 'deviance avowal'.

However, the unkindest cut of all for Goffman comes from the 'out-group' philosophy of a 'good personal adjustment', whereby the individual is asked to see him or herself from the point of view of the wider society of normals. It is here that we see most clearly Goffman's essentially moral stance and his concern for human dignity. As he eloquently puts it:

The nature of a 'good adjustment' is now apparent. It requires that the stigmatized individual cheerfully and unselfconsciously accepts himself as essentially the same as normals, while at the same time he voluntarily withholds himself from those situations in which normals would find it difficult to give lip service to their similar acceptance of him. ... It means that the unfairness and pain of having to carry a stigma will never be presented to them; it means that normals will not have to admit to themselves how limited their tactfulness and tolerance is; and it means that normals can remain relatively uncontaminated by intimate contact with the stigmatized, relatively unthreatened in their identity beliefs. ... The stigmatized individual is asked to act so as to imply neither that his burden is heavy nor that bearing it has made him different from us; at the same time he must keep himself at that remove from us which ensures our painlessly being able to confirm this belief about him.

... A *phantom acceptance* is thus allowed to provide the base for a *phantom normalcy*.

(1968b: 146–8)

The stigmatized individual is thus placed in the midst of a complex and contradictory discussion of what he or she ought to think of him or herself, a debate surrounding ego identity. For Goffman this is the stigmatized's fate and destiny.

A final issue in Goffman's analysis of stigma now needs to be raised. In true Goffmanesque style there is a twist to the tale. His penchant for mentioning 'troubling truths' about us all is clearly evident when we are led to realize that the blind, the crippled, the deaf, the prostitute, the homosexual, the ex-mental patient, the ex-convict, the member of a racial or religious minority, and many others, are not the only ones who experience stigmatization. For as Goffman notes, norms of identity breed deviations along with conformance. Stigma management is a general phenomena, a process which occurs wherever there are identity norms. The dividing line between normality and stigma is not as clear cut as one might first have imagined. The lifelong attributes of an individual may mean that he or she has to play the stigmatized role in almost every social situation, and yet few of us are totally without discrediting attributes. We are led to realize that 'stigma involves not so much a set of concrete individuals who can be separated into two piles, the stigmatized and the normal, as a pervasive two-role social process in which every individual participates in both roles. ... The normal and the stigmatized are not persons but rather perspectives' (Goffman 1968b: 163–4). This provides Goffman with a rationale for claiming that if we are to refer to the stigmatized individual as 'deviant' we might more profitably regard him or her as a 'normal deviant'. The logic behind this argument suggests that secondary deviation refers primarily to 'the extreme of a graded series of moral adaptations found among "normal" persons, as well as those with ... stigma' (Lemert 1967: 41).

Goffman, interactionism, and the issue of theory

As is traditional within interactionist studies, the issue of selfhood and identity is of fundamental importance for Goffman. However, as the foregoing discussion illustrates, his treatment of this issue is essentially unique. On the one hand, he seems to press the sociological perspective on societal determination to its ultimate conclusion. This is manifest in his acknowledgement of the power of society to define and determine an individual's very sense of being, since an individual's identity derives from the 'definitional workings of society' in all its reified glory. Yet on the other hand, he seems to resist this ultimate conclusion by championing the little ways in which the self 'resists the pull', 'our sense of being a person can often come from being drawn into the wider social unit; our sense of selfhood can arise through the little ways in which we resist the pull' (Goffman 1968a: 280). Role distance, impression management, secondary adjustments, passing and information control, covering, and so on, can all be seen as those little ways in which the individual holds off from fully embracing the identity (spoilt or otherwise) accorded him or her by society. In Goffman's scheme of imagery man is at one and the same time a *determined* and *determining* being.

A standard criticism of the interactionist perspective in general, and of Goffman's sociology in particular, is that it is astructural and apolitical, in short that it has a microscopic bias. There have been some general attempts to rescue Goffman here (Collins 1980; Rogers 1980; Goffman 1983) but even so such criticisms do not hold water. This is because interactionist studies do not claim to adhere to such levels of analysis in the first place, making such criticism inappropriate (Plummer 1979). More fundamentally, concerning the issue of stigma, interactionism offers, perhaps, the most fruitful perspective with which to understand such a processual phenomenon, bringing its sensitive and insightful concepts to bear on one of the most painful of human experiences, and, at the same time, serving to illuminate some of the methods by which such individuals cope with such a precarious existence. Goffman, with his keen Chicago-trained sociological eye, has contributed a great deal to such understanding, a contribution to 'human consciousness' (Freidson 1983).

One of the most distinctive features of Goffman's sociology is the proliferation of concepts which Lofland (1970) attributes to the 'conceptually impoverished' symbolic interactionist tradition in the early 1950s. This brings me to the question of why I have used the notion of the *analysis* and not the *theory* of stigma when referring to Goffman's work. This is because I do not believe Goffman's sociology can be conceptualized as a theory. Rather, as Lofland (1980) has noted, Goffman is more concerned with spinning out elaborate conceptual webs with which to catch the essence of social life than he is with linking concepts together in a theoretically meaningful way. Thus Goffman's sociology, following Simmel, represents, at least partly, a 'formal sociology'. In many ways it resembles those characteristics associated with interactionism generally; the concern with descriptive categories of interaction and an explicit lack of theorizing (Rock 1979). In a letter to Phil Strong, Goffman states: 'I am impatient for a few conceptual distinctions (nothing so ambitious as a theory) ... casting one's endeavour in the more respectable forms of the mature sciences is often just rhetoric. In the main I believe we're just not there yet' (Strong 1983: 349); concepts, yes, theory, no. Freidson takes up a similar line of reasoning in discussing the intense individual humanity and style of Goffman's work. He states: 'I believe that Goffman's work lives and will live not as a contribution to the development of systematic sociological theory but rather as a contribution to human consciousness' (Freidson 1983: 361). I agree.

Having painted in broad brush strokes Goffman's analysis of stigma, let us now turn to a consideration of the importance of stigma for medical sociology and to how Goffman's analytical framework has been extended and applied in this domain.

The importance of stigma for medical sociology

Goffman's definition of stigma encompasses a rather broad range of conditions, representing 'a graded series of moral adaptations'. However, it can be seen straight away that the obvious value of his analysis for medical sociology lies in its applicability as a conceptual framework, a prototypic blueprint for the analysis of stigmatizing illness conditions at the interactional level. Indeed even a cursory scan of the medical sociological literature in this area reveals the profoundly important contribution Goffman has made. *Stigma* is combed for insights and mined for hypotheses both by theorists and empirical researchers working within the discipline. In what follows I wish to consider the importance of stigma and Goffman's analysis of this phenomenon for medical sociology at both an analytical and empirical level.

The work on stigmatizing illness conditions and the range of research interests is vast. For example Schneider and Conrad (1980, 1981) and Scambler (1984; Scambler and Hopkins 1986) have focused on the problems of perceiving and coping with epilepsy, while Higgins (1980) has done the same for deafness. Rief (1975) has shown how ulcerative colitis sufferers develop strategies to manage embarrassing incidents in social interaction and the constraints on their time imposed by the illness itself. Birenbaum (1970) and Hilbourne (1973) have developed Goffman's work on 'managing a courtesy stigma' and 'disabling the normal' respectively. Scott (1969, 1970) has studied the role of health agencies and bureaucracies in the construction and moulding of particular conceptions of blindness and the socializing effect they have upon their clients. Also there have been some interesting developments within the field of medical anthropology. Hopper (1981) has studied how diabetes, itself stigmatizing, has certain consequences which are themselves stigmatizing such as special diet, impotence, amputations, blindness, and unemployment. Ablon (1981) has looked at the role of a self-help group in the USA involved in the destigmatization of dwarfism, and Knudson-Cooper (1981) has studied the problem of psychosocial adjustment to severe burn injuries in childhood. To this may be added Hunt's (1966) collection of autobiographical essays concerning stigmatization of handicapped people.

However, in order to appreciate the value of stigma for medical sociology it may be useful to start by delineating its analytical importance.

Stigma and illness: some analytical conceptions

Fabrega and Manning (1972) have distinguished four major dimensions along which illnesses vary: the *duration* of the disease episode; its reversibility or *curability*; the degree of discomfort, incapacity, or *disability* incurred, and its potential for self-degradation or *stigmatization*. From this four main types of disease and illness careers can be differentiated, which Field (1976) terms: (1) 'short-term acute illness' such as influenza; (2) 'Long-term non-stigmatized illness' such as carcinoma of the stomach or myocardial infarction; (3) 'long-term stigmatized illness' such as multiple sclerosis, poliomyelitis, or leprosy; and (4) 'mental illness', for example schizophrenia.

Thus it can be seen that one important way of ordering illness conditions is by the degree of stigmatization attached to them. As Fabrega and Manning note concerning the difference between long-term non-stigmatized and long-term stigmatized illness, 'the physiologically determined symptoms, the general subjective sense that one is "physically" ill, and the experienced disability may be identical [in both cases]' (Fabrega and Manning 1972: 107). The difference lies in the social definition of the illness as stigmatizing. It is the degree of 'spoilage' stemming from an illness, the way in which illness is perceived and responded to that is important here. As we move from short-term acute illness, through long-term illness conditions to mental illness the degree of stigmatization increases. Mental illness is perhaps the most stigmatizing of all illness labels primarily because 'it is not possible to disassociate the self from the [mental] disease. ... The manifestations, as it were, become the self or person' (Fabrega and Manning 1972: 110). Mental illness is perceived as a 'total moral state' reflecting the sick person's ontological essence. It often becomes a 'master-status' with existing roles, such as familial and occupational, undergoing drastic reinterpretations. As Goffman states concerning the ex-mental patient, 'once he has a record of having been in a mental hospital, the public at large, both formally, in terms of employment restrictions, and informally, in terms of day-to-day social treatment, consider him to be set apart; they place a stigma on him' (Goffman

1968a: 309–10). Edgerton (1967) draws a similar conclusion in his study of the plight of the mentally retarded.

Freidson's (1965, 1970) discussion of stigma, and its place within his social taxonomy of illness types based upon lay reactions, is instructive. He states that:

> If we follow Goffman's discussion of stigma, we see it as a *societal reaction* that 'spoils' normal identity. ... As the term itself implies, the societal reaction, although ambiguously, attributes moral deficiency to the stigmatized ... one's identity is permanently spoiled. ... Essentially, I believe it can be said that while many of those stigmatized are not held responsible for their deviance, the assignment of stigma in essence *withholds legitimacy* from the privileges they seek and imposes special obligations on them.
>
> (Freidson 1970: 235–6).

Freidson goes on to note:

> For 'normal' illness, many normal obligations are suspended; only the obligation to seek help is incurred. But in the case of the stigmatized, a complex variety of new obligations is incurred. Whereas in the former instance the burden of adjustment (through permissiveness and support) lies on the 'normals' around the sick person, the burden in the latter lies on the stigmatized when he is around 'normals'.
>
> (1970: 236)

Freidson (1970) provides a classification of types of legitimacy adhering to illness states. While, for Freidson, certain acute illnesses are thought to be 'conditionally legitimate', and certain chronic illnesses are considered 'unconditionally legitimate', stigmatized illnesses, such as epilepsy and leprosy, are regarded by lay populations as 'illegitimate'. This is because they are not treated as an acceptable kind of 'deviance' even though they may still be thought of as illnesses.

Thus certain conditions of the body or mind are, as Scambler (1984) has suggested, perceived as a 'threat to social order'. This is so, first, in Goffman's terms, because of their failure to conform to cultural norms of identity or being, 'the individual is judged as an essentially "imperfect being": the nature of his or her "offence" is perhaps best characterized as "ontological"' (Scambler 1984: 208). Of course, the second major threat to social order, as Goffman has highlighted, is that certain stigmatizing illness conditions may violate 'cultural norms governing routine social intercourse' (Scambler 1984: 209).

What emerges from the above discussion is that stigma, the degree of 'spoilage' to identity resulting from an illness, is a key variable in the social construction of illness (Field 1976). Following Goffman's pioneering statement we see that it is an imputed condition which relates to a violation of norms of 'identity' or 'being'. Thus it may be expected to vary fairly independently of any biophysical reality and points to an important aspect of the social experience of illness. Furthermore, it is a societal reaction which may, via negative stereo-typical beliefs and attitudes, serve to pattern the individual's behaviour and self-conception in a self-fulfilling manner, facilitating permanent incumbency of a stigmatizing role status. This line of reasoning has been taken up by Freidson (1965), for example, who argues that disability is a form of 'social deviance'. However, it has been most controversially applied to the area of 'mental illness' by Scheff (1966), who holds that labelling is *the* most important causal factor in its production.

It would seem therefore that the concept of stigma is of funda-mental analytical importance for an understanding of the social dynamics and construction of illness, in that certain illness conditions constitute roles which may permanently dominate an individual's life. They act as 'master-statuses', *vis-à-vis* the temporary incumbency of the Parsonian sick role, due to social processes of negative stereotyping or stigmatization associated with such role incumbency. This results in the formation of stigmatized or 'deviant' illness careers/trajectories. Goffman's analysis of stigma is important here, as it draws attention to the crucial role of the societal reaction in spoiling identity and imput-ing 'moral inferiority'. However, Goffman's major concern, as the earlier discussion emphasizes, is with the problems of negotiation and adaptation to the social and physical environment once a stigmatizing label has been conferred, problems pertaining to the management of stigma in everyday life. It is in this sense that his analysis seems to have important ramifications for work in the area of chronic illness and disability, as it facilitates an understanding of the socially stigmatizing consequences of such illness and the modes of management and adaptation in everyday life. Let us look at the importance of inter-actionism for the area of chronic illness and disability.

Interactionism, chronic illness, and disability

Bury (1982) suggests that medical sociologists working within the field of chronic illness and disability have drawn upon two contrasting theoretical traditions. The first derives from Parsons's (1951) analysis of illness and the sick role. On the one hand, this has led to a debate about the relevance of the sick role for understanding chronic illness. On the other hand, and more positively, there have been attempts to separate and develop the 'deviance' and 'adaptive' perspectives stem-ming from Parsonian theory (Gallagher 1976; Gerhardt 1979) in order to facilitate a consideration of chronic illness conditions. The second tradition, pertinent to us here, is that of symbolic interactionism, focusing upon issues of meaning, identity, and the management of long-term (stigmatizing) illness and disability. As Locker (1983) suggests, the concept of adaptation feeds into many of the concerns of this second tradition. The focus is upon the problems encountered by the chronically ill and disabled in their encounters with 'normals' and the way in which social interaction is managed by the discredited and discreditable in order to mitigate stigmatization and identity spoilage. Obviously Goffman's analysis fits in here, together with the work of Davis (1963, 1964) and its elaboration by others such as Edgerton (1967), Scott (1969), and Safilios-Rothschild (1970). More recently there has been an extension of this approach by Strauss (1975), Weiner (1975), and Locker (1983).

Thus it can be seen that one of the major implications of Goffman's analysis concerns its usefulness as a conceptual framework, an analytical scaffold, for understanding the interactional problems pertaining to chronic stigmatizing illness and disability. I now want to look in more detail at the linkages between Goffman's analysis and other work in this area and to highlight the manner in which it has been drawn upon and developed.

Illness, disability, and interactional malaise

As we have seen, Goffman suggests that the ambiguity and potential for social tension and disruption surrounding 'mixed contacts' can lead to rejection or withdrawal by either interactant, and that if interaction does proceed it is usually strained, ambiguous, uncomfortable, and anxiety-laden. Davis takes up this point in describing the problems that physically handicapped people typically face:

> Whether the handicap is overtly and tactlessly responded to as such or, as is more commonly the case, no explicit reference is made to it, the underlying condition of heightened, narrowed, awareness causes the interaction to be articulated too exclusively in terms of it. This, as my informants described it, is usually accompanied by one or more of the familiar signs of discomfort and stickiness: the guarded reference, the common everyday words suddenly taboo, the fixed stare elsewhere, the artificial levity, the compulsive loquaciousness, the awkward solemnity.
>
> (1964: 122–3)

Davis's discussion relates to what Goffman (1972) has elsewhere termed 'other-consciousness' as a type of interactional malaise. Similarly Safilios-Rothschild notes, concerning physically disabled people, that

It is unfortunate for the disabled, in the light of the importance it has for them, that their interaction with the non-disabled is usually strained by ambiguities and emotional reactions ... [these] interactions ... are anxiety-laden, tend to cause emotional discomfort and usually take on the form of 'stereotyped, inhibited, and over-controlled' experiences.

(1970: 122)

Scott (1969) too draws on Goffman's analysis in his study of the discredited blind, in which he found that four features of interpersonal interaction affect their socialization as 'blind men'. These are (1) the stereotyped beliefs of 'normals' introduced into the interaction; (2) the stigma attached to blindness, leading 'normals' to regard the blind as their physical, psychological, moral, and emotional 'inferiors'; (3) the fact that the conduct of such interaction is profoundly distrubed by the blind due to the critical importance of eye contact in human communication; and (4) the fact that these relationships are ones involving the social dependency of the blind on the sighted inter-actant(s). For Scott, these stereotypical beliefs – which involve lay notions of 'helplessness', 'dependency', 'docility', 'aestheticism', 'serious-mindedness', and 'melancholia' – and the stigma associated with blindness, implying 'inferiority', impose certain uniform be-havioural expectations upon the blind which they cannot ignore. Indeed some become what Scott terms 'true believers' and accept such stereotypes, internalizing them as part of their self-concept. They may also have to cope with stereotypes of blindness held by health pro-fessionals which, Scott suggests, is another important socializing factor.

Albrecht, Walker, and Levy (1982) have also taken up this point concerning 'ambiguity in social interaction' and tested its explanatory potential for the perceived social distance their respondents expressed towards various stigmas. For example they found that Goffman's distinction between stigmas of the body and character was a useful one, as their respondents expressed greater social distance from mentally ill people and from the alcoholic than they did from physi-cally disabled persons. Most importantly they found that the perceived disruption to social interaction caused by a stigma, rather than the attribution of responsibility, was the most frequent reason given for differential social distance from individuals with various types of stigmas. This was especially so for physically disabled people, thus lending empirical support to Goffman's analysis. Various respondents stated: 'We are usually afraid of those things which we don't under-stand and things that are new or foreign to us'; 'The person doesn't know how to cope and feels uncomfortable with the disabled'; and

'They don't know what, if anything, they should do to help' (Albrecht, Walker, and Levy 1982: 1,324).

If Goffman's analysis of the ambiguity surrounding social inter-action is one area which has been taken up and developed in relation to stigmatizing illness conditions, so too has his discussion of the various stigma management and coping strategies discussed earlier.

Coping with stigmatizing illness conditions

Following Goffman, we can divide those individuals with stigmatiz-ing illness conditions into the discredited and the discreditable. Physically handicapped people, for example, are typically discredited and are faced with the problem of managing tension as discussed above. However, the person with epilepsy, for instance, is typically discreditable, the condition has 'stigma potential', and will have to manage information about him or herself. But just how useful is this distinction and Goffman's discussion of the various strategies for managing such problems? How has it been developed and applied within medical sociology? It is to these questions that I shall now turn, focusing specifically on long-term illness and disability.

Concerning the 'discredited' physically disabled, Davis (1964) has delineated three stages which they typically pass through when build-ing up a relationship with normals: first, he suggests there is 'fictional acceptance', whereby they are ascribed a stereotypical identity upon which a minimal acceptance is premised; the second stage is one of 'breaking through' this fictional acceptance, the individual encourag-ing the normal to 'identify with him ... in terms other than those associated with imputations of deviance' (Davis 1964: 128); finally there is an 'institutionalization of the normalized relationship', when the individual attempts to sustain and secure a definition of him or herself as normal. This temporal process Davis terms 'deviance dis-avowal' or 'normalization'. Such a strategy of normalization is the analogue of Goffman's concept of 'covering' as a mode of stigma management.

Similarly Strauss (1975) takes up many of Goffman's insights in his analysis of chronic illness and refers in this context to a basic strategy of 'normalization' concerning interaction with others and style of life. One of the main dimensions of 'normalization' relates to the strategies chronically ill people attempt to develop in order to minimize stigma-tization and problems of 'identity spread', in which one attribute of the individual is taken to characterize the whole person. Such tactics include hiding the symptoms, such as covering them with clothes or concealing trembling hands in one's pockets, or minimizing their impact on interaction by drawing attention away from them. Strauss, too, discusses the strategy of 'passing' mentioned earlier, in order to avoid playing the stigmatized role entirely. He adds, however, that the psychological costs may be high and that there may be severe financial penalties for failure to conceal some chronic illnesses, such as losing one's job, over and above the social penalties. Strauss also points out that withdrawal from social relationships and social isolation are unfortunate sequelae of chronic illness. Strauss extends Goffman's analysis by focusing upon problems of daily living such as the prevention of medical crises, the control of symptoms, and problems of managing therapeutic regimens, time, illness trajectories, and social isolation. The basic framework focuses upon key problems, basic strategies, and changes in the organization of family life – recently extended by Locker (1983) – which is then applied to conditions such as rheumatoid arthritis, ulcerative colitis, and emphysema, amongst others. However, we can see here how Goffman's analysis informs contemporary work in this area.

Another extension of Goffman's approach is Edgerton's (1967) study of mentally retarded people, in which he documents movingly how such individuals, who were well aware of the stigma of being mentally retarded, attempted to pass as normal. However, they were usually unable to do so, their lives were lived under the guise of competence, with 'normals' participating in a 'benevolent conspiracy' to maintain its fragile appearance.

Perhaps the best way in which to illustrate the importance of stigma, and Goffman's analytical and conceptual framework for medical sociology, is to focus upon the work done on a specific long-term stigmatizing illness condition. By doing so we can see clearly how Goffman's analysis relates to work in this area. Let us look at some of the research on epilepsy.

Scambler (1984) found that in his London study based on interviews with ninety-four adults with epilepsy, his respondents were almost all extremely upset when the diagnostic label of epilepsy was 'officially' confirmed by their doctor. This stemmed from two related perceptions: first, there was a general awareness that a 'doctor's diagnostic utterance ... had in an important sense made them into epileptics' (Scambler 1984: 213), in the sense that it 'officially' confirmed the condition; and second, they perceived epilepsy 'first and foremost as a stigmatizing condition; they felt they had been ascribed a status that would, or could, distance them from or even lead to their rejection by normal people' (Scambler 1984: 213). Although accepting medical expertise, such individuals often attempted to negotiate a change of diagnosis. However, once applied, individuals suffering epilepsy – an attribute 'discreditable' to one's personal identity – typically faced problems of information control. In this context

Scambler makes a distinction between 'felt' and 'enacted' stigma. The former partly concerns 'the shame associated with being epileptic. People felt ashamed fundamentally because they saw "being epileptic" as amounting to an infringement against norms relating to "identity" or 'being"' (Scambler 1984: 215). But more fundamentally it involves the fear of being discriminated against due to cultural 'unacceptability' and 'inferiority'. Enacted stigma refers to actual discrimination of this kind. Scambler suggests that felt stigma, although not omnipresent, was much more disruptive of the lives of his respondents than enacted stigma. How do individuals cope with and manage such existential problems?

Schneider and Conrad (1981) propose a typology of modes of adaptation to epilepsy, based upon their depth interviews with eighty people with epilepsy in the USA, which will be useful to consider here. Essentially they are strategies for managing or controlling the social and personal implications of epilepsy, which are closely related to those discussed by Goffman more generally. A key distinction is between what Schneider and Conrad term *'adjusted'* and *'unadjusted'* modes of adaptation. Adjusted persons with epilepsy are those 'able to successfully neutralize the actual or perceived negative impact of epilepsy on their lives' (Schneider and Conrad 1980: 214). They go on to delineate three subtypes of adjusted adaptation.

First, there is the *pragmatic* type, whereby the individual attempts to minimize the impact of epilepsy for both ego and alter, although the existence of epilepsy is rarely denied or concealed:

> By following what might be called a course of 'reason' in daily habits and medication, being open about epilepsy to those who 'need to know' e.g. employers, official agencies, close friends and associates, while keeping a knowing eye on the possibility of others' negative judgements were they to know, the pragmatist manages a 'normal' existence.
>
> (Schneider and Conrad 1981: 215)

The second subtype of adjustment is the *secret* type. Here, epilepsy is often managed by 'elaborate procedures' to control and conceal information about what is perceived to be a 'stigmatizing, negative or "bad" quality of self' (Schneider and Conrad 1981: 215). This type of information control technique is akin to Goffman's notion of passing as a stigma management strategy. The authors draw on Goffman's notion of 'presentation of self' when they note: 'An important part of concealing one's diagnosis of epilepsy is managing one's performance before others so as to avoid disclosure. The secret epileptic ... sees him or herself passing as a social normal until the stigmatizing label of the medical diagnosis becomes public' (Schneider and Conrad 1981:

215). The scope for this secret adaptation ranges from occasional 'selective concealment' to 'total secrecy'. This subtype of adjusted adaptation was the *'first-choice'* strategy for Scambler's (1984) respondents in his study. However, he adds the caveat that considerable stresses associated with 'felt' stigma attach to such a strategy. In this context West (1985), in his study of families containing a child with epilepsy, notes that for most of the parents epilepsy is a 'courtesy stigma', and that 'concealing' is a major possibility for them. In this sense they may function as 'stigma coaches' (Schneider and Conrad 1980) unwittingly encouraging a sense of stigma in their child.

The third subtype of adjustment Schneider and Conrad term *'quasi-liberated'*. This type shares with the pragmatist a definition of self as 'having' epilepsy, but goes further by 'broadcasting' it in order to educate others, challenge lay conceptions of 'deviance' and 'moral inferiority', and free the self from a need for concealment or secrecy due to 'felt' stigma.

Concerning the 'unadjusted' mode of adaptation, Schneider and Conrad note that while the adapted response displays a sense of 'agency' or 'control', 'the unadjusted adaptation is marked by a sense of being "overcome" or "overwhelmed" by epilepsy' (1981: 217). Such individuals find the condition has a markedly 'negative' impact on their lives and do not seem to develop any stigma management strategies. The subtype here is termed *'debilitated'* and represents a clear example of

> What Hughes called a 'master status' that 'floods' one's identity and life with meanings and behaviour that figuratively constipate the social self. It is the analogue to Lemert's secondary deviation in that the debilitated response embraces epilepsy as an indelible and irrevocable threat to one's worth; it pursues epilepsy as a deviant, stigmatizing and debilitating blemish or flaw, as a 'cross to bear'.
>
> (1981: 217)

What the above discussion highlights is that, as Schneider and Conrad put it; 'To varying degrees, all seemed to be contending with problems of managing a spoiled, tainted or threatened identity; maintaining self-esteem or passing as a "normal" person' (1981: 214). It is here also that we can see the importance of Goffman's analysis for medical sociology and the manner in which it has been drawn upon and developed by researchers working within this domain in order to understand such illness conditions. However, his work has wider implications for health policy and practice, some of which will now be considered.

Wider implications: health care and health policy

Earlier I discussed Goffman's analysis of the 'good adjustment' line adopted by professional experts and the wider society. Stigmatized individuals are encouraged to accept themselves as essentially 'normal' and to work hard at attempting to fulfil ordinary standards, while at the same time being taught that they are somehow 'different'. This highlights certain moral problems inherent in such an approach which involves a stereotypical image of the 'good deviant'. As Freidson states, somewhat satirically, concerning the disabled: 'To put it crudely, he is pressed to be a "good Indian" rather than a bad one, but good or bad, an Indian he remains, and, as everyone knows, the only really good Indian is a dead one' (Freidson 1965: 81). The moral problem here revolves around the fact that, 'the idea of "adjustment" can be used in a mechanical and profoundly conservative way that rides roughshod over the unhappy individuals involved' (Freidson 1965: 95).

Furthermore this points to an important element of social control involved in the process of stigmatization and the methods developed, professional or otherwise, to deal with the stigmatized. As we have seen, people who transgress or threaten culturally entrenched normative boundaries, or in Scott's (1972) terms the 'symbolic universe', are perceived as 'deviant' and, furthermore, are stigmatized. Such persons are often 'demarcated off' from the rest of society and 'moved to its margins'. As Scott states:

> Stigma threatens the community and presents it with unpleasant problems it would rather not confront or think about. Old people, poor people, people who are blind or crippled, and those who are crazy make us uneasy; they threaten our sense of mastery of nature, and they are disruptive of routines of daily life. A community's needs relating to stigmata may be to hide them from public view, or at least to dress them up in a way that makes them more palatable to laymen or at least less offensive to them. In writing about mental hospitals, Goffman has stated the point as follows: 'Part of the official mandate of the public mental hospital is to protect the community from the dangers and nuisances of certain kinds of misconduct' ... such institutions, then, are places to which the unwanted of the community can be sent and where they can be 'taken care of'.
>
> (1970: 273)

The point is, to the extent that health professionals are involved in the process of treating and helping the stigmatized to accept their 'problem' and to make a 'good adjustment' to it, they are, albeit unwittingly, serving to perpetuate and reinforce such negative lay beliefs and attitudes. Thus they may actually reinforce the stigmatized individual's perception of him or herself as 'different'. Moreover, as Scott (1970) has shown, conceptions of stigma contained in professional ideologies 'are only partly determined by empirical knowledge derived from direct experiences with and scientific studies of stigmatized people. Their content is also determined by, and reflects, certain *social*, *cultural*, and *political* forces in the environments in which experts are immersed' (Scott 1970: 269). He has compellingly argued in his study of the blind that 'gradually, over time, the behaviour of blind men comes to correspond with the assumptions and beliefs that blindness workers hold about blindness' (1969: 119).

On a more pragmatic level, it seems that due to the medical profession's biomedical model of disease, which by its very nature denies attaching stigma to any illness, regarding it as an 'unprofessional' assignment, they may very well neglect the reality of its existence within the wider social realm. As Freidson states:

> They are too prone to ignore the fact that it does exist socially in the community, and so deny the consequences of their labelling for the individual's community life. ... What an impairment 'really' is and what one's orientation to impairments *should* be (these being consciously formulated 'professional' and agency notions) must be seen in the light of the real *social consequences* to the individual of the interaction between 'ignorant' public definitions of impairment and agency policy.
>
> (1965: 96)

Gerhardt puts the matter succinctly when she states,

> a contradictory nature of diagnosis emerges. On the one hand, it is a medical act of classification but, on the other hand, it spurs off a process of *social* classification which may often have a limiting or forbidding effect on the patient's previous social participation.
>
> (1985: 192)

What is at issue here is the need for a greater awareness on the part of doctors and health care professionals of the social and psychological ramifications of their diagnostic illness labels for their patients' lives. There is a real need to give systematic attention to the social, personal, and emotional dimensions of 'stigmatizing' illness conditions and to address the problems of personal adjustment and adaptation, in addition to the traditional concern with the disease episode and its management. The case of AIDS is a particularly good contemporary example of this need. This of course isn't news. Medical sociologists have been hammering home this point concerning the 'gulf' or 'conflict' between lay and medical worlds for some time, yet it is still an important point. For example Freidson states that 'the separate worlds of experience and reference of the layman and the professional worker are always in potential conflict with one another' (1974: 286). In this context the conflict surrounds the doctor's preoccupation with diagnosing and treating the disease episode *vis-à-vis* the patient's concern with the stigmatizing social and psychological impact of the diagnostic label and illness condition. Furthermore Goffman points to many different types of stigma. Thus it can be seen how, for instance, a physical disability, itself stigmatizing, can lead to many secondary problems which are also stigmatizing, such as unemployment or poverty (Blaxter 1976), or in the case of diabetes, special diet, insulin injections, loss of sexual activity, and blindness (Hopper 1981). Of course, I am not suggesting that doctors are altogether unaware of such problems, only that a more systematically thought out policy for dealing with such issues is necessary.

Some of the above points may also help to throw some light on why so few disease episodes are presented to the physician for diagnosis. This may be partly due to the fear that official confirmation of a 'stigmatizing' illness condition may (permanently) spoil one's identity (Field 1976). The need for a wider strategy dealing with the lay public's contribution to the difficulties such individual's encounter seems obvious. However, there is evidence to suggest that negative attitudes, at least with reference to epilepsy, may not be prevalent amongst the lay populace and that the major problem centres around the individual's fear of discrimination and 'felt' stigma (Scambler and Hopkins 1986). Here, surely, health professionals can help to mitigate such distress.

One final point is that Goffman's analysis highlights the fact that not only the stigmatized face problems, but also considerable stresses and strains are placed on their family and friends due to activity restrictions and their acquisition of a 'courtesy stigma'. This is especially the case for parents with, for example, a child with epilepsy (West 1985) or a disabled child (Voysey 1972). However, it also applies more generally to any family with a physically disabled member to care for, 'disabling the normal' (Hilbourne 1973) and leading to problems of 'managing a courtesy stigma' (Birenbaum 1970). This confirms the need for comprehensive family-based approaches to rehabilitation.

Conclusion

Drawing the above points together, it appears that Goffman's analysis of stigma serves a dual purpose. On the one hand, I have attempted to show how it links up with sociology's general concern with the phenomenon of 'deviance', especially the labelling perspective, together with his own central sociological concerns. Essentially these are (1) an interest in sources of interactional tension, disruption, and its management, and (2) a concern with the problems of the presentation of self – in this case of a discredited or discreditable self – in everyday life.

On the other hand, his analysis has ramifications for medical sociology as it draws attention to a key variable in the social construction of illness. Furthermore it serves as an important second-order framework for conceptualizing and understanding the problems of perceiving and coping with stigmatizing illness conditions in everyday life at the interactional level. His analysis provides us with a rich source of insights and hypotheses to be drawn upon and developed at both an analytical and empirical level. Thus it can be seen that Goffman's pioneering analysis of stigma links his mainstream sociological perspective to a key issue pertaining to the realm of medical sociology. Coming from such a fine sociological scholar this is something for which medical sociologists should be truly grateful.

References

Ablon, J. (1981) 'Dwarfism and social identity: self-help group participation', *Social Science and Medicine* 15(b): 25–30.

Albrecht, G. L., Walker, V., and Levy, J. (1982) 'Social distance from the stigmatized: a test of two theories', *Social Science and Medicine* 16: 1,319–27.

Berger, P. and Luckmann, T. (1967) *The Social Construction of Reality: A Treatise in the Sociology of Knowledge*, London: Allen Lane.

Birenbaum, A. (1970) 'On managing a courtesy stigma', *Journal of Health and Social Behaviour* 11: 196–206.

Blaxter, M. (1976) *The Meaning of Disability: A Sociological Study of Impairment*, London: Heinemann.

Bury, M. (1982) 'Chronic illness as biographical disruption', *Sociology of Health and Illness* 4 (2): 167–82.

Collins, R. (1980) 'Erving Goffman and the development of modern sociological theory', in J. Ditton (ed.) *The View from Goffman*, London: Macmillan.

Davis, F. (1963) *Passage Through Crisis: Polio Victims and their Families*, Indianapolis, Ind: Bobbs-Merrill.

—— (1964) 'Deviance disavowal: the management of strained interaction by the visibly handicapped', in H. Becker (ed.) *The Other Side*, Illinois: Free Press.

Dawe, A. (1971) 'The two sociologies', in K. Thompson and J. Tunstall (eds) *Sociological Perspectives*, Harmondsworth: Penguin.

Edgerton, R. (1967) *The Clock of Competence: Stigma in the Lives of the Mentally Retarded*, Berkeley, Calif: University of California Press.

Fabrega, H., and Manning, P. K. (1972) 'Disease, illness, and deviant careers', in R. A. Scott and J. D. Douglas (eds) *Theoretical Perspectives on Deviance*, New York: Basic Books.

Field, D. (1976) 'The social definition of illness', in D. Tuckett (ed.) *An Introduction to Medical Sociology*, London: Tavistock.

Fox Piven, F. (1981) 'Deviant behaviour and the remaking of the world', *Social Problems* 28 (5): 489–508.

Freidson, E. (1965) 'Disability as social deviance', in M. B. Sussman (ed.) *Sociology and Rehabilitation*, Washington, DC: American Sociological Society.
—— (1970) *The Profession of Medicine: A Study of the Sociology of Applied Knowledge*, New York: Dodd Mead.
—— (1974) 'Dilemmas in the doctor–patient relationship', in C. Cox and A. Mead (eds) *A Sociology of Medical Practice*, London: Collier Macmillan.
—— (1983) 'Celebrating Erving Goffman', *Contemporary Sociology* 12 (4): 359–62.
Gallagher, E. (1976) 'Lines of reconstruction and extension in the Parsonian sociology of illness', *Social Science and Medicine* 10: 207–18.
Gerhardt, U. (1979) 'The Parsonian paradigm and the identity of medical sociology', *Sociological Review* 27: 229–51.
—— (1985) 'Stress and stigma explanations of illness', in U. Gerhardt and M. Wadsworth (eds) *Stress and Stigma: Explanations and Evidence in the Sociology of Crime and Illness*, London: Macmillan.
Goffman, E. (1948) 'Studies in adjustment to visible injuries: evaluation of curiosity by the injured', *Journal of Abnormal Social Psychology* 43: 13.
—— (1961) *Encounters: Two Studies in the Sociology of Interaction*, Indianapolis, Ind: Bobbs-Merrill.
—— (1968a) *Asylums: Essays on the Social Situation of Mental Patients and Other Inmates*, Harmondsworth: Penguin.
—— (1968b) *Stigma: Notes on the Management of Spoiled Identity*, Harmondsworth: Penguin.
—— (1969) *The Presentation of Self in Everyday Life*, Harmondsworth: Penguin.
—— (1971) *Relations in Public: Microstudies of the Public Order*, London: Allen Lane.
—— (1972) *Interaction Ritual: Essays on Face-to-Face Behaviour*, London: Allen Lane.
—— (1983) 'The interaction order', *American Sociological Review* 48: 1–17.
Gove, W. R. (1980) *The Labelling of Deviance: Evaluating a Perspective*, London: Sage (2nd edn).
Higgins, P. (1980) *Outsiders in a Hearing World: A Sociology of Deafness*, Beverly Hills, Calif: Sage.
Hilbourne, J. (1973) 'On disabling the normal: the implications of physical disability for other people', *British Journal of Social Work* 3: 497–504.
Hopper, S. (1981) 'Diabetes as a stigmatizing condition: the case of low-income clinic patients in the united states', *Social Science and Medicine* 15(b): 11–19.
Hunt, P. (ed.) (1966) *Stigma: The Experience of Disability*, London: Chapman.
Knudson-Cooper, M. (1981) 'Adjustment to visible stigma: the case of the severely burned', *Social Science and Medicine* 15(b): 31–44.
Lemert, E. (1967) *Human Deviance, Social Problems and Social Control*, Englewood Cliffs, NJ: Prentice-Hall.
Locker, D. (1983) *Disability and Disadvantage: The Consequences of Chronic Illness*, London: Tavistock.

Lofland, J. (1970) 'Interactionist imagery and analytical interruptus', in T. Shibutani (ed.) *Human Nature and Collective Behaviour*, Englewood Cliffs, NJ: Prentice-Hall.

—— (1980) 'Early Goffman: style, structure, substance, soul', in J. Ditton (ed.) *The View from Goffman*, London: Macmillan.

Manning, P. K. (1973) 'Review of "Relations in Public"', *Sociological Quarterly* 14: 135–43.

—— (1976) 'The decline of civility: a comment on Erving Goffman's sociology', *Canadian Review of Sociology and Anthropology* 31 (1): 13–25.

Parsons, T. (1951) *The Social System*, London: Routledge & Kegan Paul.

Plummer, K. (1979) 'Misunderstanding labelling perspectives', in D. Downes and P. Rock (eds) *Deviant Interpretations: Problems in Criminological Theory*, Oxford: Martin Robertson.

Rief, L. (1975) 'Ulcerative colitis: strategies for managing life', in A. L. Strauss, *Chronic Illness and the Quality of Life*, St Louis: Mosby.

Rock, P. (1979) *The Making of Symbolic Interactionism*, London: Macmillan

Rogers, M. (1980) 'Goffman on power, hierarchy, and status', in J. Ditton (ed.) *The View from Goffman*, London: Macmillan.

Safilios-Rothschild, C. (1970) *The Sociology and Social Psychology of Disability and Rehabilitation*, New York: Random House.

Scambler, G. (1984) 'Perceiving and coping with stigmatizing illness', in R. Fitzpatrick, J. Hinton, S. Newman, G. Scambler, and J. Thompson, *The Experience of Illness*, London: Tavistock.

Scambler, G. and Hopkins, A. (1986) 'Being epileptic: coming to terms with stigma', *Sociology of Health and Illness* 8 (1): 26–43.

Scheff, T. J. (1966) *Being Mentally Ill: A Sociological Theory*, London: Weidenfeld & Nicolson.

Schneider, J. and Conrad, P. (1980) 'In the closet with illness: epilepsy, stigma potential and information control', *Social Problems* 28: 32–44.

—— (1981) 'Medical and sociological typologies: the case of epilepsy', *Social Science and Medicine* 15(a): 211–19.

Schudson, M. (1984) 'Embarrassment and Erving Goffman's idea of human nature', *Theory and Society* 13: 633–48.

Scott, R. A. (1969) *The Making of Blind Men*, New York: Russell Sage Foundation.

—— (1970) 'The construction of conceptions of stigma by professional experts', in J. D. Douglas (ed.) *Deviance and Respectability: The Social Construction of Moral Meanings*, New York: Basic Books.

—— (1972) 'A proposed framework for analyzing deviance as a property of social order', in R. A. Scott and J. D. Douglas (eds) *Theoretical Perspectives on Deviance*, New York: Basic Books.

Strauss, A. L. (1975) *Chronic Illness and the Quality of Life*, St Louis: Mosby.

Strong, P. (1983) 'The importance of being Erving: Erving Goffman 1922–1982', *Sociology of Health and Illness* 5 (3): 345–55.
Voysey, M. (1972) 'Impression management by parents with disabled children', *Journal of Health and Social Behaviour* 13: 80–9.
Weiner, C. (1975) 'The burden of rheumatoid arthritis', in A. L. Strauss *Chronic Illness and the Quality of Life*, St Louis: Mosby.
West, P. (1985) 'Becoming disabled: perspectives on the labelling approach', in U. Gerhardt and M. Wadsworth (eds) *Stress and Stigma: Explanations and Evidence in the Sociology of Crime and Illness*, London: Macmillan.

7

Habermas and the power of medical expertise

GRAHAM SCAMBLER

Introduction

Two factors which have undoubtedly inhibited medical sociologists from coming to terms with Habermas's texts, or from drawing on them to inform the construction of their own middle-range theories of health and illness, are the level of abstraction of many of his theses and the manner of their presentation. Those who have studied his work are likely to have met with further obstacles in its quite remarkable inter-disciplinary range, the complexity of the interrelationships between the various theoretical discourses it incorporates, and the fact that it is constantly evolving. The two volumes of *Theorie des Kommunikativen Handelns*, published in Germany in 1981 and the main resource for this chapter, represent the culmination of Habermas's work to date. No attempt will be made to summarize their contents here, many of which are tangential to the arguments to be advanced, but the chapter begins with a brief statement about what might be called the 'Habermasian project'. The remainder of the chapter is devoted to the development of three themes, each informed by this project: medicine's 'colonization of the lifeworld' by means of its power as an expert occupation; the distortion of communication caused by medical expertise in doctor–patient exchanges; and the social and moral possibilities of achieving undistorted communication between doctor and patient. Each theme is illustrated by reference to the changing experience of childbirth in Britain.

The Habermasian project

In his earlier writings Habermas clearly regards psychoanalysis as a model for a critical social theory (Habermas 1971). Although both his reading of Freudian psychoanalysis and his claims about its suitability as a model for a critical theory of society have rightly been questioned (see Keat 1981), it will be helpful to open this section with a summary of his argument. Psychoanalysis, he maintains, is essentially concerned with interpreting a patient's cognitions and feelings; interpreting the meaning of the content of dreams, for example, is a core aspect of therapy. Psychoanalysis, then, has a strong hermeneutic dimension. Interpretive work falters, however, when repressions block off access to the patient's unconscious. At this stage the analyst draws on psychoanalytic theory to construct plausible explanations – explanations which, like those found in the natural sciences, involve causal connections. These explanations are appropriate, Habermas argues, because the analyst is dealing with what has happened to the patient rather than with that which is under her control. In so far as the therapy is successful the need for theoretically informed causal explanations diminishes: the patient is increasingly able to bring her behaviour under autonomous control. In these circumstances psychoanalysis again becomes primarily hermeneutic.

For Habermas the goal of psychoanalytic therapy is to change behaviour 'by the very process of transmuting what happens to the individual into what the individual makes happen' (Giddens 1985: 126). His contention is that a critical theory of society should likewise be geared to emancipation. Marx's theory lacks this emancipatory potential: it can account for productive knowledge but not for reflective knowledge. It therefore requires reformulation (Habermas's initial intention was that the critical theorist become the 'psychoanalyst of the working class' – Roderick 1986: 59). In general terms Habermas argues that a critical social theory must acknowledge that a genuinely emancipated society is one in which individuals actively control their own lives, through an enhanced understanding of their material and psychosocial circumstances.

Another key aspect of Habermas's early theory is that there is no one form that all knowledge takes; rather knowledge can take three basic forms, reflecting three – 'knowledge-constitutive' – interests. He defines these interests as 'quasi-transcendental': they have a transcendental function, as conditions of knowledge, but are naturalistically grounded (that is, 'anthropologically rooted strategies for interpreting life experience'). In all societies people have to engage with the material world, through 'labour', in order to survive. This generates an interest in the prediction and control of external forces (hence the 'empirical-analytic sciences'). They are also committed to 'interaction' with others, giving rise to an interest in communication and meaning (hence the 'historical-hermeneutic disciplines'). And finally, people in all societies are confronted by 'domination', either by nature or in social relations. This leads to an interest in emancipation – 'an interest in the reflective appropriation of human life, without which the interest-bound character of knowledge could not itself be grasped' (Held 1980: 255) (hence 'critical theory').

The extent of Habermas's current allegiance to the arguments adduced in *Knowledge and Human Interests* (1972), and to the theory of cognitive interests in particular, is debatable. Some arguments have certainly undergone revision and others have been superceded. In order to appreciate the shift of emphasis in his work in the 1970s it is helpful to refer to the relationship between psychoanalyst and patient once more. Repressions clearly have the effect of misshaping what the patient says to her therapist; in Habermas's terminology, communication between the two becomes 'systematically distorted'. But what, then, are the criteria of 'undistorted communication'? And precisely what implications does the pursuit of undistorted communication through psychoanalysis have for a critical theory of society? As Giddens suggests, two arguments advanced by Habermas, each relating to language use, are especially pertinent here (Giddens 1985: 128). The first is that communication through language necessarily involves speakers in making implicit 'validity claims'. And the second is that the use of language presupposes the possibility of achieving a rational consensus amongst users with regard to both the truth of statements and the correctness of norms (that is, an 'ideal speech situation') (Habermas 1979).

When one person speaks to another she implicitly (or occasionally explicitly) raises four validity claims: (1) the utterance is 'comprehensible'; (2) its propositional content is 'true'; (3) it is 'appropriate' (or justified); and (4) it is spoken with 'sincerity'. Undistorted communication occurs when a speaker is in a position to defend all four validity claims. This situation can be contrasted with communication between a psychoanalyst and a patient, which may be systematically distorted. Giddens gives the following examples. What a patient says in free association may be, at least for a time, quite incomprehensible. The propositional content of fantasies may be false. Inappropriate or unjustified claims may be made – for example blaming others for events for which they could not reasonably be held responsible. And attempts may be made, consciously or otherwise, to mislead or deflect the psychoanalyst during therapy. On Habermas's reading, the aim of psychoanalysis would be to enable a patient to liberate herself from all factors inhibiting the successful defence of validity claims in routine dialogue (Giddens 1985: 129).

According to Habermas, only two of the four validity claims – those concerning truth and appropriateness or justification – can actually be defended *in* dialogue, that is by means of verbal elaboration and argument; he describes these as 'discursively redeemable'. Validity claims involving the comprehensibility and sincerity of an utterance can be 'shown' to be justified only by rephrasing what is said and through consistent behaviour (for example keeping promises) respectively. Habermas's controversial treatment of truth warrants further discussion here because it incorporates his concept of an ideal speech situation.

Validity claims concerning truth are mostly implicit. It is only when such a claim is contested by another that a speaker is compelled to invoke the concept of truth directly. To defend the truth of an utterance is to support it with factual evidence and logical argument, to demonstrate that it is 'warranted'. 'Truth refers to agreement or consensus reached by such warrants. A statement is "true" if any disputant faced by those warrants would concede its validity. Truth is the promise of a rational consensus' (Giddens 1985: 130). But how can a rational consensus be distinguished from a consensus deriving from tradition or power? Habermas maintains that a rational consensus is one which is secured solely 'by the force of the better argument'; and that the conditions allowing for a rational consensus are those of the ideal speech situation. An ideal speech situation refers to 'a situation of absolutely uncoerced and unlimited discussion between completely free and equal human agents' (Geuss 1981: 65).

A speaker 'anticipates' an ideal speech situation on entering discourse. In attempting to construct a reasoned argument she must assume that the outcome of debate will be determined by the force of the better argument alone. The ideal speech situation is in this sense constitutive of the meaning of discourse. Each utterance involves 'the anticipation of a form of life in which truth, freedom and justice are possible'. Although the ideal speech situation is rare in practice, it can serve as a standard for the critique of systematically distorted communication. Thus the objective of a critical theory of society – normatively and non-arbitrarily grounded in the ideal speech situation – is to achieve emancipation from systematically distorted communication or 'ideology', that is from 'those belief systems which can maintain their legitimacy despite the fact that they could not be validated if subjected to rational discourse' (Schroyer 1973: 163). Through such engagement are patterns of domination exposed.

It only remains in this highly selective survey of the Habermasian project to note that Habermas has recently tried to link his ever-changing theories of cognitive interests and language use (that is, his 'universal pragmatics') to theories of personal and cultural evolution. He argues, against the relativist, that 'procedurally the canons of rationality – that is to say, the modes of reaching warranted conclusions – are the same everywhere' (Giddens 1985: 132). This makes it possible for both individuals and cultures to be located on scales of evolutionary development using 'cognitive adequacy' as the criterion; cognitive adequacy refers to the range and depth of the defensible validity claims available. With reference to individuals, Habermas draws on Piaget's theory that there are three stages of cognitive development in children, representing a progressive expansion of their learning capacities. With reference to cultures, he maintains that there are likewise three stages of development or evolution which might be said to correspond to Piaget's stages of cognitive development: the 'mythical', the 'religious-metaphysical', and the 'modern'.

For Piaget the higher levels of cognitive development signify a 'decentration' of an egocentrically distorted understanding of the world. Individuals move from a narrow preoccupation with their own immediate needs to an enlarged awareness of a world independent of themselves and of the needs of others. According to Habermas, cultures (or 'world-views') undergo an analogous process of transformation. Traditional cultures are dominated by myth: they tend to be 'closed' and refractory to change. Forms of social organization are the product of long-established practice rather than rational argument. Indeed the institutional conditions for reasoned public engagement and debate are lacking. Rationality is expanded, however, with the emergence and spread of global religions like Buddhism, Hinduism, Islam, and Christianity, which are broader-based and less restricting than myth. Like Weber, Habermas sees religion as contributing, in turn, to the 'rationalization' of culture culminating in modern occidental capitalism. But he differs from Weber in that he associates this rationalization with the further expansion of rationality. Modern capitalism, he argues, is characterized by 'post-conventional' cognitive domains. And post-conventional forms of social organization, unlike those in the now 'disvalued' mythical and religious-metaphysical cultures, are based on warranted principles (Habermas 1984 vol. I: 68). This does not mean that Habermas is uncritical of modern capitalism – far from it – but he does see undeniable gains in the potential for human enlightenment. Schmidt aptly observes that he constructs a defence of this potential for enlightenment based on an 'enlightened suspicion of enlightenment' (Schmidt 1982: 18). It is to a fuller consideration of Habermas's analysis of rationalization and rationality in modern culture that the next section turns.

Medical expertise and the 'lifeworld'

Two of Habermas's multiple distinctions are especially important at this juncture. The first is between two types of rationalization, involving 'purposive-rational' and 'communicative' action. And the second is between the concepts of 'system' and 'lifeworld'. Each will be discussed briefly as a prelude to a more detailed account of their relevance to contemporary medical practice. Purposive-rational action, according to Habermas, can be regarded under two different aspects – the empirical efficiency of technical means and the consistency of choice between suitable means. Actions and action-systems can be rationalized in both respects. The rationality of means requires technically utilizable, empirical knowledge. The rationality of decisions requires the explication and inner consistency of value systems and decision maxims, as well as the correct derivation of acts of choice.

(Habermas 1979: 117)

As Bernstein points out, rationalization processes of this type closely correspond to Weber's *Zweckrationalitat*, the form of rationalization which he regarded as fundamental to modern culture (for an extended discussion of Weber's theories, see Brubaker 1984). The advance of the empirical-analytic sciences and of decision and game theory in recent decades has made this type of rationalization very conspicuous (Bernstein 1985: 21).

Communicative action is linked internally to the reason embodied in speech, since it is oriented towards the achievement of an agreement or consensus based on the intersubjective recognition of validity claims (that is, concerning comprehensibility, truth, appropriateness, and sincerity). The rationalization of communicative action involves

extirpating those relations of force that are inconspicuously set in the very structures of communication and that prevent conscious settlement of conflicts, and consensual regulation of conflicts, by means of interpsychic as well as interpersonal communication. Rationalization means overcoming such systematically distorted communication in which the action-supporting consensus concerning the reciprocally raised validity claims – especially consensus concerning the truthfulness of intentional expressions and the rightness of underlying norms – can be sustained in appearance only, that is counterfactually.

(Habermas 1979: 119–20)

In his most recent work Habermas introduces the concept of lifeworld as a correlate of the concept of communicative action. Members of a community normally share a lifeworld. It refers to the distinctive, pre-reflexive form of background assumptions, convictions, and relations which function as a resource for what goes into explicit communication. 'But the moment this background knowledge enters communicative expression, where it becomes explicit knowledge and thereby subject to criticism, it loses precisely those characteristics which lifeworld structures always have for those who belong to them: certainty, background character, impossibility of being gone behind' (Habermas 1986: 109). The lifeworld is the medium, or 'symbolic space', within which culture, social integration, and personality are sustained and reproduced (Thompson 1984: 288).

The lifeworld may be contrasted with the concept of system, which pertains to material rather than symbolic reproduction. Social systems, most notably the market economy and the state apparatus, follow functional imperatives and serve as formally organized systems of action based on what Habermas calls 'steering media' (that is, money and power). While the lifeworld is seen in terms of communicative action, social systems are seen in terms of purposive-rational action. These concepts of system and lifeworld, which are interrelated but cannot be reduced to one another, provide the key to Habermas's theory of social or cultural evolution. He draws a distinction between system rationalization, involving purposive-rational action, and the rationalization of the lifeworld, involving communication action. System rationalization leads to a growth in differentiation and complexity (that is, an expansion of markets and of political and administrative organization). The rationalization of the lifeworld leads to an increase in the scope of communicative action and to a growth of communicative rationality. This distinction enables Habermas to re-formulate what Wellmer labels the 'paradox of rationality'. This states that the rationalization of the lifeworld is a precondition and starting-point of system rationalization, which then becomes more and more autonomous from the normative constraints of the lifeworld, until finally system imperatives begin to instrumentalize the lifeworld and threaten to destroy it (Wellmer 1985: 56). In Habermas's own ter-minology, system rationalization threatens a 'colonization of the lifeworld'.

Habermas argues that strictly there is no paradox of rationalization, in that 'there is no logical, conceptual, or historical *necessity* that systemic imperatives *must* destroy the lifeworld' (Bernstein 1985: 23). It is true that in modern culture system rationalization has indeed prevailed, colonizing, and hence deforming, the lifeworld. Roderick summarizes:

> Under the selective pressure of the system imperatives of capitalist modernization, social rationalization did in fact take place in a one-sided, distorted and crisis-ridden way. The capitalist economy and the modern administrative state privileged the value sphere of science for its functions of power and control, and thus they one-sidedly imposed the hegemony of scientific-technological rationality over the other value spheres.

> (Roderick 1986: 133)

This is the dark side of modern culture, which absorbed almost all the attention of Weber, Lukàcs, and the early Frankfurt School. But there is also a bright side to modern culture, namely the rationalization of the lifeworld. This allows for a critical appropriation of what has hitherto been taken-for-granted in the lifeworld, and enhances the objective possibility of achieving genuine rational consensus – a rational conduct of life based on free and equal discussion rather than force. In brief, rationalization in modern occidental capitalism has been *selective*. The challenge Habermas lays down is to work towards communicative rationality in order to obtain 'a proper balance' between the legitimate demands of system rationalization and the communicative rationalization of the lifeworld (Bernstein 1985: 24).

In the remainder of this section attention is focused on specific ways in which medical expertise may be said to have colonized the lifeworld. It is important to remember, following Habermas, that this is a contingent and not a necessary process. Nor, despite its conspicuous presence in all contemporary capitalist societies, has its course been uniform. Consider, for example, the professionalization of medicine, a crucial precondition for the establishment of medical expertise as a source of power. Sociological work on the professions originated with, and was for a long time monopolized by, Anglo-American theorists; not surprisingly, it reflected their interest in the dominant professions in Britain and the USA, particularly medicine and law (Freidson 1983). But the professionalization of medicine in Britain and the USA differed markedly from equivalent processes on the European continent. Anglo-American associations of physicians skilfully exploited opportunities presented by the expansion of economic markets under modern capitalism. The state was called upon to provide a framework for private exchange relations, but it had no role either in determining the substance of medical work or in regulating the content of physicians' exchange relations with their clientele. It was essentially passive. In European societies, however, the professionalization of medicine was typically initiated and shaped by a centralized bureaucratic state, which exerted considerable influence both on institutional forms of medical work and on the cultural orientations of physicians (Rueschemeyer 1986). Clearly no theory of system rationalization in relation to medicine, and of the consequent colonization of the lifeworld, could be regarded as mature unless it had the means to accommodate highly significant inter-societal variations within modern occidental capitalism, of which the differing roles of the market economy and state apparatus in the professionalization of medicine is but a single example.

What follows is no more than preliminary spadework for such a theory. Concentrating on the current situation in Britain and to a lesser extent the USA, it is argued that system rationalization in the sphere of health and illness has indeed led to a medical colonization of the lifeworld. The argument is thematic and begins by considering aspects of the relationship between expert occupations like medicine and power. Medical expertise is in part founded upon, and generally justified or legitimized in terms of, what Freidson calls 'formal knowledge'. Formal knowledge is the higher knowledge of modern culture; it is distinct from both routine everyday knowledge and non-formal specialized knowledge. 'Originally rooted in arcane lore and in texts in ancient languages known only to a few, higher knowledge is now still expressed in terms unfamiliar to and impenetrable by the many and discussed by techniques of discourse that are opaque to outsiders' (Freidson 1986: 3). Freidson points to Weber's concept of *Zweckrationalitat* as best characterizing the nature of formal knowledge. For this may be substituted Habermas's system rationalization, also involving the growth and spread of purposive-rational action. Formal knowledge, Freidson continues,

> is manifested most obviously in technology but also in law, the management of institutions, the economy, indeed, in the entire institutional realm of modern society. It is intimately associated with the accounting and management methods that developed with capitalism and the administrative methods of developing predictable social order that rose along with the modern state in the form of 'rational-legal bureaucracy'.
>
> (1986: 3–4)

But above all else, he adds, it is associated with the rapid rise of modern science and the application of scientific method to technical and social problems.

The use of formal knowledge to order human affairs constitutes an exercise of power, 'an act of domination over those who are the object' (Freidson 1986: 6–7). In *Toward a Rational Society* (1971) Habermas argues that the growth of formal knowledge, increasingly rapid since the Second World War, has served to pre-empt much political decision-making and democratic participation. But he insists that there is nothing inevitable about this. Technology and science are a threat to democracy only when used inappropriately, as 'ideology', to address problems or justify decisions and actions which are not technical or scientific (that is, which do not properly answer to the professional competence of specialists) (Habermas 1971: 61). When they are used inappropriately they may provide an unwarranted but politically effective legitimation for the undemocratic exercise of power.

> Under such circumstances political decisions are not subject to popular debate because they are presented as 'technical' decisions. People are not allowed to choose among a variety of alternatives

because the issue is presented as a technical one that involves the necessary use of the 'one best method'.

(Freidson 1986: 8)

A number of critiques of modern medicine combine the charge that medical expertise has become increasingly technocratic and un-accountable with some version of the thesis of medical imperialism, involving a progressive 'medicalization' of everyday life. While this thesis is potentially compatible with, and might perhaps be profitably incorporated in, the Habermasian theory of system rationalization and the colonization of the lifeworld, it should be recognized at the outset that the case for medical imperialism has sometimes been overstated (Strong 1979: 205–8). The literature on changing medical attitudes towards pregnancy and childbirth contains such 'overstatements' – for example when reference is made to a mythical golden age of 'natural' childbirth prior to its twentieth-century medicalization (MacIntyre 1977). But it also contains potent evidence of a medical colonization of the lifeworld, and, for this reason, is an appropriate resource for illustrating the arguments advanced in this section.

There is no doubt that childbirth has become safer for both mother and child, if safety is assessed in terms of maternal and perinatal mortality rates. This is true for all modern capitalist societies, although there has been considerable variation between (and within) societies in the speed and extent of reductions in mortality. The mortality statistics for England and Wales are not particularly impressive when compared to those of some other western societies (for example Sweden), but they do reflect the general trend to increased safety. In 1901 48 women died for every 10,000 live births; in the mid-1980s, one woman does. In 1931 one baby in every sixteen was stillborn or died in the first week of life; in 1982 the figure was one in eighty-seven (Doyal and Elston 1986: 187). There are competing theories as to why these significant reductions in mortality have occurred. Some argue that social factors like improved family income, housing, and diet over the duration of women's lives have had a crucial effect. But the theory favoured by the medical profession, and reflected in recent government reports, is that it is the development of comprehensive medical services, affording widespread access to medical expertise, which have been critical. It follows from this theory that further reductions in mortality are largely dependent on increased resources for antenatal, obstetric, and perinatal medical services, and of course on women's use of these services.

The merits and otherwise of these opposing theories will continue to be debated. What is incontrovertible is that medical – and predomi-nantly male – control over pregnancy and childbirth has increased to such an extent that women who do not submit to it are regarded as irresponsible, gambling with the health, well-being, and even lives, of their babies. Clearly, as Oakley ironically observes, 'childbearing is too important to be left to women' (Oakley 1986: 232). Wagner (1986), writing on behalf of the WHO Regional Office for Europe, discerns at least seven factors relevant to physicians' achievement of control or power over the experience of birth. First, they have redefined birth as a medical problem, as a process which is either pathological or potentially so; and 'whoever defines the problem controls the solutions'. Second, they have secured the 'hospitalization' of birth; and on their own territory of the hospital they have long exerted near absolute control. Third, they have come to dominate other birth attendants, like midwives; although midwives are still responsible for about 75 per cent of normal deliveries in hospitals in England and Wales, they usually work under physicians' supervision. Fourth, physicians have retained control over the prescription of drugs and the use of machines and procedures now associated with childbirth. Fifth, they have continued to govern the distribution of research funds and, hence, 'the generation of new knowledge about pregnancy and birth, what shall be studied, how it should be studied, and how the results should or should not be disseminated'. Sixth, they have largely dictated government policy on birth care. And finally, they have over time managed to convince the non-medical population, including government, that only they are in a position to evaluate their own activities. Wagner, a physician himself, adds: 'This peer review clearly has a built-in conflict of interest. Nowhere in the world, to my knowledge, has peer review been adequate in controlling the excesses of the medical profession' (1986: 196–7).

Two related aspects of birth are selected for examination here. Both have excited controversy, arguably because they epitomize the process of medical colonization. They concern the switch from the home to the hospital as the typical location for childbirth (that is, the growth of territorial power), and the increasing emphasis on the active management of labour and childbirth (that is, the growth of technological power). It was in 1927, when the proportion of all live births occurring in institutions of one kind or another stood at 15 per cent, that the Registrar General in Britain first noted the potential importance of place of delivery; tentative reference was made to a growing individual recognition of the superiority of institutional treatment. By 1932 the proportion of institutional births had risen to 24 per cent and the Registrar General again referred to the advantages of institutional over home deliveries. The trend towards hospital confinement has since continued in Britain, although the gradient of increase has not been particularly stable. The proportion of hospital deliveries had reached two-thirds by the mid-1950s, and in 1959 the Cranbrook

Report recommended a figure of 70 per cent. It claimed that women appeared to prefer hospital confinement and that avoidable maternal deaths were still occurring in the home. The Peel Report in 1970 noted that the proportion of hospital births had by then exceeded 80 per cent and stated: 'There seems to be a gradually increasing appreciation in the profession and amongst the general public that confinement in hospital is the safest arrangement, irrespective of considerations of finance or convenience' (Peel Committee 1970: 39–40). The report recommended 100 per cent hospital confinement. By 1972 the proportion of hospital deliveries had topped 90 per cent, and it has since exceeded 99 per cent (Oakley 1986: 215–17).

Two particular observations need to be made about this seemingly inexorable process. First, influential groups within the medical profession, most notably obstetricians, have always been in the vanguard in calling for hospital confinement. In 1944, fifteen years before Cranbrook, the Royal College of Obstetricians and Gynaecologists advocated a 70 per cent hospital delivery rate; and as early as 1964 the same body anticipated Peel by arguing for a 95 per cent rate (Oakley 1986: 218). Throughout this period, not surprisingly, there was a steady rise in the number of consultant obstetricians – an increase of more than a quarter between Cranbrook and Peel, for example – and a commensurate increase in consultant unit beds. It is axiomatic that the assertions that the hospital is the safest place of birth, and that hospital confinement therefore accords with the true interests of mother and baby, were consonant with the advancement of the material and other interests of the obstetricians themselves.

The second observation focuses on the key claim that the hospital is the safest place for delivery. Few would dispute the advisability of hospital deliveries for a small sub-population of high-risk women, perhaps 10–15 per cent of the total. But the case for hospitalization for the large majority of low-risk women has certainly not been made. After extensively reviewing the research literature, Campbell and Macfarlane unambiguously state that 'there is no evidence to support the claim that the safest policy is for all women to give birth in hospital'. Amongst their other pertinent conclusions are the following: that the statistical association between the increase in the proportion of hospital deliveries and the decline in the crude perinatal mortality rate 'seems unlikely to be entirely or even mainly explained by a cause and effect relation'; that the perinatal mortality rate is 'very low' for women who have planned home deliveries, although somewhat higher for those having unplanned home deliveries; that there is some evidence that morbidity may be higher amongst mothers and babies delivered and cared for in hospitals in general, and consultant obstetric units in particular, than amongst those remaining at home;

and that most women who have experienced both hospital and home births prefer the latter (Campbell and Macfarlane 1986: 681–2). In short, not only is there no 'scientific' evidence to justify a policy of majority, let alone 100 per cent, hospital confinement on the grounds of improved safety, but also it may even be the case that there are health advantages accruing to low-risk women having their babies at home. Moreover, most women clearly derive more satisfaction from home births. It is in this context that the recent remark by the President of the American College of Obstetricians and Gynaecologists that home delivery constitutes 'the earliest form of child abuse' should be appraised (quoted in Oakley 1986: 219).

The transfer of the birth experience from the home to the hospital has been accompanied by a growing emphasis on the active management of labour and childbirth. It is instructive to compare changes in rates for caesarian section in Denmark and the Netherlands in this respect. In Denmark between 1960 and 1980 hospital deliveries rose from 50 per cent to 99 per cent, while in the Netherlands over the same period they increased from about 28 per cent to 67 per cent. The caesarian section rate in both societies stood at 2 per cent in 1960; it had risen to 11 per cent in Denmark by 1980, while in the Netherlands it had increased to only 4 per cent (Scherjon 1986). In England and Wales the figures are similar to those for Denmark. The caesarian section rate increased slowly from 4.7 per cent in 1962 to 5.3 per cent in 1972, and then more rapidly to 10.1 per cent in 1982. The rate for forceps delivery increased steadily from 8.1 per cent in 1962 to 13.2 per cent in 1977, and then decreased to 10.3 per cent in 1982. These increases in the rates for caesarian section and forceps delivery are partly explicable in terms of the dramatic rise in the rate of induction in hospitals. This stood at 13.4 per cent in 1964, trebled to 39.4 per cent in 1974, remained at approximately 37 per cent until 1978, and then nearly halved to 18.8 per cent in 1982. Comparable data for other aspects of obstetric management, such as the use of anaesthetic, analgesic or other drugs, foetal monitoring, and ultrasound scanning are not available (Tew 1986).

Two comments on the trend to active obstetric management are in order here. The first concerns safety again. Hospital confinement is entirely appropriate for certain high-risk women because it facilitates active management should this be or become necessary. But active management is no longer confined to such cases: it has become commonplace. There has been a growing tendency to define more and more risk factors, with the result that all women are now perceived and treated 'as if' they are high-risk (Graham and Oakley 1981). This fundamental perception of women as at risk legitimizes as well as promotes hospitalization and active management. ('Risk is the bludgeon used to scare not only women but also politicians and health care providers' – Wagner 1986: 200–1.) 'Indeed, the expectation of complications becomes self-fulfilling, as different interventions and technologies take their psychological and physiological effect' (Young 1983: xiii).

In his excellent discussion of high technology medicine, Jennett suggests that modern obstetrics, like other specialized branches of medicine, makes 'routine' use of a family of technologies, some of which have never been properly evaluated, and all of which are appropriate only for specific subgroups of patients. He concentrates on foetal monitoring, noting that it would seem to provide an obvious way of checking on a baby during labour and might be expected to lead to an earlier recognition of distress and to more timely interventions (and its use does lead to an increased proportion of operative deliveries). But, he adds, randomized control trials have so far failed to demonstrate 'a convincing increase in the well-being of infants when such monitoring is widely applied', which prompts him to suggest that a mother's monitoring of the frequency of foetal movements might be quite adequate in low-risk cases (Jennett 1986: 138–9). Tew is more scathing about the general over-use of technology. The main conclusion of her statistical review of the admittedly limited data available is that the trend to obstetric intranatal intervention which has accompanied progressive hospitalization has 'made birth less safe, not more safe, for the vast majority of cases' (Tew 1986: 671). At the very least it can be said that the case for 'routine' active management on the grounds of safety is 'scientifically' unproven.

The second comment has to do with the discernible reduction in some aspects of active obstetric management, especially induction, over the last decade. There are a number of factors behind this decline in the induction rate, including, for example, documentation of its costs, as well as its benefits, in a period of deepening economic depression. Also important has been organized consumer opposition. The strength of women's feelings can be seen in the results of Cartwright's survey in the mid-1970s when the induction rate was at its peak. Four out of five of the 2,378 mothers surveyed wanted to be able to exercise effective choice regarding the medical management of their pregnancies and labours. Of those who had had their babies induced 78 per cent wished not to repeat the experience, and 93 per cent of those who had had their babies spontaneously expressed the wish to do so again (Cartwright 1979: 107). The theme of women's dissatisfaction with and resistance to medical control – leading, in Habermasian terms, to an organized defence of the integrity of the lifeworld – is taken up again in some detail in the final section of the chapter.

An attempt has been made in these last paragraphs to show how medical expertise, deriving both power and legitimation from its roots in formal knowledge (that is, science and technology), has effected a colonization of the lifeworld in relation to pregnancy and childbirth. Concentrating on the significance of territory and technology, it has been argued that system rationalization, involving the expansion of purposive-rational action, has gone too far; indeed, in important respects it has got out of control. It is not possible to justify the very substantial medicalization of the birth experience that has occurred in Britain and elsewhere on the grounds of safety − the criterion invariably cited by obstetricians and narrowly defined by them in terms of reduced maternal and perinatal mortality. Moreover, it is quite inappropriate that so many of the pivotal decisions surrounding the bringing of a baby into the world have been redefined as technical and usurped by physicians in their roles as experts or agents of formal knowledge. As far as birth is concerned it is clear that 'a proper balance' between the legitimate demands of system rationalization and the communicative rationalization of the lifeworld has yet to be achieved.

Medical expertise and distorted communication

The current imbalance between system rationalization and the rationalization of the lifeworld is reflected in the great majority of studies of communication between physicians and patients. Central to many of these is the concept of patient compliance, and it is generally taken for granted that patient compliance is a valid measure of medical care. As Mishler points out, 'it requires a shift in perspective and some reflection to recognize that the concept incorporates a medical bias' (1984: 49). It is revealing that although in several influential studies a high proportion of patients have reported that physicians did not fulfil their expectations, physicians have not as a result been described as 'non-compliant' with patient expectations. Only patients are non-compliant. 'The term non-compliance is used in a way that makes it equivalent to deviance, and it is this deviance from the unquestioned norms and values of medicine that provides the basis for interpretation and analysis' (Mishler 1984: 50).

In his own research Mishler attempts to break with this medical bias. He distinguishes analytically between the 'voice of the lifeworld' and the 'voice of medicine'. The voice of the lifeworld refers to the patient's contextually grounded experiences of everyday events and problems. Her reports of these are expressed from the perspective of what Schutz called the 'natural attitude'. The voice of medicine reflects a technical interest and issues from the perspective of the 'scientific attitude': 'the meaning of events is provided through abstract rules that serve to *decontextualize* events, to remove them from particular personal and social contexts' (my emphasis) (Mishler 1984: 104). Mishler draws on Habermas's early writings to explore the interaction of these two voices in physician–patient communication. It is inter-action characterized by conflict. He suggests a substitution of Habermas's concept of symbolic (or communicative) action for the voice of the lifeworld, and his concept of purposive-rational action for the voice of medicine. And he goes on to argue that the physician's attempt to dominate or control communication with the patient typi-cally has the effect of absorbing and dissolving the patient's self-understanding of her problems into a system of purpose-rational action (that is, the framework of technical medicine). Current clinical practice, he asserts, is based on and incorporates an asymmetrical power relationship between physician and patient. 'Achieving humane care is dependent upon empowering patients' (Mishler 1984: 193).

The general literature on the dominance physicians exercise over patients, and on the strategies they adopt to do so, is extensive and cannot be reviewed here. But it is worth emphasizing that the conflict Mishler regards as characteristic of physician–patient interaction is not always overt. Lukes (1974) distinguishes between one-, two-, and three-dimensional analyses of power. The one-dimensional analysis views power as something that can be measured by studying decision-making and registering whose decisions prevail. The two-dimensional analysis recognizes that the study of overt conflict may fail to uncover all those contexts in which power has been exercised. Thus especially powerful individuals may use their power to prevent the more awkward or threatening concerns of others from reaching the decision-making agenda. An absence of overt conflict may indicate a false or manipu-lated consensus rather than a true one. The three-dimensional analysis argues that a yet more subtle exercise of power involves influencing, or even determining, what others want. In this event it may be known that power has been exercised because individuals have demonstrably acted against their own interests, even though they may express satis-faction with the outcome. 'What one may have here is a *latent conflict*, which consists in a contradiction between the interests of those exer-cising power and the *real interests* of those they exclude' (Lukes 1974: 24–5).

Lukes insists on the possibility of achieving a three-dimensional analysis of power – 'an analysis that is at once value-laden, theoretical and empirical' (1974: 57). Habermas would of course concur. As was apparent in the outline of the Habermasian project at the beginning of the chapter, he sees it as precisely the function of a critical theory of society to expose the inconspicuous or hidden exercise of power or domination. Moreover, his recent extension of his own and others' analyses of speech acts into a 'formal pragmatics' contains pointers as to how this might be accomplished. It is convenient to start by recalling Austin's influential distinction between 'locutionary', 'illocutionary', and 'perlocutionary' speech acts (Austin 1962). Through locutionary acts the speaker says something – expresses a state of affairs. Through illocutionary acts she performs an action in saying something, normally by means of a performative verb in the first person present (for example 'I promise you that "p"'). And through perlocutionary acts she produces an effect on the hearer. Habermas characterizes Austin's three acts in the following 'catchphrases': 'to say *something*, to act *in* saying something, to bring about something *through* acting in saying something' (Habermas 1984 vol.1: 288–9).

Habermas begins by defining 'communicative action' as linguistically mediated interaction in which all speakers pursue illocutionary aims unreservedly in order to arrive at 'an agreement that will provide the basis for a consensual coordination of individually pursued plans of action'. And he contrasts communicative action with 'strategic action', which occurs when at least one speaker aims with her speech acts to produce perlocutionary effects on her hearer(s). Perlocutionary effects ensue 'whenever a speaker acts with an orientation to success and thereby instrumentalizes speech acts for purposes that are contingently related to the meaning of what is said' (Habermas 1984 vol. 1: 289). Thus communicative action is 'action oriented to understanding', and strategic action is 'action oriented to success'.

This requires some qualification. Simple imperatives – requests and demands – are illocutionary acts with which the speaker 'openly' declares her aim of influencing her hearer(s) (and with which she connects a power claim). In such instances the speaker pursues illocutionary aims unreservedly but none the less acts with an orientation to success rather than understanding. This can be termed 'open strategic action'. When speakers employ speech acts for perlocutionary purposes, this can be termed 'concealed strategic action'. In the case of either open or concealed strategic action 'the potential for the binding (or bonding) force of good reasons – a potential which is always contained in linguistic communication – remains unexploited'. This potential is fulfilled only in communicative action, when illocutionary acts express *criticizable validity claims*. In the context of communicative action all comprehensible speech acts raise criticizable validity claims concerning truth, appropriateness (or justification) and sincerity. Speakers can 'rationally motivate' hearers to accept their speech acts because they can assume the 'warranty' (*Gewähr*) for providing, if necessary, good reasons that would stand up to hearers' criticisms of validity claims.

Communication 'pathologies', as Habermas calls them, can be conceived as the product of confusion between actions oriented to understanding and actions oriented to success. Situations of concealed strategic action may involve either conscious or unconscious deception. In cases of conscious deception at least one of the participants acts with an orientation to success, but allows others to assume that all the presuppositions of communicative action are being satisfied. This 'manipulation' has already been touched upon in connection with perlocutionary acts.

> On the other hand, the kind of unconscious repression of conflicts that the psychoanalyst explains in terms of defence mechanisms leads to disturbances of communication on both the intrapsychic and interpersonal levels. In such cases at least one of the parties is deceiving himself about the fact that he is acting with an attitude oriented to success and is only keeping up the appearance of communicative action.

(Habermas 1984 vol. 1: 332)

This can be described as unconscious deception or 'systematically distorted communication'. The diagram below locates manipulation and systematically distorted communication in Habermas's theory of communicative action.

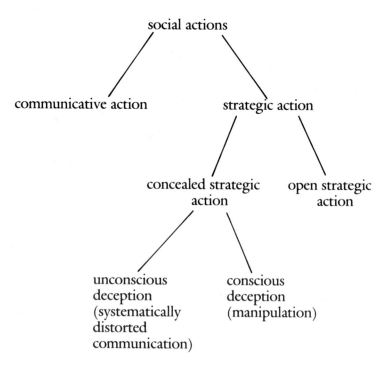

What implications does Habermas's formal pragmatics have for the analysis of physician–patient communication? Two points need to be made before this question is addressed. First, although Habermas argues that his formal pragmatics constitutes an essential point of departure and 'guide' for empirical-pragmatic investigations, there is no denying that such investigations are in their infancy. And Habermas admits to the rich and daunting complexity of everyday communications compared with the strong idealizations of his formal pragmatics. Thus the true potential of his analysis has yet to be tested. Second, currently available transcriptions of communications between physicians and patients are too crude to be convincingly used to explore the potency or otherwise of Habermas's formal pragmatics (Mishler 1984: ch. 2).

As these somewhat negative comments suggest, attempts to draw on Habermas's formal pragmatics to analyse physician–patient communication can at this stage be only tentative and provisional. This certainly applies to what follows. The arguments adduced elaborate on earlier themes on pregnancy and childbirth, and it is convenient to begin by noting Graham and Oakley's (1981) comparison of the conflicting frames of reference of physicians and mothers on reproduction. Conflict manifests itself, they claim, in four principal contexts. First, women generally view pregnancy and childbirth as normal processes. Physicians tend to treat them as pathological or potentially so. Second, most women see themselves as possessing knowledge and expertise about their own bodies and lives. Physicians appear to believe that all useful knowledge about pregnancy and childbirth, extending to 'the entire symptomatology of childbearing', is medical knowledge; their formal knowledge affords them the only true expertise. Third, women typically wish to retain control over what happens, especially during childbirth. Physicians usually act as if all the key decisions are for them to take. Some women resent the use of technology during birth because it involves a loss of personal control and clashes with their perception of childbirth as an essentially normal process. Physicians see technology as an important resource in containing a potentially pathological process. And fourth, women often complain about unsatisfactory communication. Questions are difficult to ask and, if asked, are frequently ignored or interpreted as requests for reassurance. Physicians tend to perceive mothers' questions as evidence of anxiety rather than requests for information, and either fail to respond at all or resort to vague or trivial answers if pressed (Graham and Oakley 1981: 56–71).

Following Mishler, the conflicting frames of reference of physicians and mothers are here referred to as the voices of medicine and the lifeworld respectively. And the discussion focuses on Graham and

Oakley's fourth arena of conflict – 'the communication gap'. The main thesis proferred is that one of the most profound implications of system rationalization for physician–mother communication is the domination of the voice of the lifeworld by the voice of medicine via open and concealed strategic action.

It is important to recognize the context in which communication between physicians and pregnant women typically occurs. Graham and Oakley emphasize that the women they interviewed, in York and London respectively, saw 'a different face at every clinic visit'. More-over the antenatal clinics in both locations resembled assembly lines, 'if only because a small number of doctors must see a large number of patients in a short space of time'. In the London clinic the average time per encounter was 3.9 minutes (Graham and Oakley 1981: 66–7). A research team in Australia has suggested that women attending antenatal clinics in public hospitals undergo a form of 'processing', with little opportunity to establish relationships with the physicians and other health professionals they meet (Shapiro et al, 1983: 145). These background or contextual circumstances are clearly more pro-pitious for purposive-rational action and the voice of medicine than they are for communicative action and the voice of the lifeworld.

It is rare for the preconditions for communicative action to be fully realized in encounters between physicians and pregnant women, al-though there are likely to be moments of partial realization. Paradoxi-cally, dialogues in which the preconditions seem to have been most fully realized – when, for example, both physician and patient express satisfaction with process and outcome – may be most indicative of physician dominance (that is, in accordance with Lukes's three-dimensional analysis of power). This is perhaps most often the case when physician and patient share an uncritical faith in the salience and comprehensiveness of medical or obstetric expertise based on formal knowledge. Physician *and patient* adopt the voice of medicine. In this context the question of open strategic action or manipulation on the physician's part may simply not arise. It of course remains a central function of the critical theory of society advocated by Habermas to expose instances of systematically distorted communication when they do occur by showing that the satisfaction of physician and patient is born of a false or non-rational consensus which derives from the power of medical expertise and may not accord with the patient's true interests.

Open strategic action and manipulation by physicians can be more readily illustrated by reference to published material on physician – patient encounters than can systematically distorted communication. Consider the following interchange recorded by Graham and Oakley (1981: 62–3). A registrar has done an internal examination of a woman towards the end of her first pregnancy, and comments:

Physician:	It'd be difficult to get you off now – I think you ought to come in for the rest and to do some water tests and then we can start you off. The baby isn't growing as fast as it was.
Patient:	What do you mean, come in?
Physician:	Really it's a matter of when you come in, Sunday, I should think, and then stay in.
Patient:	Stay in until it's born, you mean.
Physician:	Yes.
Patient:	I don't fancy that very much.
Physician:	If you'd been ready I would have started you off today. You see on the ultrasound it's not growing as well as it was, and on the water tests the oestriols are falling – it's not bad, but you should come in and have some water tests, get some rest, and then we can start you off sometime next week probably, when you're ready.
Patient:	If my husband wanted to come and talk to you about inducing me, can I make an appointment for him?
Physician:	I don't think anything your husband said would affect our decision one way or the other.
Patient:	No, but he would like to talk to you.
Physician:	Yes, well he can talk to whoever's on duty, but there's nothing he can say that will affect us: it's a medical question.
Patient:	Yes, but he'd still like to talk it over, find out what's going on.
Physician:	What it amounts to is that we won't be browbeaten by the *Sunday Times* (a reference to two articles published shortly before this encounter).
Patient:	No, I understand that.
Physician:	If we explained to everyone, and everyone's husband, we'd spend all our time explaining. I think you've got to assume if you come here for medical attention that we make all the decisions. In fact I think you should come in today, but I've already been browbeaten into saying Sunday, which is another forty-eight hours.

The registrar starts by giving a rudimentary account of why he wants to induce labour. This is offered in 'lay' language (for example 'start you off' for induction). It is apparent that his decision is made and he has no wish to discuss it. When the woman resists, he introduces 'technical' terms – 'water' tests become 'oestriol' tests. Graham and Oakley write: 'Technical language in explanations is reserved for cases where a doctor wants to encourage a patient to agree to a particular procedure (and perceives her as unwilling to do so)'. This is an example of manipulation, where the physician employs speech acts for their perlocutionary effects. Graham and Oakley go on to note that while women in their studies who objected to induction all met with 'hostility', women who explicitly or implicitly requested an induction met with a different response: 'in some cases the patient's request was granted, but even when it was not, the plea for induction was accepted as legitimate patient-behaviour'. They suggest that women who ask for an induction are subscribing to two important norms in obstetric practice: 'the idea that technological childbirth is "good" childbirth, and the notion that while the doctor's superior expertise may be challenged by *refusing* medical decisions, it is *confirmed* by polite requests for them; "begging for mercy" is how doctors often described such requests' (Graham and Oakley 1981: 63; see also Oakley 1980). Returning to the dialogue, it is clear that when the registrar's attempt to manipulate his patient fails, he quickly – and confidently – resorts to open strategic action, with the connected power claims becoming more and more explicit.

There is insufficient space to illustrate further the potential of Habermas's formal pragmatics for exposing and analysing the power exercised by physicians through their dialogues with pregnant women (Oakley's writings are probably the best available source for additional material). But hopefully enough has been said to demonstrate that a programme of empirical pragmatic investigations of speech acts, based on Habermasian foundations and utilizing the kind of sophisticated techniques of transcription commended by Mishler, would be a worthwhile sociological investment. That there is a need for systematic study of the dominance of the voice of medicine over the voice of the lifeworld caused by excessive system rationalization would seem to be incontrovertible.

Maintaining the integrity of the 'lifeworld'

Giddens observes that the basic theme of all Habermas's work is 'an endeavour to reunite theory and practice in the twentieth century' (Giddens 1985: 124). And Habermas does indeed attempt to apply his latest reformulation of critical theory to contemporary political struggles. He pays special attention to the 'new protest movements', and tentatively links these movements both to the crises identified by critical theory and to the emancipatory thrust of the theory. He argues that conflict in modern industrial societies is no longer centred on distribution. Roderick's summary draws heavily on Habermas's own words:

The 'new conflicts arise in areas of cultural reproduction, social integration, and socialization' and are 'manifested in sub-institutional, extra-parliamentary forms of protests'. These protests are directed at the question of how 'to defend or reinstate endangered life styles, or how to put reformed life styles into practice'. Thus, 'the new conflicts are not sparked by problems of distribution, but concern the grammar of forms of life'. Unlike the 'old politics' which centres on questions of economic, social, domestic and military security, the 'new politics' centres on questions of equality, individual self-realization, the quality of life, participation and human rights.

(1986: 135)

Habermas sees a critical theory of society as directed primarily at movements associated with the new politics. Those directly involved, he suggests, tend to be at the periphery of the production process. They also tend to be members of the new middle class, young, and with experience of higher forms of education. He lists the following: the peace movement, the anti-nuclear and environmental movement, minority liberation movements, the movement for alternative life-styles, the tax protest movement, religious fundamentalist protest groups, and the women's movement. These otherwise heterogeneous movements share one characteristic: they can all be understood as 'resistance to tendencies to colonize the lifeworld' (Habermas 1981: 33–5). Not all of them, of course, are progressive or have emancipatory potential. Habermas distinguishes between those which adopt an 'offensive' posture, sponsoring new forms of social life and community, and those which adopt a 'defensive' posture, supporting traditional ways of life and property relations. And he further distinguishes between progressive offensive movements which remain at the level of 'particularistic' demands, and progressive offensive movements which pursue radical social change from a 'universalistic' perspective. The women's movement, he claims, is currently the only progressive offensive movement with a universalistic viewpoint. In general terms, he sees the 'practical intentions' of a critical theory as involving 'encouraging an "offensive" and universalistic posture on the part of these heterogeneous groups, as well as aid in focusing the struggle against a one-sided capitalist rationality that denies the possibility of constructing a society of undistorted communication and free and equal participation' (Roderick 1986: 136).

What relevance do these ideas have for medicine in general and obstetrics in particular? In the course of his consideration of high technology medicine Jennett lists five main reasons why the deployment of technology may be deemed inappropriate. First, it may be 'unnecessary', because the desired objective can be achieved by simpler means. Second, it may be 'unsuccessful', because a patient's condition is too advanced to respond to treatment. Third, it may be 'unsafe', because the complications outweigh the probable benefit. Fourth, it may be 'unkind', because the consequent quality of life is not good enough, or of insufficient duration, to have justified treatment. And fifth, it may be 'unwise', because it diverts resources from treatments that would yield greater benefits to other unknown patients (Jennett 1986: 174). Although Jennett makes reference elsewhere to physician accountability, it is interesting that he omits a sixth reason from his list – 'unwanted'.

A number of consumer or user organizations have emerged to articulate the wants of pregnant women, and most have come to challenge the appropriateness of hospital and technological childbirth on Jennett's criteria. Jennett himself writes: 'There can be little doubt that the retreat from technology in obstetrics, together with increasing willingness to acknowledge the preferences of mothers, has occurred in response to consumer pressure' (1986: 139). The earliest user organizations were formed in Britain and the USA in the late 1950s and early 1960s. The experience of the Association for the Improvement of Maternity Services (AIMS) is fairly typical. It was founded in 1960, initially to campaign for women's right to hospital deliveries at a time when the demand for hospital beds exceeded supply; but more recently it has moved on to criticize hospital childbirth and to defend women's right to home confinements. Allied organizations include the Maternity Alliance and the National Childbirth Trust. Mention should also be made of the suspension of Wendy Savage, a consultant obstetrician in London, for allegedly being a 'danger to her patients': it was claimed that she was too liberal in her rejection of the role of technology in childbirth. Suspended from clinical practice in April 1985, she was exonerated after a public inquiry into her competence in February 1986, and finally reinstated in July 1986, ironically one month after her election as a Fellow of the Royal College of Obstetricians and Gynaecologists. Mrs Savage's ordeal at the hands of her 'orthodox' male colleagues attracted national media coverage and provided an important temporary focus for women's resistance to medical – and largely male – control of the birth experience. User groups converged and campaigned vigorously in conjunction with sympathetic women, health professionals, and colleagues in Tower Hamlets and elsewhere *for* Wendy Savage and her model of practice and *against* the power of a highly questionable obstetric orthodoxy (Savage 1986).

User organizations like AIMS, the Maternity Alliance, and the National Childbirth Trust may be said to constitute an alternative perinatal service movement in Britain. Similar movements exist in the USA and other European countries. They appear to be strongest in countries where the official services emphasize clinical, especially technological, and near 100 per cent hospital-based care; where continuity of care – by the same person or a small team – is lacking within the official system; and where the status of midwives in relation to obstetricians has been devalued or is under threat (Houd and Oakley 1986: 21). It is generally appropriate, following Habermas, to classify such movements as progressive offensive movements which have as yet remained at the level of particularistic demands. Moreover it might plausibly be argued that, despite being put under pressure, physicians have actually consolidated their control over pregnancy and childbirth of late by *appearing* to be responsive to some of the less threatening of the demands made of them. By publicly agreeing that the hospital environment should be more 'home-like' and more open and accessible to relatives, for example, physicians have given an impression of accountability without giving any ground on the *real* issue of the total hospitalization of birth. The capacity of physicians to manoeuvre to retain power in the face of user protests should not be underestimated (Arney and Neill 1982).

The alternative perinatal service movement is part of a wider consumer health movement in Britain (Houd and Oakley 1986: 19). But its potential is unlikely to be fully realized unless its specific goals are subsumed under the general goals of an increasingly international women's movement. This seems to be happening. Wagner writes: 'With regard to the role of women in gaining more control over birth, I suspect that the one thing that the medical establishment was not prepared to reckon with was the women's movement'; and he adds that 'whenever I have witnessed a confrontation between the women's movement and the medical profession, the women always seem to prevail in the long run' (Wagner 1986: 204). Habermas is surely correct both when he defines the women's movement as a progressive offensive movement with an agenda for radical change issuing from a universalistic stance, and in his estimation of its significance in the new politics.

Wagner goes on to list five counterbalances to power over birth based on medical expertise. By far the most important is the role pregnant women themselves can play in taking control of their own births and birth care. Wagner stresses 'informed choice' as a key issue here, and draws attention to the need for 'community epidemiology' in maternity care: communities should have full access to information on their own maternity services – for example on local obstetric intervention and perinatal mortality rates – and the power to monitor and control them. He cites the Community Health Councils in Britain as 'a feeble start in this direction'. A second counterbalance is a strong independent midwifery service. A third is the courts, which Wagner reluctantly sees as providing the only currently effective procedure for complaints against physicians. A fourth is the public health authorities, which are increasingly sponsoring 'unbiased, scientific evaluations of services' and following them up with recommendations concerning practice. And the final counterbalance is the general public through its elected representatives. Wagner regards all of these as of growing significance throughout western Europe and the USA (Wagner 1986: 203–7). Most are predictable correlates of the kind of rationalization of the lifeworld that Habermas commends and that the women's movement is likely to play a part in furthering: it is a rationalization promising gains in the scope of communicative action and in communicative rationality.

Conclusion

An attempt has been made here to indicate the nature of the Habermasian project and to suggest three related ways in which it might clarify important foci of concern in medical sociology. It has been argued that system rationalization in relation to medicine has had undesirable as well as desirable consequences: most notably it has led to a colonization of the lifeworld; that systematically distorted communication and manipulation by physicians are aspects of this process of rationalization; and that system rationalization needs to be balanced by an accelerated rationalization of the lifeworld most likely to be triggered by the pioneering resistance work of ad hoc but converging pressure groups (currently analagous to a form of 'guerrilla warfare' – Wilding 1982: 144). To preserve an element of continuity illustrative material was taken throughout from the literature on the birth experience.

It is perhaps as well to end by recalling and highlighting two of the chapter's principal lacunae. First, the use made of Habermas's work has been not only selective but also largely uncritical. This reflects less a comfortable satisfaction with all the theses and arguments assembled therein than it does a lack of space to do anything but offer simple summaries. There is no question either that some of Habermas's arguments are provisional, suspect, or flawed, or that he would accept as much himself (witness, for example, his recent backtracking on the crucial notion of the ideal speech situation). Second, the themes addressed here clearly raise more theoretical problems than they solve. To take a single example, the narrow treatment of the power deriving from medical expertise needs to be set in the much broader context of the genesis and expansion of what the editor of the *New England Journal of Medicine* has called 'the new medical-industrial complex' in modern capitalism (Relman 1980). It was beyond the scope and intent of the chapter to do more than touch on such issues, as it was to explore the undoubted and real achievements of system rationalization in medicine generally, and in obstetrics in particular.

Acknowledgements

I am grateful for the comments of Annette Scambler and Ray Fitz-patrick on a draft version of this chapter.

References

Arney, W. and Neill, J. (1982) 'The location of pain in childbirth', *Sociology of Health and Illness* 7: 109–17.

Austin, J. (1962) *How To Do Things With Words*, Oxford: Oxford University Press.

Bernstein, R. (1985) 'Introduction', in R. Bernstein (ed.) *Habermas and Modernity*, Cambridge: Polity Press.

Brubaker, R. (1984) *The Limits of Rationality: An Essay on the Social and Moral Thought of Max Weber*, London: Allen & Unwin.

Campbell, R. and Macfarlane, A. (1986) 'Place of delivery: a review', *British Journal of Obstetrics and Gynaecology* 93: 675–83.

Cartwright, A. (1979) *The Dignity of Labour? A Study of Childbearing and Induction*, London: Tavistock.

Doyal, L. and Elston, M. (1986) 'Women, health and medicine', in V. Beechey and E. Whitelegg (eds) *Women in Britain Today*, Milton Keynes: Open University Press.

Freidson, E. (1983) 'The theory of professions: state of the art', in R. Dingwell and P. Lewis (eds) *The Sociology of the Professions*, London: Macmillan.

—— (1986) *Professional Powers. A Study of the Institutionalization of Formal Knowledge*, Chicago Ill: University of Chicago Press.

Geuss, R. (1981) *The Idea of a Critical Theory. Habermas and the Frankfurt School*, Cambridge: Cambridge University Press.

Giddens, A. (1985) 'Jurgen Habermas', in Q. Skinner (ed.) *The Return of Grand Theory in the Human Sciences*, Cambridge: Cambridge University Press.

Graham, H. and Oakley, A. (1981) 'Competing ideologies of reproduction: medical and maternal perspectives on pregnancy', in H. Roberts (ed.) *Women, Health and Reproduction*, London: Routledge & Kegan Paul.

Habermas, J. (1971) *Toward a Rational Society*, London: Heinemann.

—— (1972) *Knowledge and Human Interests*, London: Heinemann.

—— (1979) *Communication and the Evolution of Society*, London: Heinemann.

—— (1981) 'New social movements', *Telos* 57: 194–205.

—— (1984) *The Theory of Communicative Action, vol. 1, Reason and the Rationalization of Society*, London: Heinemann.

—— (1986) 'The dialectics of rationalization', in P. Dews (ed.) *Habermas: Autonomy and Solidarity*, London: Verso.

Held, D. (1980) *Introduction to Critical Theory: Horkheimer to Habermas*, London: Hutchinson.

Houd, S. and Oakley, A. (1986) 'Alternative perinatal services', in J. Phaff (ed.) *Perinatal Health Services in Europe*, London: Croom Helm.

Jennett, B. (1986) *High Technology Medicine: Benefits and Burdens*, Oxford: Oxford University Press.

Keat, R. (1981) *The Politics of Social Theory: Habermas, Freud and the Critique of Positivism*, Oxford: Blackwell.

Lukes, S. (1974) *Power: A Radical View*, London: Macmillan.

MacIntyre, S. (1977) 'Childbirth: the myth of the golden age', *World Medicine* 12: 18.

Mishler, E. (1984) *The Discourse of Medicine: Dialectics of Medical Interviews*, Norwood, NJ: Ablex.

Oakley, A. (1980) *Women Confined*, Oxford: Martin Robertson.

—— (1986) *The Captured Womb*, Oxford: Blackwell.

Peel Committee (1970) (Standing Maternity and Midwifery Advisory Committee) *Domiciliary Midwifery and Maternity Bed Needs*, London: HMSO.

Relman, A. (1980) 'The new medical-industrial complex', *New England Journal of Medicine* 303: 963–70.

Roderick, R. (1986) *Habermas and the Foundations of Critical Theory*, London: Macmillan.

Rueschemeyer, D. (1986) *Power and the Division of Labour*, Cambridge: Polity Press.

Savage, W. (1986) *A Savage Enquiry: Who Controls Childbirth?*, London: Virago.

Scherjon, S. (1986) 'A comparison between the organization of obstetrics in Denmark and the Netherlands', *British Journal of Obstetrics and Gynaecology* 93: 684–9.

Schmidt, J. (1982) 'Jurgen Habermas and the difficulties of Enlightenment', *Social Research* 49.

Schroyer, T. (1973) *The Critique of Domination*, New York: George Brazillier.

Shapiro, M., Najam, J., Chang, A., Keeping, J., Morrison, J., and Western, J. (1983) 'Information control and the exercise of power in the obstetric encounter', *Social Science and Medicine* 17: 139–46.

Strong, P. (1979) 'Sociological imperialism and the profession of medicine: a critical examination of the thesis of medical imperialism', *Social Science and Medicine* 13A: 199–215.

Tew, M. (1986) 'Do obstetric intranatal interventions make birth safer?', *British Journal of Obstetrics and Gynaecology* 93: 659–74.

Thompson, J. (1984) 'Rationality and social rationalization: an assessment of Habermas's theory of communicative action', in J. Thompson, *Studies in the Theory of Ideology*, Oxford: Polity Press.

Wagner, M. (1986) 'Birth and power', in J. Phaff (ed.) *Perinatal Health Services in Europe*, London: Croom Helm.

Wellmer, A. (1985) 'Reason, Utopia and the "Dialectic of the Enlightenment"', in R. Bernstein (ed.) *Habermas and Modernity*, Oxford: Polity Press.

Wilding, P. (1982) *Professional Power and Social Welfare*, London: Routledge & Kegan Paul.
Young, D. (1983) 'Preface', in D. Young (ed.) *Obstetrical Intervention and Technology in the 1980s*, New York: Haworth Press.

8

Rationalism, bureaucracy, and the organization of the health services: Max Weber's contribution to understanding modern health care systems

SHEILA HILLIER

During the First World War a harassed health service administrator working for the Reserve Military Hospitals Commission in Heidelberg snatched a moment to write a letter to a friend:

> There are forty-two hospitals in the district, nine of which I had to organise and am administering disciplinarily and economically largely by myself. My duties here do not permit me to be away for any great length of time. Since the beginning of the War I have had two Sundays off, and am in the office or hospitals from 8 a.m. to 7 or 8 p.m. every day.

> (Marianne Weber 1975: 535)

Max Weber ordered linen, organized schoolchildren to deliver the post, dispensed charitable funds, bemoaned nursing amateurs and praised professional nurses, regulated catering, promoted physiotherapy, and disciplined the sexual inclinations of young male orthopaedic patients by a series of evening lectures on history, bookkeeping and the differences between the Russian and German agrarian constitutions. After a year, his loose amateur administration, supported by fellow-academic volunteers, was replaced by an ordered bureaucratic one, and Weber's final report to his military superiors displays his view of the necessity of records, reports, and regulations. What he had experienced confirmed his belief in the limitations of 'administration by dilettantes' and the importance of professional bureaucratic administration. It was to an examination of this phenomenon that he devoted a significant proportion of his major work *Economy and Society*, published in 1920.

Weber's general project

Rationality as a secular trend

It would, however, be otiose to argue that Weber's wartime encounters with chaotic organization formed the basis of his life's project. *Economy and Society* represents the development and integration of many themes which he worked on throughout his career, and the work encompasses an enormous range.

Weber's work offers an interpretation of human history in terms of the dynamic effects of religious ideas, economic structures, and human action and interests, and his particular concern is the transition to modernity in the west. He identifies as a key feature in the change the extension of 'rationality' into the western forms of economy, state administration, law, and scientific activity. Indeed 'rationality' has been described as the *'idée maîtresse'* in Weber's work (Brubaker 1984: 1).

For Weber, the modern western world was decisively different because of its specific and peculiar rationalism (Schlucter 1981). He eschewed the postulation of inevitable world processes in history and, in particular, tried to divest himself of the Enlightenment notion of inevitable moral progress which characterizes Comte, Hobhouse, Durkheim, and Marx (Tenbruch 1980). His personal social vision, which he was at pains to try and separate from his scientific sociological work, regarded the development of rationality as having the potential of both liberation and imprisonment. The change promised the freedom from dark, threatening, irrational, and instinctive action or the repressiveness of tradition, towards the more perfect, more ordered control of the individual by the 'iron cage' of bureaucracy-rationalism's most perfect administrative form.

The important epistemological break which distinguished the west, Weber had previously described in *The Protestant Ethic and the Spirit of Capitalism*, which he produced as a compensation for, rather than a rejection of, materialist interpretations of history. Here, he emphasizes the role of ascetic Protestantism as one important factor in the birth of modern rationalism. The rigorous self-discipline of that religion produced individuals who constantly scrutinized their way of life in a methodical and calculated way, producing a spirit with an affinity towards the economic form of capitalism (Howe 1978). This insight is a demonstration of Weber's underlying methodological premise that all forms of social action – including rational action – are the actions of individuals, and that social situations and developments are to be explained in terms of ends sought by individuals who are placed external to a given situation, rather than in it. It is a principle of Weber's type of analysis that individuals are historical *subjects* rather than the *objects* of historical development (Touraine 1974).

Weber's view of the methodological primacy of individual action, the individual as the 'atom' of sociological analysis, has been challenged. In particular his argument that this approach was a value-free position and necessary to the study of concrete social organizations has been disputed. Such discussions are beyond the scope of this chapter, which is eclectically concerned to show the relevance of Weber's concept of rationality, and to consider what importance his identification of a secular trend of rationalization has for our understanding of modern health care systems. How far may modern health care organization be seen as an example of the rationalizing process? Below, the contribution of bureaucracy, described by Weber as the most rational form of social organization, to the organization of health services and health institutions is examined. Rationalization in other areas related to health and illness are also considered, particularly technocratic dominance, and the nature and limits of rationality in medicine.

Values and rational action

Weber's view of his own work was that he was engaged in the objective description of social systems, albeit by drawing together the patterns evoked in subjective meanings. He was, he believed, describing reality, sequences, trends, and social configurations. He was not concerned, as a result of his work, to tell 'what we shall do and how shall we live'. In his view this could not be scientifically determined. One could not say how society ought to be, but could have as an object of study the answers that others have given to these questions.

Despite these views, Weber undoubtedly possessed a moral vision which is expressed in ambivalence towards the various effects of rationality in the modern western world. Weber does have a notion about 'humanity', and how it is to be developed and preserved. Although he does not present a view of the ideal society, he has an idea of the 'fully human' personality, which is a logical development of his emphasis upon individual action. The truly human person is one who is guided by reason, who transforms impulses and desires into a systematic life plan, exercises choice, and can improve the world. Such a view encompasses both normative and empirical components, and embodies what Weber thinks distinguishes 'human' (which is a concept to which he is more sympathetic than 'social') life from natural events (Max Weber 1964). Therefore to be fully human action must be rational, free, and meaningful, the result of conscious deliberate choice without coercion or accident. He concludes that for many this is not a possibility, a view he shares with Nietzsche (Brubaker 1984: 98). Hence it follows that Weber is pessimistic about the future of 'human' society. The force of reason produces social structures which carry within them the seeds of repressive social control. A further problem is that there are multiple rationalities, or 'value spheres' as Weber calls them, which compete for acceptance. Is it possible to know which one is correct?

> There are rationalisations of economic life, of technique, of scientific research, of military training, of law and administration. Furthermore each one of these fields may be rationalised from many different ultimate points of view and towards many different ultimate ends and what is rational from one point of view may well be irrational from another.
>
> (Max Weber 1922: 26)

This provides the ultimate paradox. Competing rationalities emerge as part of the overall process of rationalization, but are not reducible one to another. 'Love thy enemy always' is a moral precept, but not a political one. Finally, individuals have to choose – and their choice is essentially non-rational. These arbitrary choices display the *limits* of rationality for they cannot themselves by rationally explained. Value conflicts are irreconcilable, and therefore, Weber would argue, a fully rational human society – 'a good society' – is not identifiable from a scientific point of view. The scientist has nothing to offer in terms of policy judgements, but can offer guidance only when a given and fairly limited goal is decided upon (Brubaker 1974: 55–60). He was also innovative in pointing out that many so-called 'technical' problems, when unpicked, reveal value conflicts.

This exposition – rather than critical examination – of Weber's views on values and rationality would be incomplete without a description of his types of rationality; it is in a close examination of the concept that we experience Weber in all his irritating, paradoxical, and multifaceted richness. In a skilful summary, Brubaker enunciates sixteen apparently different meanings of the word 'rational', among which are deliberate, systematic, calculable, quantitative, impersonal, consistent, rule-governed, and purposeful (Brubaker 1984: 2). These multiple meanings, however, display Weber's understanding of the range of phenomena which emerges as a genotypic unity, despite the fact that his applications of the concept to various phenomena were not co-ordinated systematically.

Weber describes four types of action. Two can be described as non-rational, in the sense that they are not the result of deliberate choice. These are *traditional* action, guided by habit, and *affectual* action, produced by powerful emotions. A further two, however, are types of rational action, and the distinction between them is illuminating. The first is *wertrational* action, which is undertaken as a result of belief in the ultimate or intrinsic value of acting in a certain way. The second is *zweckrational* action, which is calculation of the appropriate action to be taken to achieve a desired end. A relevant example might be the following: the parents of a mentally handicapped teenage girl might refuse to sterilize her because by so doing they would be removing her basic right to procreate. This would be an example of *wertrationalität*. The parents of another such girl might agree to her sterilization on the grounds that the consequences of a pregnancy might be too difficult for her and those who care for her to cope with. This would be *zweckrationalität*. Both decisions invoke values of a different nature and are examples of competing rationalities. The refusal to sanction abortion, because human life is sacred (*wertrationalität*) contrasts with the view that there are situations where the consequences of pregnancy would be damaging, therefore abortion is necessary (*zweckrationalität*). A *wertrationalität* position would suggest that health services should exist because aiding the vulnerable is good in itself. A *zweckrationalität* argument would say that a good health service ensures a healthy and productive population.

It was Weber's contention that in modern society, *zweckrational* action, precisely because it is calculable and predictive, becomes the pre-eminent form. Further, *zweckrational* action is capable of assessment not only by the individual actor, but also by the observer, as to how far the particular action is effective in producing or avoiding certain consequences. This is not true of *wertrational* action, where the performance of the action is also simply its evaluation – it is good in itself. To the *wertrational* actor, the saving of a life is simply that. To the *zweckrational* actor, the saving of one life rather than another, or the consideration of the means or consequences of so doing, can also be externally assessed as to their effectiveness or appropriateness. But this assessment can only be of a limited nature. In Weber's view, the danger is that problems which are questions of value (*wertrationalität*) become defined as technical questions (*zweckrationalität*).

Rationalism and scientific medicine

Established rationality

The rationality of western culture, according to Weber, possesses one distinctive trait. Weber suggests that only the west has developed a rational physics, chemistry, and astronomy. The work of Needham on the nature and growth of Chinese science challenges this view significantly, discussing the scientific heritage to which China has contributed (Needham 1948). However, Needham observes that there was no rise of modern science in the sixteenth and seventeenth centuries in China as occurred in Europe and, in particular, Puritan England.

In a now famous essay Robert Merton, following Weber, has considered the particular part played by Puritanism in the scientific revolution (Merton 1938), which linked religious and scientific radicalism. Merton describes the factors in Calvinistic theology, especially the broad support given to experimental science, which were conducive to the growth of science. The parallel with capitalist development and Weber's thesis of the 'protestant ethic' is obvious. The argument of Merton, later supported by Hill (1964), has been criticized on the grounds that its definitions of Puritanism/Calvinism are too imprecise for the generalizations made about scientific development.

The details need not concern us so much here; for the general point is that the theoretical development of science and its practical application has been a distinctive feature of the west, which has pervaded the whole of life. How far has this been true of medicine? Harvey's publication of *De Motu Cordis* in 1628, which detailed his discovery of the circulation of the blood, was an important paradigm shift. He wrote the book as a result of clinical observation and experiment, and capped his observations with a quantifiable estimate of the amount of blood pumped by the heart in an hour – an amount which would be impossible if the old theory of blood occurring as the result of nourishment was correct. This introduced a new way of looking at the human body, seeing it as an internal world, with its own circular forms of motion. Harvey's approach exhibited the analytic/mechanical approach to the body, consolidated by Descartes. The latter's philosophy supported the independence of mind and body, which allowed the body to become the object of scientific enquiry and to be examined and understood in the same way as the rest of the world.

The enormous growth of laboratory sciences in the latter half of the nineteenth century finally removed mystery from the human body, by the convincing victory of the mechanistic paradigm, which viewed the body as a series of interrelated parts and no longer possessed of a vital spirit which gave it life (Figlio 1977). Illness would therefore be defined as the failure of the workings of mechanical systems, specifically caused and for which some appropriate intervention, itself usually a product of scientific experiment and observation, would be undertaken.

This picture of the development of modern medicine, which utilizes the discoveries of materialist science to demystify the body, or, as Koch did, to identify disease-producing agents, is one which would satisfy Weber. Rationalization in the west has resulted in the process of 'intellectualization', in the displacement of magical and religious world views, and has given force to the idea that everything can potentially be known and understood. The whole *raison d'être* of scientific research in medicine is that 'there is no mystery', and that the application of science in medicine has gradually produced more and more knowledge about disease processes and the means of controlling them successfully. This kind of development must be distinguished from the contribution of the medical profession itself. The realization that the phenomena of everyday life can be controlled and predicted demystifies the world. But, Weber argues, it also robs it of all irrational elements, the orgiastic, ecstatic, sexual, revelatory, and metaphysical.

Competing rationalities in medicine

Many current criticisms of medicine take the view that the mechanistic paradigm adopted by scientific medicine, despite many apparent successes, is in some sense 'wrong' because it individualizes sickness and fails to consider the social factors which produce ill-health (Doyal and Pennell 1979). The limited paradigm of modern medicine has made it largely ineffective in dealing with the modern disease burden of chronic disease; improvements in health which have occurred, for example the eradication of many infectious diseases, owe relatively little to the activities of doctors (McKeown 1976). A further argument suggests that medical *practice* is often ineffective; for example it is claimed that patients do not comply with treatment, fail to keep appointments, and do not respond to their own bodily symptoms by seeking medical treatment, mainly because doctors are unable to clarify their instructions, are poor communicators, and (most importantly) do not share the same framework of understanding as their patients.

The thrust of much current medical sociology and psychology is framed as a response to these problems: medicine is enjoined to understand the social conditions which produce disease, and doctors are instructed to improve their communication skills. They are encouraged to understand more about their patients' social contexts in order to improve their awareness of how patients perceive and experience illness (Byrne and Long 1984). The consultation becomes one key aspect of medical practice and the patient an active participator. It is no longer the clinical observations that can be made of the patients which form the fundamental data of diagnosis and treatment, but the information about personal problems and difficulties which the patient supplies. As Armstrong says, 'illness [is] transformed from what [is] visible to what [is] heard' (1983: 339). By this process, experience itself becomes codified; mystery is removed not only from the body, but also from the patient's behaviour through knowledge of his biography and social experience.

These approaches can be seen as examples of the growth of competing rationalities to the dominant medical paradigm. The Marxist view concentrates upon the need for the clearer elucidation of the disease-producing features of modern capitalist or industrializing societies, and implicitly suggests, as do many other writers who do not espouse a fully Marxist analysis, that the greatest gains in health will be made by a better understanding of macro-sociological factors in illness, the results of which can be applied at the level of populations. The micro-sociological view holds that increasing knowledge about and awareness of 'the patient's view' may improve doctors' diagnostic and treatment skills, and patient's satisfaction and compliance. Further, the nature of clinical practice itself, and the scientific basis of medicine, could be transformed by a new conceptual framework which, incorporating patients' rationalities and events or life changes experienced by them, would alter the understanding of the relationship between experience and biological lesion – to produce a truly psychosomatic medicine. Such an approach does not indicate a flight from rationality, but its extension.

Using Weber's terms, the paradigm shifts that are urged upon medicine are *zweckrationalität*, implying the ability of individuals to calculate experience methodically; self-interest and self-focus become profoundly important as the basis of a more 'rational' form of practice, and the means by which it is judged. Both process in the doctor–patient relationship, and the outcome of the process, can be appraised.

Consequently there has been a growth in *measures* of health and illness which incorporate social and psychological factors and extend the traditional biomedical approach. They include subjective assessments by patients. Examples are the ADL (Activities of Daily Living) index (Katz and Akpom 1976), the Sickness Impact Profile (Bergner and Gibson 1981) and the Nottingham Health Profile (Hunt and MacEwan 1980). One of the most sophisticated attempts in understanding the social aetiology of illness – in this case depressive illness – is exemplified by the complex codification of life events and chronic difficulties offered by Brown and Harris (1978). A classification of the experimental 'stages' of dying has been widely regarded as an important contribution to the care of terminally ill patients (Kubler-Ross 1970).

The existence of 'irrationality' in health and illness – medicalization

Illich (1975) has argued that medicine has undermined the human processes and natural capacities by which people respond to experiences such as birth, death, pain, fear, and suffering. It has reduced people's confidence in their own abilities to deal with such matters, believing that scientific expertise is more reliable. By implication, increased knowledge and understanding of both the biological and sociological aspects of these critical events represents a blunting of some prior human ontological response. He goes further than Weber – who of course never considered the problems of health and illness directly – by suggesting that the process of increased understanding by the application of rationality is a wholly negative one. For Weber at least, traditional or instinctual approaches also have their dangers and their dark side. The process of rationalization may well be a creative and liberating one, rather than repressive, and this is certainly the view of those who espouse a more 'humane' medicine.

Weber equated irrationality with the primitive and traditional. The belief in magic, the other-worldly, and the divine were all examples of 'irrational' thought. Later writers would suggest that the rationality of thought in non-literate societies, even where directed (in Weberian terms) to some irrational end like a magical transformation, is quite complex. It is now suggested that what is observed is not irrational practice, but practice carried out on the basis of a different system of classification (Horton 1970). This is particularly true in cases of healing (Levi-Strauss 1968).

Medicalization is profoundly linked with an external calculable environment, produced in the spheres of science, technology, law, and administration. Weber would probably regard the 'medicalization' commented upon by Illich as the outcome of the developing tendency to produce predictability in human life, which is now to include the previously uncharted areas of patient experience. Widening the discussion represents an extension of the rationality process. It is not a return to beliefs in mystical or magical healing processes, nor to a fully 'personalized' medicine, where each case is unique. It is an example of the further disenchantment of the world as intellectual process dissects and classifies human experience, in a new 'biographical medicine'.

Alternative medicine

The growing interest in what are termed 'alternative medicines' might suggest a growing 'disenchantment with disenchantment', a sign of popular doubts about the ability of modern medicine to cure, palliate, or console. In Britain in 1980 there were nearly 30,000 alternative healers (more than the number of general practitioners), of whom about 20,000 were spiritual or religious healers who eschew quasi-scientific explanations of their effectiveness. For their recognition by the medical establishment, alternative medicines would have to justify themselves experimentally, by controlled trials to rule out the 'irrational' placebo effect, regarded by most experimenters as an irritating contamination of the rationally constructed clinical trial (British Medical Association 1986). At present there appears little willingness to seek to join 'orthodox' medicine, since presumably demand for alternative healing can be sustained without the imprimatur of formal medical recognition, and for spiritual and religious therapists such recognition may have little meaning.

Health beliefs – 'irrational' survivals?

Studies of how people think about health, illness, and disease, especially the causes of diseases, suggest that magical and spiritual beliefs, as well as beliefs which incorporate ideas from an earlier and now displaced theory of disease aetiology, still exist. Magical medicine – beliefs in the power of amulets, signs, colours, particular prayers recited in a particular way – are not apparently of great public importance. Yet nurses' uniforms are usually blue, doctors' coats white, and ward staff will react with horror if a mixed bunch of red and white flowers are brought on the ward or if new babies are dressed in an inappropriate colour. Although these may be no more than trivial examples of the vestigial remains of colour magic, they still persist.

Research indicates that many people in the west hold views about health and illness that are broadly congruent with scientific medicine, but at the same time classify them in different ways as well. They may have a broader concept of the causes of illness, which incorporates ideas about social factors like occupation, 'stress', catastrophic events – for example loss and 'broken heart'. They may describe ill health as a loss of functional capacity in areas deemed to be salient, or as an imbalance, with health being perceived as a state of equilibrium. Ill health, it is thought, can result from the loss of such equilibrium by improper diet, lack of sleep, the invasion of a germ, a poison, or disagreeable food; the bodily system can 'run down', as in heart disease, or become 'blocked' by constipation (Herzlich 1973: Helman 1978; Chrisman 1977). Many of these theories are quite sophisticated, often combining a rational causality with less clearly elucidated elements of energy, balance, and force.

Obviously these ideas have implications for what people regard as appropriate action about health and illness. For example if cancer is a mysterious illness which can strike anyone, then emphasis on personal responsibility for preserving health, by avoiding smoking for example, appears less forceful when set against personal experiences. People cannot see why some women develop breast cancer when others do not, or if the risks of life-style are so great, why heavy smokers do not always die of cancer. The *zweckrational* concept of probability, which raises the level of uncertainty, if applied to people's everyday experience, not only demands a puritanical commitment to a regulated existence, but also cannot guarantee survival, until survival has occurred. This parallels the 'salvation anxiety' of the ascetic Calvinist. One might regard lay concepts of health and illness as an important defence against the *zweckrational* medicalization of everyday life.

Elements of lay beliefs might well be appropriated to the practice of medicine (the paradigm expansion referred to above), especially those of a quasi-rational character. But the rationalist approach has its limitations. How do doctors confront a patient's belief that serious illness is a punishment for wrong-doing, which may be that person's solution to the question 'why me?' It should be noted that it may be more consoling for a patient to believe in illness as punishment, for which reparation can be made, than to carry the heavy burden of personal responsibility for illness produced by behaviour (for example smoking) which cannot now be undone. Even laying the blame elsewhere – the tobacco industry, an occupational process – merely reinforces the patient's powerlessness and view of himself as passive victim or dupe.

Charismatic authority

Illness, pain, and death do present existential challenges, because, as Weber would suggest, our rationalizing culture seeks to equate meaning with understanding, usually understanding in terms of cause. Events in life cannot simply be accepted but should be prevented, alleviated, and controlled. Those able to undertake such activities and to satisfy these particular wants may be seen to be endowed with a special gift, which Weber would argue legitimizes their power. This he calls charisma: 'a certain quality of an individual by virtue of which he is considered extraordinary and treated as endowed with supernatural, superhuman, or at least specifically exceptional powers or qualities' (Max Weber 1978a: 241). Weber treats this concept in a many-sided way, but suggests that each society produces its own form of charismatic leader – warrior, prophet, king, or doctor. Charisma need not simply be embodied in a single individual but may become a depersonalized form of power, held for example by priests, independent of their personal qualities, or, it could be said, by doctors. Belief in medicine, or the special powers and attributes of doctors, especially when these extend far beyond specific functions, could be regarded as profoundly irrational. It matters not that the object of such belief, scientific medicine, may be regarded as rational, or indeed that the achievement of health through its administration could be a *wertrational* goal.

People who practise medicine will informally discuss the importance of their own credibility *vis-à-vis* the patient, and even admit to the
importance of 'the will to live' or the healing power which resides in
the doctor as an accredited social role. Balint describes this as 'the drug
[called] doctor' (Balint 1957).

Indeterminacy and rationality

Writers on the existence of professions often discount the importance
of charisma and irrational beliefs about the powers of doctors, prefer-
ring instead to discuss economic and political factors which have
encouraged the development of medicine as a dominant profession.
While much of this is undoubtedly correct, and explains the particular
configuration that occurs in the west, nevertheless the special significance of doctors and medicine in modern human life may bear some
relation to the former's expertise, regarded as similar to magical or
priestly power, which gives them access to the means of controlling
particular threats. Power resides not in what doctors know but what
they are believed to know. This power may be described as the exercise
of indeterminacy and, although balanced by the *zweckrational* knowledge of technique, is *itself* non-rational. It is an important part of
doctors' professional image, and is a corrective to the view of a doctor
as one who merely carries out technical procedures efficiently and
expertly (Jamous and Peloille 1970). Indeterminacy is not calculable
nor replicable, and it therefore possesses charismatic potential.

There seem to be some grounds for arguing that what Weber calls
'irrationality' still exists. As rationalization progresses, one would expect the significance of the indeterminate, the charismatic, and the
fearful to decline. It may be this process which we are witnessing at
the moment in western medicine. Such a change is associated with
other events in the organization of medicine and health care, and it is
to an examination of these other factors producing 'disenchantment'
that we now turn.

The bureaucratic organization of medicine and health care

Health services are, generally speaking, bureaucratically organized.
This is, however, a matter of degree. Where health services are allied
with or are an aspect of the structure of the state, where there is some
concept of or commitment to national planning, then the bureaucratic
form predominates. It is extensive in the United Kingdom, in state
socialist societies, and in the newly developing health services of the
Third World. In other countries bureaucratic organization is minimal,
as a large proportion of health services are dispensed by individual

practitioners, with bureaucracy being more characteristic of the public health services and the administration of medical/social programmes.

Weber wrote extensively on the nature of bureaucracy, which he saw as the prime example of institutional rationalization. He generally used the term to refer to an administrative body of appointed officials. The characteristics which he ascribed to bureaucracy – centralization, hierarchy, the separation of work-place from living place, the 'office', special qualifications, permanent salaried employment, and the construction of written records to which access is restricted – were found in the ancient empires of Egypt, Rome, Greece and China, in the medieval Islamic empire and European city states and kingdoms. But it reaches its purest and most extensive form in the west, where its development is intimately linked to the growth of modern capitalism (Bendix 1966).

Bureaucracy is a type of legal-rational domination. The rationality of its structure, based upon formal law, is the basis of its power. All systems of domination make some claim to their legitimate right to exercise power. In the case of rational-legal authority, the claim is based on the view that laws will be arrived at or enacted by a proper procedure and that those formulating or enacting them will have arrived at their position of power not by inheritance, chance, or favouritism, but as a result of legal and generally recognized procedures – for example a formal examination. Officials are not self-interested. Their conduct is governed by specific rules which restrict them to certain areas of competence, and the application of laws and rules is therefore free from irrational discrimination or ignorance. The most appropriate form of administration for legal-rational domination is the bureaucracy, the impersonal power of officialdom.

Charismatic domination, where a leader legitimizes his position by the demonstration of extraordinary powers, or traditional domination, where power is based on the rightness of inherited status, both carry the threats of institutional instability, the former because it depends so much on personal qualities, the latter because it is characterized by favouritism and personal dependence. Although Weber characterizes three 'ideal' (that is ahistorical) types of domination, his notion of the development of increasing rationality suggests that charisma is routinized in traditional societies and then radically transformed under the growth of modern industrial capitalism and bureaucracy, where legal-rational authority predominates (Weber 1978a: 246, 1,121). The predictability and consequent stability of legal-rational domination is one reason for its ascendancy.

Weber suggests a further reason for the importance of bureaucracy is that its rational administrative character gives it a technical supremacy over all other forms of organization.

The fully developed bureaucratic apparatus compares with other organisations exactly as does the machine with the non-mechanical form of production. Precision, speed, unambiguity, knowledge of the files, continuity, discretion, unity, strict subordination, reduction of friction and material and personal costs – these are raised to the optimum point.

(1978a: 973)

Elsewhere Weber remarks

it would be sheer illusion to think for a moment that continuous work in any field can be carried out except by means of officials working in offices ... for bureaucratic administration is, other things being equal, and always from a formal technical point of view, the most rational type.

(1966: 337)

The growth of bureaucracy is both a product of and a contribution to the modern financial economy. The central imperatives of production and competition and the pressure for profits means that *calculability* in economic matters is indispensable. 'Today it is primarily the capitalist market economy which demands that the official business of public administration be discharged precisely, unambiguously and with as much speed as possible' (Max Weber 1978a: 26). Capitalism itself uses rational accounting procedures and is profoundly calculable. Even production itself is bureaucratized with hierarchy, specialized production, and scientific management. Thus bureaucracy as an organizational form not only permeates the organs of state, which therewith support capitalist development, but is also a feature of capitalism.

Weber argues that the marriage between capitalism and bureaucracy reflects the affinities of each. Predictability, calculability, and above all impersonality, the complete elimination of love, hatred, and all purely personal, irrational, and emotional elements which escape calculation, are the special virtues which make bureaucracy so attractive to capitalism. However, the bureaucratic phenomenon, as an expression of growing rationality, is a pervasive feature of *all* forms of modern organization. The importance with which Weber endows bureaucracy as an all-embracing feature of modern industrial societies contrasts with Marx's analysis, which suggests that capitalist relations of production are fundamental.

Weber says: 'in comparison with all other historical bearers of the rational order of life, bureaucracy is distinguished by its much greater inescapability'; he notes that those who seek to avoid this form of organization are 'equally subject to bureaucratisation. Even in the case of revolution or occupation by an enemy the bureaucratic machine will normally continue to function, just as it did for the previous government' (1978b: 602). The forward march of bureaucracy is irresistible.

That bureaucracy is a central organizing principle in all modern societies was stated by Weber in an excursus on state socialism, in which he noted: 'if under socialism a comparable level of technical efficiency were to be achieved, it would mean a tremendous increase in the importance of specialised bureaucracy' (Weber 1978a: 225). Therefore capitalism is only one precondition for the development of modern bureaucratic domination.

It is not our purpose here to examine the differences between Marx and Weber on the question of bureaucracy. For Marx, bureaucracy was a purely parasitic form of administration, and since the state itself was merely a tool of the bourgeoisie, the task of its administration was to consolidate and perpetuate the system of class domination (Miliband 1969). Under socialism the tasks performed by officials would change, become demystified and simplified, and the concern of all citizens – truly public administration. However, as Weber drily noted in 1917, 'what is advancing is not the dictatorship of the workers but of the officials' (Andrewski 1984).

If bureaucracy represents a rationalizing force in society, what are the consequences?

> Once fully established, bureaucracy is amongst those social structures which are hardest to destroy. Bureaucracy is *the* means of transforming social action into rationally organised action. Therefore, as an instrument of rationally organising authority relations, bureaucracy was and is a power instrument of the first order for one who controls the bureaucratic apparatus.
>
> (Max Weber 1978a: 987)

Weber notes that state bureaucracy would rule alone if private capitalism were eliminated. It has enormous coercive power. He writes passionately of the threat to individual freedom which bureaucracy poses: 'It is busy fabricating a shell of bondage which men will perhaps be forced to inhabit some day, as powerless as the fellahs of ancient Egypt ... how can one possibly save any remnants of individualist freedom?' (1978a: 1,403).

Although in Weber's theory individual actors are essentially creators of the social system, resulting forms can impose a domination upon them. Bureaucracy is

> a machine that we are already caught up in, and the great question is ... what can we oppose to this machinery in order to keep a portion of mankind free from this paralleling out of the soul, from this supreme mastery of the bureaucratic way of life.
>
> (quoted in Mitzman 1971)

Both Brubaker (1984) and Mommsen (1974) point out that one idea that is implicit in Weber's theory is the growing predominance of *zweckrational* (instrumentally rational) systems of orientation through the growth of formal bureaucracy. *Zweckrational* thought is not hampered by the weight of tradition or emotion, or by ultimate value commitments, and is the product of conscious and calculable decision; it is oriented towards the satisfaction of immediate wants which are already 'given' by the social agenda. *Zweckrational* action is therefore conservative, for it does not question ultimate values, but merely seeks to achieve ends which are already defined, in the most efficient manner possible. This rules out the possibility of 'chosen' wants appearing as values to be achieved practically.

Bureaucracy, because it is a formally rational system, will tend to favour *zweckrational* action, both because it does not threaten the existing structure by any awkward questions – it is concerned with 'how?' rather than 'why?' – and because the technical superiority of rational procedures provides a continuity which makes the organization self-perpetuating, increasing its possibilities of control. *Wertrational* issues are too difficult to handle, and would disrupt organizational and administrative continuity.

Our question then becomes – to what extent do health services display bureaucratic features, and to what degree is the tendency suggested by Weber, for *zweckrational* action to drive out *wertrational* action, to be observed? The discussion will be confined largely to the British National Health Service and its development since 1948.

Hospital organization

The assumption that is made throughout Weber's writing on bureaucracy as a formal rational structure is that it is simply the best form of organization and the most efficient. In this he contrasts with both earlier and later writers who regarded bureaucracy as wasteful, inefficient, and far from rational (Albrow 1970). Studies of bureaucracy in the health field have used Weber's work to examine the modern hospital. It seems fair to say that research on hospitals and other organizations has contributed some exceptions to the ideal type he described. It has been suggested that the features of bureaucratic organization, rules, precision, and reliability, may be interpreted in such a way as to produce conflict, organizational stasis (Merton 1952). Officials can oppose changes which, for example, political ministers see as necessary. It does seem that Weber's analysis gives the impression of automatons working in a monocratic order, whereas other writers have suggested that informal relationships contribute more to the functioning of organizations than regulatory and hierarchical principles of activity (Blau and Scott 1963). Some go further and suggest that health organizations in particular are structures of bargaining and influence which are socially constructed in terms of the meanings actors attach to the organization. Far from being regulated collectivities, they are characteristically open-ended, and their formal structure merely masks the degree of negotiation which occurs. In the hospital, affective and traditional forms of action (irrational in Weber's terms), as well as rational goal-oriented action, take place (Silverman 1970; Strauss 1963).

The critique is further strengthened by the observation that doctors, whose work is professionally autonomous, are 'of' the organization but not 'in' it. It is suggested that organizations in which professionals predominate cannot usefully be regarded as bureaucracies at all. A better perspective might be to consider the ways in which doctors negotiate power and control in a situation where they are all theoretical equals (Bucher and Stelling 1969). Such an argument takes for granted, however, that the professionals *are* the key figures in hospital organization, whereas this may be less true of hospitals for the chronically ill than acute general hospitals. Further, the notion of negotiation implies that all organizational members are equally free to negotiate, which is simply not the case. Authority and control are exercised hierarchically within nursing *and* medicine from senior to junior staff, and even the theoretically equal competing senior doctors find it difficult to overcome the superiority of status which attaches to certain specialties over others.

Some writers have found it easier to understand hospital organization in terms of organizational goals, and this perspective allows for Weber's concept of rationally oriented action to be utilized. In fact the distinction between *wertrationality* and *zweckrationality* is implicit in the tension which Goffman observes between 'humane standards' and 'institutional efficiency' (Goffman 1961). It could be argued, using Weber's distinction, that the possession of techniques either for curing patients or controlling them can be *zweckrational* in orientation. In an acute hospital instrumental action could mean that ward routines and technical procedures become ends in themselves. An example would be the induction of childbirth, to fit in with the time staff prefer to work, or the refusal to give pain-killing drugs in the preparation room, since pain is allowed to be expressed only in the delivery room (Rosengren and de Vault 1963). In a chronic mental hospital there are many examples of organizational rules which encourage 'batch living' producing the phenomenon known as 'institutionalization' (Wing and Brown 1970).

Coser has noted that where there is a *wertrational* aim, for example

patient therapy, yet no developed *zweckrationalität* (means) to produce it, two possible outcomes are likely: ritualism and retreatism
(Coser 1963). Where staff undertake ritualistic behaviour, they adopt
a minimum of instrumentality, which is rigidly applied. Wards and
patients are kept very clean, patients are fed regularly, and duties
carried out in a clearly circumscribed way. Patients are essentially the
objects of processing. Sometimes staff give up the effort, they 'retreat',
patients are neglected, and wards become dirty. The organization
then becomes in Weber's term 'irrational and anarchic'.

Empirical studies indicate the value of the *wertrational/zweckrational*
distinction: in Weber's view both forms would be important. The
discussion of dire consequnces of *zweckrationalität* in hospital organization is better developed than the argument which stresses the *need* for
zweckrational action, and the circumstances that can result from over-
generalized Utopian goals which are unreachable. This situation
leaves participants free to act in purely personal, even irrational ways,
including sadistic behaviour towards patients.

Although Weber's concepts of the rational bureaucracy and types of
rational actions do not form the definitive framework for the study of
the modern hospital, they enjoy a certain utility which may be particularly important in understanding organizational failure and conflict.

Rationality, bureaucracy, and health policy in the NHS

Bureaucratic regulation of the form and delivery of health services is
not a new phenomenon. Throughout early and medieval times in both
Orient and Occident the growth of the city and the establishment of
bureaucracies concerned with public health were everywhere extant
(Ackernecht 1985; Mei 1971; Needham and Lu 1970). The development of the modern state extended these activities. Foucault notes that
the founding of the *Hôpital General* in Paris in 1656 marked an
administrative restructuring of a variety of existing institutions and
the introduction of the concept of internment (Foucault 1961).

The mercantilist administrators of seventeenth- and eighteenth-
century Europe produced plans for national health based on the
collection of statistics, and Frank's 'System of Medical Police' was
published in 1779. Slowly health bureaucracies developed in the
German states. In France after the Revolution hospitals were national-
ized, with *conseils de santé* set up in all the major cities (Rosen 1974).

By the nineteenth century France's pre-eminence in hygiene and
systems of medical care was transferred to Britain, the wealthiest
industrial nation. By the formation of local boards of health after 1848
Britain became the world leader in public health. Her successive

history, culminating in the founding of the National Health Service a century later, is among other things a history of the increasing bureaucratization of health services. The NHS represented an attempt to apply the principles of rational administration to the efficient and fair distribution of health care in Britain to all those in need (Klein 1983). In Weber's terms its inception was a triumph for the winning combination of instrumental and value rationality. A *wertrational* aim – improving health and accessibility to health care for all – with a *zweckrational* means – an organized health service.

A number of writers have suggested, however, that the final form which the NHS took was rather irrational, the result of conflict and bargaining amongst pressure groups (Eckstein 1960; Willcocks 1967). The structure was in fact tripartite, with general practitioners retaining an independent status, some preventive services managed by local authorities, and hospitals managed by regional boards whose geographical and technical administrative scope bore little relation to the other two branches. General practitioners were the main channel of referral to hospital, yet were 'outside' the system. The medical profession retained an important independent voice in policy-making, and control over resources, as well as technocratic dominance over their style of work. The 'medical model' of illness, the idea that disease results from a pathological process within the body, remained unquestioned.

Weber has been criticized for his failure to understand the role and power of 'free professions' like medicine. In his experience the professional was a technical expert subordinated to the bureaucratic machine (Giddens 1972); in fact, professions, at least in the west, are groups which have evolved occupational control and enjoy considerable independence (Johnson 1972). Therefore any bureaucratic structure which is associated with them will be aware of their influence. For Weber the importance of professions lay mainly in their expertise, which contributed to the overall process of rationalization. His analysis would show the mutuality of interest between bureaucracies and professional groups, and would perhaps predict the way in which the growth of bureaucracy in the health services led, in the initial stages, not to the demise of professional dominance but to the rationalization of such dominance and its formal institutionalization. The eradication of competition for patients, and the provision of large-scale resources, particularly hospitals, in the early years of the NHS lends support to this view. In the absence of other powerful conflicting perspectives, the NHS bureaucracy assumed quite early on a minimal instrumental character, seeking to carry out, albeit with a far from perfect form of administration, an agenda largely set by the profession.

It can be argued that the NHS, as a bureaucratic legal-rational form, derives much of its considerable legitimacy from its supposed ability to apply rational impersonal calculations to a given end – equitable treatment in response to need. Yet much evidence has accumulated over the years to show that this end has not been achieved. There are major inequalities in health and in the allocation of health care resources regionally, between health service sectors – for example acute care and care for chronically sick and mentally ill people – and between hospital and community services. These inequalities have been extensively documented. This would seem to indicate profound irrationality and bureaucratic failure (Townsend and Davidson 1982; Brotherston 1976; OPCS 1983; Morgan, Calnan, and Manning 1985; Ham 1985).

For some writers the problem is easily explained. It is their contention that because the NHS is a structure in a capitalist state it plays a part both in producing favourable conditions for capitalist accumulation and in maintaining social order and control. State provision of health services is one way in which the state defrays the cost of labour power to capital, and particular repressive ideologies concerning health and the causes of disease are reproduced by its health care agencies. The health service, as an instrument of class domination, will concentrate its efforts on caring for the most economically productive sectors of the population (Gough 1979; Navarro 1976). Finally, however, a fiscal crisis develops when the demand for health services outstrips resources (O'Connor 1973).

Since its inception the NHS has been described as 'short of money'. It seems a limited perspective to suggest that the financial and administrative changes which the NHS has undergone, especially since a major reorganization in 1974, can be seen as occurring *solely* as a response to capital's requirements for the restructuring and cutting of public spending. It is equally important to consider the independent bureaucratic impetus to use existing resources more efficiently and to exercise greater control over the workings of the health service.

If one considers the development of the NHS since 1948, two features stand out. One is the gradual attempt to rationalize allocations, and the frustrations which this attempt encounters; the other is the dynamic relationship between *wertrationalität* and *zweckrationalität*. It is to an examination of these two developments that we now turn.

Controversially it might be suggested that the NHS as a rational bureaucracy really developed in 1974. Up to that point its structure represented a compromise with the traditional form of medical authority. Throughout the 1960s administration in other areas of the civil service and local government was the subject of several government reports which stressed the need for organizational change to improve efficiency. The NHS was in receipt of more money, and expenditure rose 16 per cent between 1968 and 1978 (Klein 1983: 67). This greater expenditure paradoxically crystallized the fear that resources would always be inadequate to deal with the burden of illness. It also became clear that some client groups, the elderly, the physically and mentally handicapped, and the mentally ill, were less well provided for and that the egalitarian aims of the service were not being met (Ham 1985: 25).

Planning norms, based on achieving an equitable share of resources, were introduced, and in 1970 a new formula for allocating resources to the regions was introduced. However, these redistributional aims foundered on the fact that the acute hospital-based specialties were still able to dominate the demands for resources.

In 1974 the NHS was reorganized with the aim of unifying health services under one hierarchically organized authority (although general practitioners still remained outside the system); the reorganization was dedicated to improving management and co-ordinating links between health and social services. National priorities and goals were set. For the first time, the medical profession was given a role in management; the idea was that at each managerial level multidisciplinary teams would work to achieve consensus, bearing in mind the need to plan services for disadvantaged groups and to control expenditure. It was shortly after this reorganization that the first cash limits were introduced, in 1976. The 1974 reorganization has been described as the 'managerial zenith'.

By stressing consensus over planning, the reorganization sought to avoid confronting a central issue – that both redistributional or equity aims and the objective of expenditure control (themselves potentially in conflict) foundered on the question of clinical autonomy: 'the existence of clinical freedom undoubtedly reduced the ability of the central authorities to determine objectives and priorities and to control individual facets of expenditure' (Expenditure Committee 1971).

Alford (1975) has described how health services contain three sets of interests – dominant, challenging, and repressed. From its inception the NHS had been characterized by the pre-eminence of the professional monopolizers – the doctors – but these have been increasingly challenged by 'corporate rationalizers' such as health planners, managerial experts, and health economists. The third 'repressed' group consists of the community of users, who have so far made relatively little impact, except in so far as they have become a propaganda vehicle for either of the other two groups.

Corporate rationality in the NHS began with an emphasis on rational planning in the 1960s. It developed into a philosophy of managerialism, focused on the efficient and equitable use of resources in the 1970s. In 1976 the Resource Allocation Working Party

(RAWP) began to set targets for the redistribution of resources away from the richer regions to the poorer ones, but because this was largely a geographical formula of allocation its impact on sectoral inequalities was limited. While the objectives of the corporate rationalizer could still ostensibly be regarded as *wertrational*, the emphasis on financial control has tended towards an increasing instrumentality.

The rise of the corporate rationalizer can also be seen in the challenge that has been mounted to professional definitions of health and doctors' role in producing it. The work of McKeown (1976) demonstrated the major role of improved nutrition, clean water, and environmental sanitation in reducing deaths from infectious disease and in increasing life expectancy. The dominance of the medical model of disease, which largely ignores the behavioural and environmental determinants of ill health, has come under scrutiny, and this has led to a renaissance of the concept of prevention as a crucial alternative means of controlling the causes of ill health. Since the allocation of resources is related to definitions of health, changing these could be a potent force in switching resources away from the personal and acute services, which are largely controlled by doctors.

Even if such a large-scale reallocation does not take place, the further organizational changes which have occurred as a result of the Griffiths management inquiry are crucial for the NHS. The Griffiths Report recommended a system of management with one general manager at each level, replacing the team. This, it was felt, would give clearer direction and better financial control (DHSS 1984). Recently the necessity of hospital doctors becoming budget-holders with personal responsibility for what they spend has been stressed, and the emphasis here is on 'responsibility' rather than freedom. Performance indicators which cover clinical services, finance, manpower, and estate management have been operationalized, and health authorities are encouraged to compare costs per case, waiting lists, and length of stay (DHSS 1983). Clinical practice is increasingly evaluated in terms of the efficiency and effectiveness of types of treatment and care.

These developments are, on the one hand, the result of increasingly stringent financial controls, which give rise to the suspicion that balancing the books is the major objective of NHS policy. On the other hand they represent the triumph of *calculability* in the functioning of a rational bureaucratic organization. In practice, it becomes increasingly difficult to know where instrumentality ends and value considerations begin.

A formidable rational challenge has been made by the cost/benefit concepts of health economics. Economists take as their starting-point the notion of scarcity, and believe that there will always be competition for resources. Therefore in evaluating health procedures the following cost/benefit principles apply:

'Only do those things where benefit exceeds cost; do not do those things where costs exceed benefits' (Mooney 1986: 16). Cost/benefit analysis has its problems. Not all costs can be calculated; while the cost of an elderly person in a hospital bed can be assessed, it is more difficult to see the costs to that patient's relatives (particularly the female ones) if that elderly person is nursed at home. As for benefits, like better care, comfort, and quality of life, these involve social, political, and moral judgements and few so far have been robustly confident enough to make these. In the first section of this chapter subjective assessments of health were discussed; measures of health status, however, need not contain a subjective component. Rather they may contain an objectively judged 'subjective' component. The assessment of quality of life is not a neutral technical tool, but it can *appear* so. This process of valorization carries potential for *zweck-rationality*. Weber himself remarked: 'I do not believe questions of universal importance can be dealt with like questions of economics, or become the object of special disciplines like political economy'.

Must we then conclude that all attempts to measure, compare, and assess, which seem increasingly to characterize the operations of the health service, are dangerous, and that in the end *zweckrationality* drives out *wertrationality*, change becomes impossible, and values take second place to formal operations? Consider the position where a doctor says that the only duty is to the individual patient, and the clinical freedom to choose the best is the only value. This would indeed be value-rationality. Weber would describe it as an example of the 'ethic of conviction', which cares only for the realization of a particular goal without regard to consequences. He contrasts this with the ethic of responsibility, which does not reject all forms of rational calculation. This ethic combines the most promising elements of both types of rationality which have been discussed above: 'ends determined in a *wertrational* manner to be pursued with means selected in a *zweckrational* manner ... scientific rationality [should] serve reason ... the calculating attitude of *zweckrationalität* can be subordinated to the pursuit of ends chosen in a *wertrational* manner' (Brubaker 1984: 109).

Only by combining the two is the best outcome achieved, and the liberating potential of rationality overcomes the threat of repression inherent in a bureaucratically organized, legally dominant system. But to those who assume that technical means alone will guide us to correct answers Weber issues the following warning:

We know of no scientifically ascertainable ideals. We must not and cannot promise a fools paradise and an easy road to it, neither in thought nor in action. It is the stigma of our human dignity that the peace of our souls cannot be as great as the peace of one who dreams of such a paradise.

(Weber 1909)

References

Ackernecht, E. (1985) 'Some remarks concerning bureaucracy and medicine', *Gunerus* 42: 221–9.

Albrow, M. (1970) *Bureaucracy*, London: Macmillan.

Alford, R. (1975) *Health Care Politics*, Chicago Ill: University of Chicago Press.

Andrewski, S. (1984) *Max Weber's Insights and Errors*, London: Routledge & Kegan Paul.

Armstrong, D. (1983) *Political Anatomy of the Body*, Cambridge: Cambridge University Press.

Balint, M. (1957) *The Doctor, his Patient and the Illness*, London: Pitman Medical.

Bendix, R. (1966) *Max Weber, an Intellectual Portrait*, London: Methuen.

Bergner, M. and Gibson, B. (1981) 'The sickness impact profile', in L. Eisenberg and A. Kleinman (eds) *The Relevance of Social Science to Medicine*, Dordrecht, Holland: Riedel.

Blau, P. and Scott, R. (1963) *Formal Organisations*, London: Routledge & Kegan Paul.

British Medical Association (1986) *Alternative Therapy*, London: BMA.

Brotherston, J. (1976) 'Inequality in health: is it inevitable?', in C. O. Carter and J. Peel (eds) *Inequalities in Health*, London: Academic Press.

Brown, G. W. and Harris, T. (1978) *The Social Origins of Depression*, London: Tavistock.

Brubaker, R. (1984) *The Limits of Rationality: An Essay on the Social and Moral Thought of Max Weber*, London: Allen & Unwin.

Bucher, R. and Stelling, J. (1969) 'Characteristics of professional organisations', *Journal of Health and Social Behavior*, 10: 2–13.

Byrne, P. S. and Long, B. E. (1984) *Doctors Talking to Patients*, London: HMSO.

Chrisman, N. J. (1977) 'The health seeking process: an approach to the natural history of illness', *Culture Medicine and Psychiatry* 1: 351–77.

Coser, R. (1963) 'Alienation and social structure', in E. Freidson (ed.) *The Hospital in Modern Society*, New York: Free Press.

DHSS (1983) Performance Indicators, National Survey for 1981.

—— (1984) Griffiths Report, Health Circular 84 13, Implementation of the NHS Management Inquiry Report, London.

Doyal, L. and Pennell, I. (1979) *The Political Economy of Health*, London: Pluto Press.

Eckstein, A. (1960) *Pressure Group Politics*, London: Allen & Unwin.

Expenditure Committee (1971) Employment and Social Services Sub-committee, minutes of evidence, 31 March 1971, HC 323 ii, London: HMSO, quoted in Ham 1985.

Figlio, K. (1977) 'The historiography of scientific medicine – an invitation to the human sciences', *Comparative Studies in Society and History* 19: 265–73.

Foucault, M. (1961) *Histoire de la Folie*, Paris: Librarue Plon.

Giddens, A. (1972) *Politics and Sociology in the Thought of Max Weber*, London: Macmillan.

Goffman, E. (1961) *Asylums: Essays on the Social Situation of Mental Patients and Other Inmates*, Harmondsworth: Penguin.

Gough, I. (1979) *The Political Economy of the Welfare State*, London: Macmillan.

Ham, C. (1985) *Policy-Making in the National Health Service*, London: Macmillan (2nd edn).

Helman, C. (1978) 'Feed a cold, starve a fever – folk models of infection in a London suburban community', *Culture Medicine and Psychiatry* 2: 107–37.

Herzlich, C. (1973) *Health and Illness*, London: Academic Press.

Hill, C. (1964) 'Puritans, capitalism and the scientific revolution', *Past and Present*: 29 December.

Horton, R. (1970) 'African systems of thought and western science', in M. Young (ed.) *Knowledge and Control*, London: Macmillan.

Howe, R. H. (1978) 'Max Weber's elective affinities: sociology within the bounds of pure reason', *American Journal of Sociology* 84: 366–85.

Hunt, S. M. and MacEwan, J. (1980) 'The development of a subjective health indicator', *Sociology of Health and Illness* 2: 231–46.

Illich, I. (1975) *Medical Nemesis*, London: Calder/Boyars.

Jamous, H. and Peloille, B. (1970) 'Professions or self perpetuating systems? The French University Hospital system', in J. A. Jackson (ed.) *Professions and Professionalisation*, Cambridge: Cambridge University Press.

Johnson, T. (1972) *Professions and Power*, London: Macmillan.

Katz, A. and Akpom, C. (1976) 'A measure of primary sociological functions', *International Journal of Health Services* 6: 493–508.

Klein, R. (1983) *The Politics of the National Health Service*, London: Longman.

Kubler-Ross, E. (1970) *On Death and Dying*, London: Tavistock.

Levi-Strauss, C. (1968) 'The sorcerer and his magic', in *Structural Anthropology*, Harmondsworth: Penguin, 167–86.

McKeown, T. (1976) *The Role of Medicine*, Oxford: Nuffield.

Mei, J. (1971) 'Public works and community health in ancient China', papers on China, vol. 24, East Asian Research Centre, Cambridge, Mass: Harvard University Press: 1–15.

Merton, R. K. (1938) 'Science technology and society in seventeenth-century England', *Osiris* iv: 360–632.

—— (1952) 'Bureaucratic structure and personality', in R. K. Merton *et al.* (eds) *Reader in Bureaucracy*, Illinois: Free Press of Glencoe: 361–71.

Miliband, R. (1969) *The State in Capitalist Society*, London: Weidenfeld & Nicholson.

Mommsen, W. (1974) *The Age of Bureaucracy*, Oxford: Blackwell.

Mooney, G. (1986) *Economics, Medicine and Health Care*, London: Harvester.

Morgan, M., Calnan, M., and Manning, N. (1985) *Sociological Approaches to Health and Medicine*, London: Croom Helm.

Navarro, V. (1976) *Medicine under Capitalism*, London: Croom Helm.

Needham, J. (1948) *Science and Civilisation in China*, 7 vols, Cambridge: Cambridge University Press.

Needham, J. and Lu Gwei djen (1970) 'Hygiene and preventive medicine in ancient China', in *Clerks and Craftsman in China and the West*, Cambridge: Cambridge University Press: 340–79.

O'Connor, J. (1973) *The Fiscal Crisis of the State*, London: St James Press.

OPCS (Office of Population Censuses and Surveys) (1983) *Mortality Statistics*, London: HMSO.

Parsons, T. (1958) *The Protestant Ethic and the Spirit of Capitalism*, New York: Scribners: 75.

Rosen, G. (1974) *From Medical Police to Social Medicine*, New York: Science History Publications.

Rosengren, E. and de Vault, C. (1963) 'Time and space in the obstetric hospital', in E. Freidson (ed.) *The Hospital in Modern Society*, New York: Free Press.

Schlucter, W. (1981) *The Rise of Western Rationalism – Weber's Developmental Theory*, Berkeley, Calif: University of California Press.

Silverman, D. (1970) *The Theory of Organisations*, London: Heinemann.

Strauss, A. (1963) 'The hospital and its negotiated order' in E. Freidson (ed.) *The Hospital in Modern Society*, New York: Free Press.

Tenbruch, F. (1980) 'The problem of thematic unity in the works of Max Weber', *British Journal of Sociology* 31: 313–51.

Touraine, A. (1974) 'The *raison d'etre* of a sociology of religion', in A. Giddens (ed.) *Positivism and Sociology*, London: Heinemann.

Townsend, P. and Davidson, N. (1982) *Inequalities in Health: The Black Report*, Harmondsworth: Penguin.

Weber, Marianne (1975) *Max Weber – A Biography*, New York: John Wiley.

Weber, Max (1909) in G. Roth and C. Wittick (eds and trans). (1978) *Max Weber, Economy and Society*, 2 vols, Berkeley, Calif: University of California Press (2nd edn).

—— (1918) 'Science as a vocation (Wissenschaftals Beruf), in H. Gerth and C. W. Mills (eds) (1946) *Max Weber, Essays in Sociology*, New York: Ocord University Press.

—— (1922) *Gesammelte Aufsatze zue Religionssoziology* vol. 1, Tubingen Mohr: 11–12 in 'Author's Introduction', *The Protestant Ethic and the Spirit of Capitalism* (1958) trans. T. Parsons, New York: Scribners.

—— (1964) 'Die objektivat socialwissenschaftlicher und sozialpolitischer erkentris' in E. A. Shils and H. A. Finch (eds and trans.) (1948) *The Methodology of the Social Sciences*, Glencoe: Free Press.

—— (1966) *The Theory of Social and Economic Organisation*, New York: Free Press.

—— (1974) 'Subjectivity and determinism', in A. Giddens (ed.) *Positivism and Sociology*, London: Heinemann.

—— (1978a) *Economy and Society*, G. Roth and C. Wittick (eds and trans.) 2 vols, Berkeley, Calif: University of California Press (2nd edn).

—— (1978b) *Kings and People: Power and the Mandate to Rule*, Berkeley, Calif: University of California Press.

Willcocks, A. (1967) *The Creation of the National Health Service*, London: Routledge & Kegan Paul.

Wing, J. and Brown, G. (1970) *Institutionalism and Schizophrenia*, Cambridge: Cambridge University Press.

9

Political science and health policy

RAY FITZPATRICK

Academic interest in the state as an object of enquiry has grown at the very time that political debates have intensified as to the proper role and boundaries of the state in modern life. The so-called 'crisis of the welfare state', in particular, has been subjected to enormous scholarly attention as well as more direct political argument. The concept of crisis in this context is a point of convergence for analysts of diverse academic and political persuasions, and has resulted in numerous reappraisals of the role of the state in the provision of welfare services. This chapter is concerned with the value of recent analyses of the welfare state to the area of health care in particular, where the idea of crisis is also increasingly heard. The chapter examines the framework of concepts developed by political scientists, and especially those of Claus Offe for understanding the role of the state in health care. How far such recent theoretical analyses of the welfare state apply to the instance of publicly provided health care is the focus of concern. Writers such as Offe build on and systematize a broad range of different analyses and critiques of the welfare state and these are first outlined.

The crisis in the welfare state

A wide range of commentators agree in seeing the mid-1970s as a turning point in the fortunes of the welfare state. Particularly following the Second World War, steady economic growth in western societies had been associated with the development of extensive state provision of health and social services. However, these same public institutions, previously seen as beneficial and integral to successful social development, came now to be regarded as problematic, as potentially an unsupportable economic burden inhibiting further economic growth, and worse, as a source of more pervasive damaging influences on society. The welfare state, once seen as harmoniously working in tandem with the rest of society, was identified by a variety of observers as dysfunctional and maladaptive. Discussions of the societal crisis for which extensive state involvement in welfare was seen as responsible, centred on three basically different kinds of problems posed by the welfare state. First and most important was the argument that the growth of public welfare had outstripped available resources and become economically unbearable. The proportion of the gross national product taken up by public expenditure appeared to grow uncontrollably in all western societies. At the same time economic growth often appeared seriously to falter. Public expenditure, a growing proportion of which was spent on welfare services, thus appeared to be out of control and to have damaging consequences for the economy as a whole. For various reasons Britain, the source of the very term 'the welfare state', was widely viewed as the prime example of the economic problems created by excessive levels of public expenditure devoted to welfare (Kristol 1978). Less concrete in their manifestations were two other problems emphasized in different ways by different analysts. The very legitimacy and public support for public welfare, it was maintained, had been withdrawn. Public welfare was unpopular. Thus in Britain, for example, it is suggested that the 1970s was a period in which public approval for taxation to pay for public services declined. Widely publicized 'tax revolts' in the USA were also interpreted as symptoms of a broader withdrawal of consent. The election of governments in Britain and the USA committed to reducing the public sector were widely interpreted as evidence of a sea change in public attitudes. In addition, it was maintained by others that state services were either ineffective or worse, and actually produced more social problems than they solved. The effectiveness of governments in producing improved levels of education, in eradicating poverty, or addressing problems such as inner city decline or environmental pollution was widely questioned. At another level state welfare did great harm, it was maintained, by reducing individual initiative and self-respect, family values, and the spontaneous capacity for caring by the community, and by substituting for all of these virtues a paternalistic welfare bureaucracy.

Conservative analyses

The diagnosis of a profound malady in modern societies, of which the prime symptom was as excessive level of public expenditure on welfare, was quite widely made. However, the causes of the problem and the recommendations for remedies varied. From the conservative and right wing of the political spectrum, it was argued that 'political markets' in modern democracies were responsible for excessive governmental ambitions and activities (Brittan 1977). Politicians regularly compete with each other in elections for votes. Politicians outbid each other in their promises to solve problems in this competitive political market for votes, usually advocating governmental solutions funded publicly without any need to show restraint in terms of available resources. Furthermore modern democracies encourage groups of individuals who have a shared need, problem, or concern, to gather to form organized pressure groups to lobby for public support and funding. Such varied sources of pressures to obtain further public expenditure outweigh the more diffuse and less organized interests of the general tax-payer to control the level of spending. Moreover the public sector professions, occupations, and bureaucracies become highly organized and vociferous advocates of sustained public spending and may make common cause with interest groups in expanding the role of the state (Gould 1981). The power and influence of such bureaucracies, according to such views, is increased in direct proportion to the ability to gain further public financial support, and a strong motive to advocate state solutions is thereby established. In the end competitive electoral politics, the promotion of the view that governments can and should solve problems, and the self-interested growth of public bureaucracies result in 'government overload' (King 1975), in which the expectations addressed to governments far outstrip the means available to satisfy demands, and systemic crisis may ensue. The government will be financially unable to cope, will systematically fail to achieve objectives and produce widespread disillusionment with government. Suggestions to avoid such 'overload' variously involve reducing public expenditure, withdrawal of government from direct provision of services, reducing public expectations of government, and technical economic mechanisms such as monetarism.

Marxist analyses

Thus conservative critiques share in common a pessimism with regard to the effects on society of the democratic inflation of expectations. On the left, various analysts have also diagnosed fundamental instabilities in the welfare state which must result in 'crisis' (O'Connor 1973; Navarro 1978a; Gough 1979). The reasons identified for such 'crisis tendencies', however, are quite different, as are the remedies advocated. For Marxists the welfare state has represented a major analytical problem. In many ways classical Marxism envisaged that capitalism would produce progressive deterioration in the living conditions of the working classes, out of which emiseration a revolutionary reaction might confidently be predicted. Instead the twentieth century saw the development of the welfare state. One way of explaining this unpredicted development has been to argue that the welfare state actually fulfils certain important functions for capitalism. Thus for O'Connor (1973), the modern state plays two crucial roles within capitalist societies – 'accumulation' and 'legitimation'. Accumulation refers to the activities of the state in assisting the process of profitable capital accumulation (for example investment in the infrastructure of roads, railways, and so on). Legitimation refers to the activities of the state in maintaining social harmony and making the capitalist system acceptable (for example through welfare expenditure on education and health care). Monopoly capital, according to O'Connor, is the most powerful sector of capitalist economies and is able to socialize such expenditures by transferring them to the state sector. The welfare state therefore fulfils certain important functions in the interests of capital.

However there is another strand to Marxist analyses, which emphasizes instead the real achievements obtained by the working classes in struggles to bring about the welfare state (Navarro 1978b). According to this view, pressure from subordinate social classes has frequently been the most important factor bringing about the development of state welfare services. Such services do not solely function in the interests of capital. As Gough observes of the British welfare state:

> to concentrate solely on its negative aspect, as do certain critical theorists, is to lose sight of the very real gains that a century of conflict has won. The National Health Service, comprehensive social security, and the like do represent very important steps forward and do in part 'enhance welfare'.
>
> (Gough 1979: 14)

It has been observed that Marxist analyses of the welfare state appear to involve considerable 'tight rope walking' (Mishra 1984: 71) because of the often-shifting picture of the welfare state that emerges – variously a good and a bad thing. In any case it is not surprising that the central conclusion of such Marxist analyses is that the two state functions of accumulation and legitimation are 'contradictory' (O'Connor 1973: 71). Responsibilities for securing both private profitability and the social acceptability of the system pull the state in opposite directions. However at this point in O'Connor's analysis particularly there is a convergence with the conservative analysis of 'overload', since the 'fiscal crisis' which ultimately faces governments arises from the ever-increasing gap between the pressures and expectations placed upon them on the one hand and the ability to raise revenues on the other hand. To raise public expenditure to fulfil its different responsibilities is to undermine the very viability of the private enterprise system on which the state depends. Marxist solutions to such fiscal crises and perennial contradictions of the welfare state cannot be sought within the confines of capitalism, and transition to socialism by whatever means is viewed as the only ultimately successful resolution.

Values and theories

Thus there is considerable common ground between conservative and Marxist critiques of the welfare state, particularly in so far as they view welfare institutions as unstable and economically problematic. However these two approaches clearly differ widely in the fundamental ideological positions that inform analysis. For many conservative analysts, the ideology of liberalism is the source of disillusionment with the welfare state. Personal liberty and freedom from constraint is of primary concern and institutions of any kind that might threaten personal freedom, whether state totalitarianism or welfare bureaucracy require restraint. Market forces are the only mechanism that reliably protect the individual against 'vested interests'. Liberty is also central to the ideological core of Marxism but is closely identified with another value – equality. The main social mechanism inhibiting liberty and equality is that of the unequal distribution of economic power perpetuated by a capitalist economic system. In turn liberalism views the state with suspicion as a potential source of oppression. Marxists are more varied and may view the state as a potentially liberatory mechanism as well as a mechanism that supports capitalism.

Such contrasts arise out of fundamentally divergent values. However as George and Wilding point out (1976: 22), 'Views on the welfare state – both favourable and unfavourable – represent a fusion of scientific evidence and of ideology'. It is important therefore to examine, in addition to their contrasting values and priorities, the respective sociological explanations of conservative and Marxist views of the welfare state. Again two contrasting tendencies or broad approaches to sociological explanation may be identified – pluralism and Marxism. The equation of conservative ideology and pluralist sociological explanation is not an exact one but significant common ground may be identified.

Classical pluralism begins its analysis from the preferences and goals of individuals who, in a democracy, will form groups on the basis of shared interests to further their goals. Such groups compete through the mechanisms of local and central government to achieve their ends. A second axiom of classical pluralism is that the power to influence decisions and resources is widely dispersed in modern democracies and that there are a multitude of determinants of power other than social class. Thus interest groups may form and have influence on the basis of occupation, ethnicity, geographical location, and so on. Pluralist analyses of the origins of welfare services emphasize the process of bargaining and negotiation that occurs among interest groups. Thus, for example, Willcocks (1967) examines the emergence of the NHS in terms of the negotiations among key interest groups – the medical profession, the government, local authorities, and the insurance societies. Particularly when the stage is reached when the precise form and details of welfare legislation are being considered, pluralists emphasize the importance of bargains and compromises within the state that may quite crucially shape the very nature of policy outcomes. Quite small numbers of actors, often in private negotiations, were involved in shaping the emergence of the NHS (Klein 1983). While the medical profession had important influences in setting some of the parameters for debate in the USA about public insurance, according to Marmor's analysis (1970) many crucial components of the eventual Medicare legislation were determined more by balances of influence among Congressional coalitions. Pluralistic bargaining within the state means coincidences of interests cannot be foreseen and therefore that outcomes are not predetermined. Thus Marmor states of Medicare that 'The outcome of 1965 was, to be sure, a model of unintended consequences. The final legislative package incorporated features which no one had fully foreseen and aligned supporters and opponents in ways which surprised many of the leading actors' (1970: 82).

Whereas classical pluralistic analyses are criticized for their naive assumptions regarding the wide dispersion of power and influence, this is not the case in what many term 'neopluralism'. According to neopluralism, 'the distorted liberal state' (Nordlinger 1981) is more heavily influenced by those interests with resources such as cultural influence or money. Thus 'big business', organized labour, and the professions are groups with particularly effective abilities to influence the state. Neopluralists are interested in the mechanisms whereby such groups exert influence within the state. Governments simply depend on successful economies and therefore have a tendency to pay particular attention to the lobbying of business (Lindblom 1977). Commonly shared values between key groups and the state may exclude certain options from consideration (Fox 1986a). Also close networks and regular contact ensure certain groups' abilities to influence government (Haywood and Hunter 1982).

Marxist explanations of the origins of the state, and of the welfare state in particular, are as diverse as those of pluralism, and some degree of simplification is equally necessary. As stated earlier, the emphasis in Marxist analyses is on the constraints upon the state imposed by a capitalist economic system, and the advantages to capitalism provided by the state. Thus if we consider health care specifically, health policies in areas such as prevention (Renaud 1975) and social inequalities in health (Navarro 1978b) are constrained within capitalism to solutions that do not threaten the capitalist order. The ideology of medicine individualizes problems rather than laying bare the social causes of ill health. Furthermore medicine may operate as an agent of social control in controlling access to legitimate absence from work. Navarro accepts that there are a plurality of interests in the health sector, but argues that the large degree of consensus and shared ground amongst élite groups results in health policy consistently favouring the 'corporate and upper middle classes' (Navarro 1975: 105).

There is some interest within Marxism in the specific mechanisms whereby such relations between capital and the state are produced. Thus Navarro emphasizes the common social class origins of élites in business and in government. Other analyses, particularly of American health care, discuss the role of capitalist foundations such as the Rockefeller Foundation (E.R. Brown 1979) in directly supporting with massive levels of capital particular forms of medicine, which, it is argued, are less likely to identify and challenge the social causes of ill health. Other Marxist analyses draw attention to a recent growth of corporate capitalist involvement in the direct provision of health care (Salmon 1984).

The second strand to Marxist sociological explanations of the growth of state involvement in health care underlines the active role of the working classes in improving their health care by demands for increased public provision. At key points in history, working-class unrest is identified as the prime reason for health care reform. The growth of trade unionism and unsuccessful social revolutions in Europe are, for example, seen as crucial antecedents of the National Health Insurance Act, 1911. There are problems with this approach. It is difficult to specify the causal relationship between social unrest and legislation twenty years later (Urry 1981: 119). Furthermore no account is taken of the fact that not all capitalists perceived their interests in terms of making such concessions. Urry (1981: 120) accuses Navarro of working with a crude conflict model of capitalism involving struggles between capitalists and workers, instead of addressing the complex reality of power blocs and class alliances. Others have found the evidence for working-class interest and pressure to bring about fundamental improvements in public health care less salient forces for change compared with perceptions of needs to repair and reform from within the health care system and the state (Walters 1980).

Two quite separate ideologies of the welfare state have been identified, conservative and Marxist, which are divided by quite different values and political principles. At the same time they converge in terms of shared diagnoses of some of the fundamental problems of the welfare state. Two sociological traditions to the analysis of the welfare state have also been delineated. They may differ in ideological assumptions but it has become more customary to distinguish them on methodological grounds. Thus Pollitt contrasts the interests of pluralism in 'the surface play of events' and an emphasis on 'the resources and tactics of institutions and groups', with the Marxist ability to offer a 'big picture' (Pollitt 1984: 144). While pluralism offers 'no overall pattern of development' Marxism is liable to be too dismissive of tactical or institutional factors. Thus they are contrasted in terms of the breadth and scale of their explanatory approach – a contrast brought out by Ham in terms of Marxism's explanatory value 'at the macro level of analysis' (1982: 153) compared with pluralism's greater explanatory ability at the level of analysis of particular decisions and institutions. Quite clearly the explanatory focuses of the two approaches differ – the economic order and social classes on the one hand, and politics and pressure groups on the other hand, being the preferred sources of explanations.

A possible convergence?

Yet it may be that the divergences of these two approaches to the analysis of the state are exaggerated. McLennan (1984: 99), for example, talks of 'pluralist Marxists' who would accept that it is no longer possible to talk of *the state*. As Jessop expresses it, 'the state comprises a plurality of institutions' (Jessop 1982: 231) so that instead of being a single purposive entity it may be pursuing a diversity of objectives. Furthermore far from being solely concerned with class interests, the state may as much be concerned with preserving its own interests. McLennan sees in such theoretical developments a more 'open-ended' Marxism, less wedded to single-mindedly tracking down the functions of the state in reproducing capitalist interests. Such tendencies are directly paralleled in neo-pluralist writers such as Nordlinger. Whereas classical pluralism tended to view the state as a neutral arena in which pressure groups compete for favourable decisions from a neutral government, Nordlinger asserts the following analytical principles:

> Look at least as much to the state as to civil society to understand what the democratic state does in the making of public policy and why it does so; the democratic state is frequently autonomous in translating its own preferences into authoritative actions, and markedly autonomous in doing so even when they diverge from those held by the politically weightiest groups in civil society.
>
> (1981: 203)

Offe's analysis of the welfare state

Thus realignments are occurring within and between the two traditions that have historically been viewed as so distant (Held 1983). A writer whose works seem particularly to reflect such changes is Claus Offe. Offe's early work (e.g. Offe 1974) was based on a systems analysis of capitalist societies. He distinguishes three subsystems within capitalist societies. At the centre is 'the political administrative system' – the various elements and activities of the state, including welfare services. There are two 'flanking systems'. First, there is the 'economic system' – the production and exchange of goods in the economy. Second, he identifies 'the normative or legitimation system' – the norms, values, and processes of socialization in society. Taxes flow from the economic system to pay for the political administrative system. Constant malfunctions within the economic system such as recessions, which are beyond individual capitalists to solve, require a flow of regulations and control from the political administrative system to the economic system. Similarly he views the normative system of values as creating demands for services from the political system which respond with welfare services. Such services create a flow of 'loyalty' from the normative to the political system. Thus the political administrative system is dependent on a flow of finances from the economy on the one hand and a flow of loyalty on the other hand. It is in these system-based terms that Offe presents the dilemmas and contradictions of the state in capitalist societies. The conflict between the state and its flanking systems is the central dynamic of Offe's analysis and he shifts attention away from classical Marxist concerns with conflicts arising primarily in the economy. Offe's analysis focuses centrally on the state and its contrasting needs to maintain accumulation in the economy and legitimation or loyalty.

Another central feature of Offe's analysis is that it avoids some of the functionalist assumptions of earlier Marxist analyses, which viewed the state as almost inevitably providing functions that favoured the capitalist economy or as necessarily allied to particular classes. The state in Offe's analysis is pursuing *self-interest in survival* in being concerned to maintain the accumulation process. The dilemmas faced by the capitalist state are perpetually present and ultimately impossible to resolve. In Offe's formulation they may be summarized by contradictory tendencies towards 'commodification' and 'decommodification', in which the state is inextricably involved. The commodity form by which things may be bought and sold is essential to capitalism and has to be promoted by the state which is dependent for its own survival on capitalism. However the very means it adopts to promote the commodity form push in the opposite direction towards 'decommodification' – the promotion of forms of life based on other principles than the commodity. By this he refers on the one hand to the need for the state to provide infrastructural services that are essential to capital accumulation but are produced in socialized rather than private form, such as roads and sanitation, but also to the development of other services such as education and health care – essential to legitimation and social integration – that are provided and presented on principles such as human need or citizenship rights. These decommodified forms are produced and distributed by criteria other than those of the market and therefore threaten to undermine the commodity form.

The capitalist state is therefore faced with persistent problems in its three subsystems, with regard to fiscal resources, administrative rationality, and mass loyalty. The infrastructural investments and public subsidies necessary for the viability of private capital create public deficit problems that threaten economic growth in the short term. The political administrative system requires long-term rational planning, which is however profoundly frustrated by the short-term shifts of policy arising from party politics, and the very scale, complexity, and differentiation of the administrative system makes rational and effective co-ordination problematic. Mass loyalty is ever precarious because the political administrative system increasingly fails to achieve publicized objectives and also because decommodification undermines discipline and respect for the commodity form. For all of these reasons, the state is involved in crisis management and indeed, because of systematic failures to address crises, Offe refers to 'crises of crisis management' (1984: 36).

The workings of the state

Offe's analysis is of importance because, more than any other analyst inspired by Marxism, he insists on the importance of examining the specific mechanisms and processes of the state, matters which are often left unanalysed on the assumption that the state always operates in the interests of capitalism and its workings are therefore of no interest. Against this view Offe makes three important points. First, the state is not a unitary, co-ordinated institution capable of acting in such a consistent way. The state is a variety of institutions, often pulling in different directions. Second, the state does not have 'the requisite foresight and analytical capacity for diagnosing the functional exigencies of capital' (Offe 1984: 102). Thus it may be argued that the British government has for too long been too concerned with the interests of financial capital as represented by city institutions to the detriment of the long-term interests of capital as a whole, particularly industrial capital (Crouch 1979). As Frankel expresses it: 'Rather than acting in an efficient, purposive manner, the reality of state administrations is their propensity for *avoiding* responsibility and crisis management. This reactive avoidance of crisis is particularly crucial when considering the capacity of bureaucracies to plan efficiently' (1982: 271). Thus a third and most important point for the purposes of this discussion is that the analysis of social policies in the welfare state should start not from the assumption that policies are responses to particular class demands or needs of capital as such.

> Social policy instead consists of answers to what can be called the *internal* problem of the state apparatus, namely how it can react *consistently* to the two poles of the 'needs' of labour and capital. . . . The problem is that of the precarious compatibility of its own institutions and performances.
>
> (Offe 1984: 104)

Social policies do have external effects on society, even though their origins have to be understood in terms of the internal problems of the state apparatus. However Offe shares with other schools of policy analysis (Pressman and Wildavsky 1973) the view that the effects of policies cannot be predicted and are heavily influenced by the conflicts and outcomes of conflicts arising at the stage of policy implementation. Social policy sets some of the themes (Offe 1984: 108) and may influence the timing of debate of particular issues, but social conflict in society determines the outcomes of social policy.

Offe examines some of the general or structural constraints and dilemmas experienced by the state by means of a distinction between two types of state activity: *allocative* and *productive*. Allocative state activities involve the use of universal rules and criteria in such areas as the levying of taxes or the administration of benefits. Once principles and criteria have been established of who is included, excluded, and with what consequences, according to Offe, allocative activities can be carried out by the state with relatively simple, bureaucratic, or legal-rational principles. Productive activities on the other hand involve the state as direct producer of, for example, health or educational services. He illustrates the distinction with the example of health. State allocative health measures would include laws obliging landlords to install adequate sanitation, or employers to install safety equipment. Also the state may define certain categories of persons or benefits to be covered by health insurance. On the other hand, state productive health activities would include the state being directly involved in provision of hospital care, medical training, or supporting medical research. Whereas allocative activities can be routinized and bureaucratized, the latter activities cannot so easily be managed. Bureaucratic principles are less appropriate for productive state activities, which in the area of health, according to Offe, are the areas in which the state becomes increasingly embroiled over time. The repetition of impartial rules would not be appropriate or useful in providing direct services like health and instead the state becomes unavoidably involved in complex decisions about the goals and purposes of health care, the efficiency and effectiveness of different means of achieving health and questions such as who should receive treatments and which treatments are appropriate.

Two alternative ways of developing and implementing policies are available to the state, according to Offe. One alternative is to adopt 'purposive rational' approaches to policy. By this he refers to the adoption of rational and technical approaches to policy in which the same efficient relationship between ends and means is adopted as is possible in capitalist industry. However purposive rational policies tend to fail primarily because of a lack of clear-cut, uncontroversial, and operational goals in state-productive activities. Health is again a good example. Whereas the production of industrial products of specifiable type and quantity is a clear and unambiguous goal for a capitalist enterprise, there is no equivalent goal in health services in terms of which technical rational policy means can be assessed. The concept of health is essentially contested, as indeed are the optimal means for achieving health. Also the kinds of goals that might be set by the state in areas such as health normally involve long-term planning, whereas the economic and political environment creates short-term turbulence that upsets any long-term rational planning. Thus, in Offe's view, health policies set by capitalist states in terms of operational programmes, with objectives stated by means of outcomes, explicit indicators, and cost-benefit analyses are doomed to failure (Offe 1975: 143).

The second alternative approach to policy formation available to the state in its productive activities is 'to allow for a highly decentralized process of political conflict and consensus to determine the production process' (Offe 1975: 139). Thus instead of either bureaucratic rules or scientific programmes, the clients and recipients would be the prime determinant of state policy. This highly participative strategy is also unlikely to succeed within a capitalist state as the very process of obtaining consensus from diverse and conflicting groups of recipients would again make long-term state planning impossible, as it is increasingly required to respond to shifting democratic pressures. It is also likely to invite more demands than the system can possibly satisfy. Experiments with such a participatory strategy are few. Nevertheless a comparative study of health policy in the USA, Australia, and Britain supports Offe's views by concluding that public participation is 'expensive, time consuming and inefficient' and is unlikely to improve 'access, equity or quality of care', even if individuals' stakes in the system are increased by participation (Bates 1983: 191).

Thus in this analysis Offe concludes that, regardless of the content of policy in state productive activities in areas such as health, the very forms in which policies are produced are likely to produce failure. Whether bureaucratic rules, scientifically determined goals, or democratic participation are the basis of policy formation, the capitalist state will find that the policy process enmeshes it in further crises.

State coping strategies

In more recent analyses Offe has focused on three particular strategies that the state may adopt in social policy to cope with its various incompatibility problems and contradictions – increasing state administrative steering capacities, the 'scientization of politics', and privatization. All are of particular interest because they are topical themes in current health policy. In many ways the strategy of increasing state administrative steering capacities takes up themes previously discussed by Offe in terms of 'purposive rational' approaches to policy. This strategy, described by Offe as 'expanding the state's horizon for conceptualizing and acting' involves increasing the ability of the state to regulate by means of improved information. Rational planning is undermined however not merely because of the factors underlined above – the ambiguous nature of goals, for example. In his later analyses Offe argues (1984: 72) that rational planning on the basis of enhanced information and monitoring can only be increased if trust and confidence are consolidated. If significant social groups dissent, rational planning founders. '"Consensus" becomes the decisive bottleneck' (Offe 1984: 72). Similar problems occur in the strategy of 'scientizing politics', by which Offe means the translation of political demands and problems into scientific issues of measurement and assessment by experts. This strategy attempts to unburden the state of demands that are scientifically illegitimate and a 'temporal buffer' is placed between the expression of demands and their subsequent resolution, by the need for expert enquiries, research, and so on (Offe 1984: 113). Thus governments attempt to avoid potentially damaging political conflict by 'non political forms of decision making' (Offe 1984: 168).

Recent developments in relation to the British NHS can be used to develop and examine Offe's ideas. One crucial issue to consider is the extent and nature of a crisis in the NHS specifically as opposed to other institutions of the British welfare state. Offe identifies three sources of crisis in the welfare state: economic, legitimation, and administrative crises. In common with conservative analyses the threat of financial crisis is ever present in the work of Offe and others.

The NHS and economic crisis

Undoubtedly expenditure on the NHS has consistently risen. In 1950 NHS expenditure was £477 million. By 1980 this figure had reached £11,494 million, an increase of twenty-five-fold (Butler and Vaile 1984). If the effects of inflation are controlled for, by calculating in terms of constant prices, the increase of spending on the NHS in this period is still two-fold (Butler and Vaile 1984: 54). Whereas in the earlier period of 1960–75 the average annual increase in real NHS expenditure was 3.4 per cent, by the later period of 1975–81 annual growth had slowed down to 2.0 per cent (Gillion and Hemming 1985). Thus despite the slowing down of growth in expenditure on the NHS, there clearly is prima-facie evidence here of the kinds of public expenditure problems identified by Offe. On the other hand, these increases have to be set against the growth in overall wealth experienced by Britain in this period. Gross Domestic Product (GDP) in the period 1950–80 more than doubled. In these terms the rise of NHS expenditure is not nearly so dramatic, taking up 3.7 per cent of GDP in 1950 and steadily rising to occupy 5.1 per cent of GDP by 1980 (Butler and Vaile 1984). These trends are not of course unique to the NHS. Thus, whereas real annual growth in NHS expenditure grew by 2.0 per cent in the period 1975–81, the figures for public expenditure on health in OECD European countries as a whole in this period show a growth rate of 2.8 per cent and in the USA growth was 3.8 per cent per annum (Gillion and Hemming 1985).

Thus if health care has become a source of state fiscal crisis, this is much more the case elsewhere than in Britain. Indeed it is widely observed that, despite real increases in NHS expenditure, the really distinctive characteristic of the NHS is the way in which funding has been so successfully controlled when contrasted with the health care systems of other comparable countries (Aaron and Schwartz 1984; Daniels 1986). It is quite difficult to be clear about expenditure on the NHS in more recent years. The Conservative government has been inimical to public expenditure, holding very firm beliefs that econ-omic growth can be sustained only by containing public expenditure. Nevertheless the government has at the same time been anxious to maintain a reputation of being responsible for growth in the NHS and has claimed a growth of 24 per cent in expenditure in the health service over the period 1979–85. The reality of such claims is diffi-cult to unravel. The parliamentary Social Services Committee argued that much of the claimed expenditure was spent on wages rather than real growth in services (McKie 1986). An authoritative report for the Institute of Health Services Management, the British Medical Associ-ation, and the Royal College of Nursing produced evidence for the view that increased expenditure by the Conservatives had been insufficient to cover costs arising from increasing demands created by demographic changes (Bosanquet 1986). The Labour opposition has also produced evidence that allowing for demographic changes, wage increases, and growing costs of medical technology, the four years between 1982 and 1986 have seen *dwindling* expenditure in the hospital and community services (Davies 1986). To such criticisms the government replies that no account is taken of the additional finance made available by cost improvement programmes (efficiency savings). Two points do emerge, however, from the complexities of such disputes about the real levels of current NHS expenditure. The government has accepted that its initial estimates of growth must be revised downwards (McKie 1986) so that there is probably some considerable overlap in realistic estimates. Such estimates are likely to support the view to be obtained from longer-term trends of quite modest growth rates in NHS expenditure. The second point relates more immediately to what such expenditure disputes reveal about the ways in which the state copes with potential crisis. Klein, from an analysis of Conservative policies toward the NHS, provocatively makes the point that 'party ideology does not predict policy' (Klein 1984: 103). Many of the more radical Conservative proposals for changing the private/public mix of funding for health care in Britain have been either dropped or watered down as the government confronted the strength of the different constituencies supporting the status quo (Klein 1984b: 104). Many policies have become more symbolic and rhetorical as a result. Symbolically important support for private practice is upheld at the same time as the government has become incrementally drawn into overall financial policies for the NHS that are less radically different from those of their predecessors. Indeed the main lesson of recent financial policies towards the NHS may be that governments see political success as dependent on a strategy of claiming credit simultaneously for financial constraint *and* growth in services. Indeed one of the greatest analytical problems for theorists of welfare state crisis is the extent to which governments routinely and successfully cope through such political strategies (Held and Krieger 1983).

The mechanisms whereby NHS costs are contained are varied and difficult to unravel but would include by comparison with, for example, North American health care, lower pay for key occupations such as medicine, lower standards of hospital catering, lower rates of elective surgical and medical procedures, a more extensive primary care sector, lower administration costs, and, crucially, central Treasury influence on the total volume of NHS expenditure (Bevan *et al.* 1980). Perhaps the most notable feature of the NHS, however, is the complex process of clinical rationing of expensive medical procedures and interventions. Renal dialysis is carried out at one-third of the rate prevailing in the USA. Coronary artery surgery is conducted at one-tenth of the rate in the USA. Aaron and Schwartz estimate that even allowing for excessive use in the USA, 'the British could perform six or seven times more bypass procedures than at present, with probable benefit to patients' (Aaron and Schwartz 1984: 28). Similar discrepancies are indicated by Aaron and Schwartz with regard to CT scanners and the use of diagnostic X-rays. It may rightly be argued that in the longer term, pressures in both countries to make more rational and appropriate use of health services will lead to a convergence in rates of use of high technology, so that British health care will not look quite so severely rationed (Jennet 1986: 46). It nevertheless remains a remarkable characteristic of the NHS that no systemic crisis has arisen in relation to the rationing of expensive medical procedures and that clinicians and society generally have accepted the need for medically defined rationing (Klein 1984a). Indeed the strategic intelligence of governments in their allocation of funds in the area suggests one major limitation of crisis theories – the ability of governments, not to resolve long-term contradictions, but to operate successfully with short-term strategies. Thus at a pre-election period – 1986–7 – the government would appear to be supplementing the scientifically derived 'allocative' rules of territorial allocation of NHS funds by both a review of the Resource Allocation Working Party (RAWP) principles (Holland 1986) and by 'one-off' payments to ease the transitional traumas of RAWP-losing but vociferous regions in the south-east.

It may be argued that the real financial crises for the NHS are being stored up for the future, especially given that growth rates under the recent Conservative government have been so modest and demographic factors such as the increasing numbers of very old people will place additional demands on the NHS. O'Higgins and Patterson (1985) attempt to model projected public expenditure in different areas, such as health and education, over the period 1983–94 under different assumptions for annual growth of GDP (varying between 1.0 per cent and 3.0 per cent per annum) and a number of different assumptions about changes in productivity, public sector wages, and demographic changes. They conclude that provided there is growth in GDP of at least 1 per cent per annum over the period modelled, there can be modest increases in public expenditure in line with changing demographic demands, without creating any kind of fiscal crisis. Hill and Bramley (1986) similarly conclude that the evidence for a public sector fiscal crisis derives more from political evaluations of the welfare state than any strong trend for public expenditure to outstrip resources. The more general point to emerge from this evidence is the need for more caution and specificity in discussions of the fiscal crisis of capitalist welfare institutions; clearly the need is for more sociologi cal sophistication in explaining the excessive success of fiscal restraint in relation to the NHS, compared with inflationary systems such as in the USA.

The NHS and legitimation

To what extent is there evidence of a crisis of state legitimation or loyalty in relation to the NHS? Levels of satisfaction with the NHS have consistently been found to be quite high. Although there may be doubts about the validity of much survey research in this area, it is hard to come to any conclusion other than that the NHS is a popular social institution which retains public loyalty. This loyalty to the institution does not mean that people uncritically accept all aspects of the NHS. Routines and rigidities in the system, such as times for waking up in-patients in the morning, and the poor quality of many basic amenities such as waiting-rooms, catering, and washing facilities provoke dissatisfaction in large numbers of patients (Fitzpatrick 1984). Other limitations reported by patients of the NHS, such as poor communication to the patient from professional staff, may be universal features of the practice of western scientific medicine. The NHS ranks very high amongst the institutions of the welfare state that survey respondents wish to see receive more public funding, even if this involves the individual's having to pay higher taxes (Taylor-Gooby 1985). Surveys appear to find that support and approval for public welfare in Britain are associated with perceptions of personal interest arising from position in the life cycle (Taylor-Gooby 1983) rather than, for example, individuals' beliefs about whether they or other groups are the main beneficiaries of public welfare institutions such as the NHS (Papadakis and Taylor-Gooby 1986). Such evidence is important because it addresses one aspect of crisis theory – namely the view that the legitimacy of the welfare state will decline amongst groups who view themselves as benefactors rather than beneficiaries of the welfare state. In support of this view of Britain, Pescosolido and colleagues (1986) found more evidence in a large-scale comparative study for resentment of the welfare state by supposed benefactors in the USA than was the case amongst British respondents. Such evidence suggests that in Britain feelings of resentment, about redistribution at least, are not a major source of delegitimation of public provision.

However, support for the NHS is not unqualified. Taylor-Gooby found that on every dimension except the standard of emergency care provided, respondents rated the private sector higher than the NHS. The private section was particularly more favourably rated than the NHS with regard to privacy, waiting lists, and staffing levels (Taylor-

Gooby 1986). Furthermore given a hypothetical choice between private and NHS health care, with the assumption that there was no difference in cost, some two-thirds opted for private care, mainly on the basis that the standard of care was better and more quickly available. Three-quarters of respondents were in favour of the principle of individuals' being permitted to contract out of the NHS to participate in private schemes. Respondents appear to be in favour of a mixed economy of welfare in which private and public options thrive. In this sense state welfare has not fundamentally undermined the commodity form.

Evidence of recent growth in private medicine may be cited as symptomatic of increased disaffection with the NHS. The early 1980s saw a rapid expansion of private provision. By 1984 7 per cent of the population was covered by private medical insurance. It might be argued that the limitations in terms of catering, accessibility, and flexibility of the state service impelled those who could afford to do so to opt for private medicine. However, there are problems with the interpretation of this trend. Most importantly the numbers of those subscribing as individuals has stabilized, and most of the increase in private insurance since 1981 has been in company-paid schemes (Mohan 1986). Those with private medical insurance continue to receive half their in-patient medical care and four-fifths of out-patient care under the NHS (Rayner 1986). Such alterations in the public/private mix of service use by privileged groups of employees cannot easily be interpreted as evidence of a widespread decline in support for the NHS.

Furthermore Taylor-Gooby's research finds no support for the thesis that public acceptance of a mixed economy of health care arises from a sense of oppression or alienating bureaucracy in the public system. For crisis theorists the oppressive influence of professions within welfare bureaucracies is a crucial notion. One of the most problematic aspects of Offe's analysis of the welfare state is his uncritical acceptance of Foucaultian notions of 'disciplinary power' (Offe 1984: 278) which, for example in Offe's discussions of health care, result in the 'destruction of the competence of clients' (Offe 1984: 276). Such views not only have to discount the popularity of welfare institutions as false consciousness, but also ignore the more striking and distressing evidence of the failures of the welfare state to address much hidden suffering and its attempts to disguise such failures behind the rhetoric of 'community care' (Walker 1982). The ability of the welfare state to reach and influence people's lives is simply overstated.

Administrative crisis

It is in the planning and administrative processes of the NHS that one may find the most likely sources of crisis tendencies. Structural changes to the NHS have regularly been perceived as the solution to inherent problems and have just as frequently been interpreted after implementation as failures. The most recent changes have emerged from an inquiry into NHS management carried out by Mr Roy Griffiths (DHSS 1984). The main recommendation of the report that has been accepted and implemented at every level of the NHS, from region to district to hospital unit, is the appointment of general managers with wide-ranging responsibilities for the management of health services, especially with regard to efficiency. Earlier experiments in reforming the NHS by means of 'managerialism' have not been particularly successful in their primary purpose (R. Brown 1979) and arguably have seriously damaged industrial relations (Carpenter 1977). However current circumstances differ from the 1974 exercise in managerialism in several important respects. First, management responsibilities are not clouded or confused by the complex process of consensus management emphasized in the 1974 reorganization. Second, more thought is being given, in post-Griffiths changes, to providing personal rewards and incentives to encourage more dynamic general management. Third, it is hoped that lines of account-ability of managers to health authority chairmen, and the role of the new NHS management board in supervision, are both clearer and more effective. Fourth, there is more widespread acceptance (rein-forced by the lengthy deliberations and recommendations of the Korner Steering Group on information needs in the NHS – Korner 1982) of the need for improved financial and medical information services which might permit managers to understand and control their environment more effectively. Lastly and perhaps most importantly, the Griffiths Report and its implementation have taken place with the positive and enthusiastic backing of a government with considerable electoral legitimacy. This has meant that the fundamental ideology behind the Griffiths Report has not been particularly strongly chal-lenged. Trade union opposition to some of the consequences of managerial control upon work conditions may be quite weak given that they are simultaneously coping with the consequences of contrac-ting out of services and a general environment of high unemployment. At the very least such considerations suggest that the upheavals ex-perienced by NHS administration over the last few years will not necessarily further deepen the 'crisis of crisis management' so widely predicted and that administrative improvements may occur.

Improved management will not produce miracles of increased efficiency and effectiveness given that the relationships between health resources and outcomes remain unmeasurable (Klein 1982). In this sense Offe's scepticism about the benefits of rationalization is well founded. Moreover the implementation of Korner data systems and the appointment of general managers cannot be expected to reduce the degree of conflict of interests between centre and periphery within the NHS. It is widely suggested that such changes are largely in the interests of the centre – the secretary of state, the DHSS, and the regions – and aimed to enhance centrist control of the NHS, the very opposite of original intentions (McClenahan *et al.* 1986). According to this view such developments may clearly be seen in Offe's terms as one aspect of the state's enhancing its administrative steering capacities as it attempts to cope with the multiple demands placed upon it. Decisions become centralized and at the same time reduced to technical processes less accessible to political demands. Nevertheless it may be simplistic to regard such developments as strategies emerging from the state to counter the contradictions of welfare capitalism. Several authors have shown that the dilemma of central versus local control of health services has been a perennial one in the NHS since its inception (Klein 1983; Hunter 1983). Other issues, such as democratic participation, territorial equality, and changing health priorities, tend to be the issues of contention behind this basic dilemma, rather than the more functional concerns to cope with fundamental contradictions identified by state crisis theories. Furthermore the centralizing tendencies identifiable in the NHS in recent years may be explained in terms of conventional pluralist conflict, avoiding the need to invoke functionalist needs of the welfare state. Many of the requirements for information and accountability expressed in recent years may be explained in terms of demands by parliamentary select committees for an increased role in the monitoring of public expenditure (Klein 1982). In other words conflicts within the state between parliament and government may be a sufficient explanation for centralizing tendencies within the NHS. In any case central versus local control may be a systemic problem in any complex health care system. In the Soviet Union, for example, the health care system is at the same time criticized for widespread bureaucratic inefficiencies that result from centralization and identified as lacking sufficient central control to overcome persistent problems in regional inequalities in provision (Ryan 1978). While administrative upheaval may persist and the NHS may not become dramatically more effective through administrative fiat, in comparative terms the NHS remains an organizational mechanism of considerable efficiency, admired for its lack of waste and duplication (Spicer 1981; Torrens 1982) and capable of providing justice in the rationing of scarce resources (Daniels 1986). As with many other aspects of crisis theory, it is clearly essential to look more cautiously and more comparatively.

A number of areas of planning and policy in the recent past show how flexibly and intelligently governments may avoid crisis. Thus high-level policy reviews of American-style medical insurance dissuaded the Conservative government from this option. Similarly the same government is not allowing the political capital to be gained from its support for the NHS to be jeopardized by too interventionist a means of supporting private medicine, especially if an over-provided private sector might require financial rescue (Mohan 1986). As with the flexible adjustment of RAWP discussed above, such political manoeuvres, particularly in anticipating media reactions, seen by Offe as doomed to deepen the state's crisis, may be viewed in quite the opposite way as normal and successful state-coping strategies. The very ambiguity and complexity of goods such as health, seen by Offe as reasons for state failure to organize long-term effective planning, may also be the very reason for short-term successful coping. It remains possible for 'contradictory' strategies to be pursued in such complex systems in ways not allowed for in crisis theories. The role of symbolic actions is seriously underestimated by crisis theory. Especially given the difficulties of assessing current expenditure, governments do not appear to have to rely on raising expenditure continuously and uncontrollably, as predicted by right and left ideologues. The lesson of the recent past is that political credit for both expenditure increases *and* control may be claimed simultaneously in the area of health, at least over the short term. The political market ultimately reasserts itself at periods approaching elections and as sensitivity to a variety of powerful voices within the health service is increased.

The work of analysts such as Offe should provoke medical sociology to take up the myriad of theoretical and empirical issues to be tackled in a *systemic* analysis of any health care system such as the NHS. Political scientists and policy analysts have been less hesitant than medical sociologists in examining the complexity and multilayered reality of health care (e.g. Fox 1986b; Klein 1983; Marmor 1984). Offe suggests ways in which analysis may be more open ended and more empirically based than the rigidities permitted by Marxist functionalism. The role of the state and its different internal components have been clearly identified by Offe and others as an important area of investigation. There may still be dangers of over-schematic theorizing in the new political economy of welfare. There are ambiguities about the scope of the term 'welfare state' and unwarranted generalizations abound about the apparently unitary phenomenon of the 'welfare state' (Carrier and Kendall 1986). Central concepts may prove disappointing. The 'contradictions' of the welfare state may often be more economically explained as persistent dilemmas and difficulties of social policy in complex societies – and with less ominous implications (Pemberton 1983). The remarkable capacities of governments in terms of 'system maintenance' cannot be ignored (Birch 1984). Stone graphically criticizes 'breakdown' theories of the welfare state in crisis, for failing to examine how the state can learn 'to walk with crutches and braces', and for failing to theorize the state's art of 'hobbling' (Stone 1984: 189). Sociologically it would appear essential to steer a course between the assumptions of conservative and Marxist ideology that the state is inherently contradictory, with a healthy expectancy that governments will adopt workable coping strategies in their crises of crisis management.

References

Aaron, H. and Schwartz, W. (1984) *The Painful Prescription*, Washington, DC: Brookings Institute.

Bates, E. (1983) *Health Systems and Public Scrutiny*, London: Croom Helm.

Berliner, H. (1975) 'A larger perspective on the Flexner report', *International Journal of Health Services*. 5: 573–92.

Bevan, G., Copeman, H., Perrin, J., and Rosser, R. (1980) *Health Care Priorities and Management*, London: Croom Helm.

Birch, A. (1984) 'Overload, ungovernability and delegitimation: the theories and the British case', *British Journal of Political Science* 14: 135–60.

Bosanquet, N. (1986) *Public Expenditure on the NHS: Recent Trends and the Outlook*, London: London Institute of Health Services Management in association with BMA and RCN.

Brittan, S. (1977) *The Economic Consequences of Democracy*, London: Temple Smith.

Brown, E. R. (1979) *Rockefeller Medicine Men: Capitalism and Medical Care in America*, Berkeley, Calif: University of California Press.

Brown, R. (1979) *Reorganising the National Health Service*, Oxford: Blackwell.

Butler, J. and Vaile, M. (1984) *Health and Health Services*, London: Routledge & Kegan Paul.

Carpenter, M. (1977) 'The new managerialism and professionalism in nursing', in M. Stacey (ed.) *Health and The Division of Labour*, London: Croom Helm.

Carrier, J. and Kendall, I. (1986) 'Categories, categorizations and the political economy of welfare', *Journal of Social Policy* 15: 315–35.

Crouch, C. (1979) 'The state, capital and liberal democracy', in C. Crouch (ed.) *State and Economy in Contemporary Capitalism*, London: Croom Helm.

Daniels, N. (1986) 'Why saying no to patients in the United States is so hard', *New England Journal of Medicine* 314: 1,380–3.

Davies, P. (1986) 'New money turns out to be dud notes', *Health Services Journal* 3 July: 881–2.

DHSS (1984) Griffiths Report, Health Circular 84 13, Implementation of the NHS Management Inquiry Report, London.

Fitzpatrick, R. (1984) 'Satisfaction with health care', in R. Fitzpatrick, J. Hinton, S. Newman, G. Scambler, and J. Thompson, *The Experience of Illness*, London: Tavistock.

Fox, D. (1986a) 'The consequences of consensus: American health policy in the twentieth century', *Milbank Memorial Fund Quarterly* 64: 76–99.

—— (1986b) *Health Policies, Health Politics: The Experience of America and Britain, 1911–1965*, Princeton, NJ: Princeton University Press.

Frankel, B. (1982) 'On the state of the state: Marxist theories of the state after Leninism', in A. Giddens and D. Held (eds) *Classes, Power and Conflict*, London: Macmillan.

George, V. and Wilding, P. (1976) *Ideology and Social Welfare*, London: Routledge & Kegan Paul.

Gillion, C. and Hemming, R. (1985) 'Social expenditure in the United Kingdom in a comparative context', in R. Klein and M. O'Higgins (eds) *The Future of Welfare*, Oxford: Blackwell.

Gough, I. (1979) *The Political Economy of the Welfare State*, London: Macmillan.

Gould, A. (1981) 'The salaried middle class in the corporatist welfare state', *Policy and Politics* 9: 401–18.

Ham, C. (1982) *Health Policy in Britain*, London: Macmillan.

Haywood, S. and Hunter, D. (1982) 'Consultative processes in health policy in the United Kingdom', *Public Administration* 69: 143–62.

Held, D. (1983) 'Central perspectives on the modern state', in D. Held, J. Anderson, B. Gieben, S. Hall, L. Harris, P. Lewis, N. Parker, and B. Turok (eds) *States and Societies*, London: Martin Robertson.

Held, D. and Krieger, J. (1983) 'Accumulation, legitimation and the state: the ideas of Claus Offe and Jurgen Habermas', in D. Held, J. Anderson, B. Gieben, S. Hall, L. Haris, P. Lewis, N. Parker, and B. Turok (eds) *States and Societies*, London: Martin Robertson.

Hill, M. and Bramley, G. (1986) *Analysing Social Policy*, Oxford: Blackwell.

Holland, W. (1986) 'The RAWP Review: pious hopes', *Lancet* 2: 1,087–90.

Hunter, D. (1983) 'Centre – periphery relations in the NHS: facilitators or inhibitors of innovation?' in K. Young (ed.) *National Interests and Local Government*, London: Heinemann.

Jennett, B. (1986) *High Technology Medicine*, Oxford: Oxford University Press.

Jessop, B. (1982) *The Capitalist State*, London: Martin Robertson.

King, A. (1975) 'Overload: problems of governing in the 1970s', *Political Studies* 13: 284–96.

Klein, R. (1982) 'Performance, evaluation and the NHS: a case study in conceptual perplexity and organisational complexity', *Public Administration* 60: 385–407.

—— (1983) *The Politics of the National Health Service*, London: Longman.

—— (1984a) 'Rationing health care', *British Medical Journal* 289: 143–4.

—— (1984b) 'The politics of ideology vs. the reality of politics: the case of Britain's National Health Service in the 1980s', *Milbank Memorial Fund Quarterly* 62: 82–103.

Korner, E. (1982) Steering Group on Health Services Information, *First Report to the Secretary of State*, London: HMSO.

Kristol, I. (1978) *Two Cheers for Capitalism*, New York: Basic Books.

Lindblom, C. (1977) *Politics and Markets*, New York: Basic Books.

McClenahan, J., Flux, R., Ijebor, L., and Mumford, P. (1986) 'Korner – preparing for the payoff', *Health Services* 25 September: 1,258–9.

McKie, D. (1986) 'Government spending on the NHS', *Lancet* 2: 1,345–6.

McLennan, G. (1984) 'Capitalist state or democratic polity? Recent developments in Marxist and pluralist theory', in D. Held, G. McLennan, and S. Hall (eds) *The Idea of the Modern State*, Milton Keynes: Open University Press.

Marmor, T. (1970) *The Politics of Medicare*, London: Routledge & Kegan Paul.

—— (1984) *Political Analysis and American Medical Care: Essays*, New York: Cambridge University Press.

Mishra, R. (1984) *The Welfare State in Crisis*, London: Wheatsheaf.

Mohan, J. (1986) 'Private medical care and the British Conservative Government: what price independence?' *Journal of Social Policy* 15: 337–60.

Navarro, V. (1975) 'The political economy of medical care', in V. Navarro (ed.) *Health and Medical Care in the U.S.: A Critical Analysis*, New York: Baywood.

—— (1978a) 'The crisis of the western system of medicine in contemporary capitalism', *International Journal of Health Services* 8: 179–211.

—— (1978b) *Class Struggle, the State and Medicine*, London: Martin Robertson.

Nordlinger, E. (1981) *On the Autonomy of the Democratic State*, London: Harvard University Press.

O'Connor, J. (1973) *The Fiscal Crisis of the State*, New York: St Martin's Press.

Offe, C. (1974) 'Structural problems of the capitalist state', in K. Von Beyme (ed. *German Political Studies*, vol. 1, London: Sage.

—— (1975) 'The theory of the capitalist state and the problem of policy formation', in L. Lindberg, R. Alford, C. Crouch, and C. Offe (eds) *Stress and Contradiction in Modern Capitalism*, Boston, Mass.: Lexington Books.

—— (1984) *Contradictions of The Welfare State*, London: Hutchinson.

O'Higgins, M. and Patterson, A. (1985) 'The prospects for public expenditure: a disaggregate analysis', in R. Klein and M. O'Higgins (eds) *The Future of Welfare*, Oxford: Blackwell.

Papadakis, E. and Taylor-Gooby, P. (1986) 'Positional satisfaction and state welfare', *Sociological Review* 34: 812–27.

Pescosolido, B., Boyer, C., and Tsui, W. Y. (1986) 'Crisis in the welfare state: public directions to welfare policies', in N. Furniss (ed.) *Futures for the Welfare State*, Bloomington, Ind: Indiana University Press.

Pemberton, A. (1983) 'Marxism and social policy: a critique of the "contradictions of welfare"', *Journal of Social Policy* 13: 289–307.

Pollitt, C. (1984) 'The state and health care', in G. McLennan, D. Held, and S. Held (eds) *State and Society in Contemporary Britain*, Cambridge: Polity Press.

Pressman, J. and Wildavsky, A. (1973) *Implementation*, Berkeley, Calif: University of California Press.

Rayner, G. (1986) 'Health care as a business? The emergence of a commercial hospital sector in Britain', *Policy and Politics* 14: 439–59.

Renaud, M. (1975) 'On the structural constraints to state intervention in health', in V. Navarro (ed.) *Health and Medical Care in the U.S.: A Critical Analysis*, New York: Baywood.

Ryan, M. (1978) *The Organisation of Soviet Medical Care*, Oxford: Blackwell.

Salmon, J. (1984) 'Organizing medical care for profit', in J. McKinlay (ed.) *Issues in the Political Economy of Health Care*, London: Tavistock.

Spicer, T. (1981) 'British and American health care systems: a comparative economic perspective', *British Medical Journal* 282: 1,334–6.

Stone, D. (1984) *The Disabled State*, London: Macmillan.

Taylor-Gooby, P. (1983) 'Legitimation deficit, public opinion and the welfare state', *Sociology* 17: 165–84.

—— (1985) *Public Opinion, Ideology and State Welfare*, London: Routledge & Kegan Paul.

—— (1986) 'Privatism, power and the welfare state', *Sociology* 20: 228–46.

Torrens, P. (1982) 'Some potential hazards of unplanned expansion of private health insurance in Britain', *Lancet* 1: 29–33.

Urry, J. (1981) *The Anatomy of Capitalist Societies*, London: Macmillan.

Walker, A. (1982) 'The meaning and social division of community care', in A. Walker (ed.) *Community Care: The Family, The State and Social Policy*, Oxford: Blackwell.

Walters, V. (1980) *Class Inequality and Health Care*, London: Croom Helm.

Willcocks, A. (1967) *The Creation of the National Health Service*, London: Routledge & Kegan Paul.

Name index

Aaron, H. 234, 236
Ablon, J. 148–9
Ackernecht, E. 69, 211
Adelstein, A. M. 104n
Akpom, C. 201
Albrecht, G. L. 153–4
Albrow, M. 209
Alexander, Franz 86–7, 127
Alford, R. 214
Andrewski, S. 208
Antonovsky, A. 104n
Arluke, A. 112
Armstrong, David 6, 44, 59, 71, 73, 94, 200
Arney, W. R. 73, 189
Ashworth, C. 3, 4, 5–6, 39, 40, 51
Atkinson, J. 38, 51
Austin, J. 181

Balint, M. 205
Bamforth, K. W. 104n
Barnes, B. 64
Barnes, H. E. 60
Barrett, M. 12
Bartley, M. 17
Bates, A. 233
Bauman, Z. 44
Baumann, B. O. 113
Becker, H. S. 89, 121, 137
Beechey, V. 15
Bendix, R. 206
Benedict, Ruth 103n
Bentham, J. 67, 68
Bergen, B. J. 73
Berger, P. 138
Bergner, M. 201

Berkman, L. 45
Bernstein, R. 170, 172
Bevan, G. 235
Bhaskar, R. 40, 51
Bilton, T. 38
Bion, W. R. 99, 104n
Birch, A. 241
Birenbaum, A. 148, 160
Blackwell, B. L. 113
Blalock, H. 46
Blane, David 5
Blau, P. 210
Blaxter, M. 104n, 105n, 160
Bosanquet, N. 235
Boudon, R. 51
Bowley, A. L. 23, 25–6
Bramley, G. 236
Brede, K. 104n
Brill, A. A. 85–6
Brittan, S. 222
Brown, E. R. 227
Brown, G. W. 46, 201, 210
Brown, J. A. C. 83
Brown, M. H. 21, 23, 24, 25
Brown, R. 239
Brown, William 83
Brubaker, R. 170, 197, 209, 216
Bucher, R. 210
Bulmer, Martin 86, 87, 88
Burgess, E. W. 68, 92, 101
Burnett, J. 26
Bursten, B. 113
Bury, M. 44, 151
Butler, J. 234
Buzzard, Sir Farquhar 78, 83
Byrne, P. S. 200

Subject index